Youth Ministry in City Churches

by Eugene C.
Roehlkepartain

Loveland, Colorado

Youth Ministry in City Churches

Credits

Edited by Michael D. Warden
Designed by Judy Atwood Bienick
Cover design by Judy Atwood Bienick
Cover photo by David Priest

Scripture quotations are from the Holy Bible, New International Version. Copyright © 1973, 1978, 1984 International Bible Society. Used by permission of Zondervan Bible Publishers.

Library of Congress Cataloging-in-Publication Data

Roehlkepartain, Eugene C., 1962-
   Youth ministry in city churches / by Eugene C. Roehlkepartain.
      p.   cm.
   ISBN 0-931529-71-9
   1. Church work with teenagers.   2. City churches.   I. Title.
   BV4447.R64   1989
   259!.23—dc20

ISBN 0-931529-71-9
Printed in the United States of America

Dedication

To Jolene,
my wife,
who helped me learn
to love the city.

Contents

Part One: Understanding Urban Youth Ministry

Part Two: Building an Urban Youth Ministry

Part Three: Leading Urban Youth Ministry

Acknowledgments

Journalist Bill Moyers once said, "A journalist is a professional beachcomber on the shores of other people's wisdom."

This book embodies the truth of that image. It would never have been written if dozens of urban youth workers across the United States had not been willing to let me "comb their beaches" by sharing their experiences, concerns, questions, ideas and programs.

The following people (listed in alphabetical order) consented to extensive interviews—the substance of which is the basis of this volume:

● Phill Carlos Archbold, associate pastor, First Church of the Brethren, Brooklyn, New York.

● Deborah Ban, staff minister with responsibilities for youth, Calvary Baptist Church, Denver, Colorado.

● John Carlson, program director, Evangelical Association for the Promotion of Education, Philadelphia, Pennsylvania.

● Dave Carver, former outreach coordinator, First Presbyterian Church of Crafton Heights, Pittsburgh, Pennsylvania. He currently lives in Rochester, New York.

● Jerald Choy, volunteer youth leader, First Chinese Baptist Church, San Francisco, California.

● James DiRaddo, urban youth ministry consultant, West Chester, Pennsylvania.

● Art Erickson, associate pastor for youth and community, Park Avenue United Methodist Church, Minneapolis, Minnesota.

● Dr. H.O. Espinoza, president, PROMESA (Proyectos Y Ministerios Evangelicos Hispanos), San Antonio, Texas.

● Wendell Fisher, youth director, Manhattan Bible Church, New York City.

● Wayne Gordon, pastor, Lawndale Community Church, Chicago, Illinois.

● Rob Grotheer, minister with youth and college, First United Methodist Church, Houston, Texas.

● Jim Hopkins, associate minister, First Baptist Church, Los Angeles, California.

● Tracy Hipps, junior high coordinator, Inner City Impact, Chicago, Illinois.

● Diana Loomis, pastor, Lafayette Park United Methodist Church, St. Louis, Missouri.

● David Miles, associate pastor of youth and missions, First Baptist Church, Flushing, New York.

● Melanie Monteclaro, youth coordinator, North Shore Baptist Church, Chicago, Illinois.

● Steve Pedigo, co-pastor, Chicago Fellowship of Friends, Chicago, Illinois.

● Marietta Ramsey, minister to youth, Bethel African Methodist Episcopal Church, Baltimore, Maryland.

● Ron Scates, associate pastor, First Presbyterian Church, San Antonio, Texas.

● Bryan Stone, pastor, Liberation Community of the Church of the Nazarene, Ft. Worth, Texas.

● Paul Tarro, director, Urban Youth Ministries, Kansas City, Missouri.

● Maria Torres-Rivera, Hispanic youth coordinator, Archdiocese of Philadelphia, Philadelphia, Pennsylvania.

● Bruce Wall, minister to youth, Twelfth Baptist Church, Boston, Massachusetts.

● Michael Walton, pastor of youth ministries, First Baptist Congregational Church, Chicago, Illinois.

● Harold Wright, minister of youth and family life services, Friendship Baptist Church, Vallejo, California.

● Bill Wylie-Kellermann, co-pastor, Cass Community Church, Detroit, Michigan.

I am deeply grateful to these people, not only for their openness and helpfulness in working with me, but also for the important ministries their names, stories and churches represent.

I also offer my thanks to the following people for their help in preparing the manuscript for this book:

● Jolene Roehlkepartain, my wife, for taking added responsibilities at home to free me for writing, and for diligently transcribing hours of interview tapes.

● Michael Walton, Art Erickson and H.O. Espinoza, for their careful critiques and useful suggestions on the manuscript's contents.

● Sally Schreiner, urban church resource exchange manager for the Seminary Consortium for Urban Pastoral Education (SCUPE), for invaluable assistance in locating resources and contacts in urban ministry.

● Michael Warden, Paul Woods, Chris Yount and Judy Bienick—my colleagues and friends at Group Books—for carefully editing, copy editing and designing the book.

● Thom and Joani Schultz and other leaders at Group Publishing, for allowing this risky dream to become a reality.

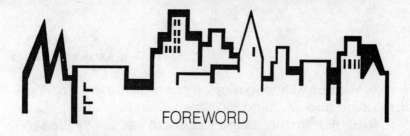

A Challenge to the Church

By Buster Soaries

Aristotle once said that "to perceive is to suffer." That's certainly the case in urban youth ministry.

Urban teenagers live in a difficult world. Some people become anesthetized to and overwhelmed by the struggles of city life. Knowing the overall urban picture can blur our vision and dull our sensitivities. But we can't help but feel the pain when we know the names, faces and places behind abstract urban statistics.

Another reaction is to give up in the face of the city's needs, accepting the conditions as inevitable and unchangeable. We often hear about the challenges of youth ministry in the city. We hear stories about incidents and conditions that seem overwhelming. Urban teenagers' needs seem so great, and people tell us that nothing can be done. So nothing is done. And a permanent underclass is created and sustained.

Neither anesthetization nor acceptance will do for those whose mission is the spreading of good news to everybody.

As the church, we are charged to share the good news with people of every age and in every condition.

In *Youth Ministry in City Churches*, Gene Roehlkepartain (I can't pronounce it either) accurately describes the situation confronting urban teenagers. He combines the discipline of scholarship and the heart of ministry to create an invaluable, balanced tool for urban youth workers.

He takes seriously our need to perceive and understand. His empirical data and his testimonies from the field are so authentic and relevant that we develop perceptions and images as we read the pages.

But the book moves beyond description. Gene offers assorted prescriptions without the arrogance that many non-urban writers convey. Too often the urban situation is portrayed as so desperate that nothing can be done. And, more often, writers offer simplistic, moralistic formulas that ignore the situation's gravity and comprehensiveness. Gene has sensitively and thoughtfully avoided both traps.

Finally, Gene stresses that to reach urban teenagers, we must see them as victims and inheritors of unjust urban conditions and institutions, as well as people who are caught in changing societal priorities and patterns. Urban youth ministry must be aware of and confront systemic challenges. This book refreshingly points to the many issues that affect kids in the city—issues for which we are all responsible.

I hope that *Youth Ministry in City Churches* won't be confined to the urban youth workers' libraries—though it should be on those shelves. This book portrays and projects the greatest challenge in America today. Thus it addresses the greatest challenge for the entire church. My prayer is that it will become mandatory reading for the whole body of Christ. And as we read, may we each identify on these pages an assignment for ourselves.

Buster Soaries is a specialist in urban youth ministry based in Trenton, New Jersey. He is former national coordinator of Jesse Jackson's Operation PUSH, and he has served as pastor of two urban churches.

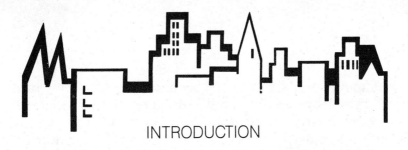

INTRODUCTION

A Critical Void

Given the great concern in North America about urban problems, it's ironic and sad how little is written about urban youth ministry. While other books have been published in the past, none are still in print. Occasional articles in religious magazines describe particular ministries, but they barely scratch the surface. Rarely—if ever—does anyone deal with the broad array of issues, concerns and needs of urban youth ministry.

Youth Ministry in City Churches was written to respond to this need. Through the book, I have tried to address several key issues and concerns:

Erasing myths. Our culture in general and the church in particular, hold to stereotypes or myths about the city that must be confronted before effective ministry can occur. I have tried to identify some of these myths and to provide correctives based on research and the experiences of urban youth ministers across the country. Chapters 2 and 3 deal specifically with many of these stereotypes.

In my research, I discovered that many urban youth workers themselves don't understand the city and the teenagers they're trying to reach. This book provides some practical tools for getting to know your city and your teenagers.

Understanding needs. Urban teenagers' needs are complex and diverse. Media reports heighten the concern by highlighting different problems at different times—illiteracy one month, gangs the next and drugs the next. Without discounting the serious attention each of these issues deserves, this book broadens the focus, discussing a variety of different needs in different cities and different urban teenagers.

Providing ideas and models. If you're like most urban youth workers, you already know many needs. You see them as you walk around the block in your community. But how can you respond effectively to those needs? I asked dozens of urban youth workers that same question. Their ideas and their stories of how their churches met the needs become a gold mine of ideas you can use in your own ministry.

Encouraging networks. One of the most common comments I heard from various urban youth workers was: "I don't know anyone else who's doing this kind of ministry. I guess our situation is unique." But I discovered that different people in different cities are struggling with similar questions, concerns and problems. I also learned that while some cities have strong networks of urban youth ministers, few people know about ministries in other cities.

This book introduces a variety of youth workers in a variety of cities and churches across the country. These people represent hundreds who are also ministering in effective and creative ways. You'll probably find at least one or two people in this book whose situations are similar to yours.

Introducing resources. No single book can provide everything needed to be effective in urban youth ministry. Yet I've tried to gather a variety of resources that will take you into areas of specialization beyond this book's scope.

Many of the resources are listed beginning on page 245. Other resources are footnoted in the text that deals with the specific issue. These resources are gathered from a variety of secular and religious sources and have proved valuable in dealing with the unique issues of urban youth ministry.

A Note about Diversity

One of the struggles in writing a book such as this one is terminology. The word "urban," for example, carries with it a great deal of baggage. Even more sensitive is the issue of identifying various groups of people, whether by income level or by racial or ethnic background.

Words have power, and a particular ethnic group's self-chosen identity is important and must be respected. Yet language also changes from one generation to the next. For example, we used to talk about Negroes; later, the appropriate term became blacks. At the time of this writing, some leaders are advocating transition to the phrase African Americans or black African Americans.

Thus, while I have tried to be sensitive to the preferences of different groups, it's sometimes difficult to be aware of and adjust to the most current and most widely accepted terminology. For this reason, I have varied my references to different ethnic groups based on my awareness of the different usages. If I offend any person or group by my word choices, please accept my apologies. The spirit of the book is one of openness, acceptance and exploration. I hope you can "read beyond" the words so the book may serve you and your ministry.

Joining the Journey

Youth Ministry in City Churches is filled with stories of youth workers who have discovered ways to meet the needs of teenagers in the city. They don't claim to have all the answers. They're struggling and learning and growing—like any pilgrim.

Yet their stories highlight the opportunities and challenges of youth ministry in the city. And while the challenges are indeed great, congregations across the country have found innovative ways to respond.

May their ideas and insights enrich you and your ministry.

PART 1:

Understanding Urban Youth Ministry

CHAPTER 1

The Call of the City

nstead of joining Boy Scouts or Camp Fire Girls, elementary kids in Chicago's Cabrini-Green housing project join gangs. The northeastern section of the neighborhood is turf for the Cobra Stones and the Vicelords; the southwestern section, for the Black Gangster Disciples.[1]

The Chicago Fellowship of Friends serves in Cabrini-Green, one of the nation's most notorious government housing projects. Of the almost 9,000 residents, 5,800 are young people. Approximately 93 percent of the families are single-parent.[2]

The church's pastor, Steve Pedigo, began the church by coaching a basketball team of inner-city teenagers in the late 1970s. By building trust and relationships with the young people, he gradually formed a youth group that became the core of the church. Today the church has 50 to 60 young people active in its program—many of them taking leadership roles with the younger children.

●

Nine out of 10 members of First Church of the Brethren in Brooklyn, New York, are Hispanic. Eighty percent of the 170 members are domestic workers or in low-paying service jobs.

This small church has dedicated itself to helping young people find a better life. It has a tutoring program for kids from elementary to high school, and it provides funds for clothing, books and food when teenagers need help to stay in school. Church leaders visit schools to check youth group members' progress, then they report to parents who might otherwise never know.

Hoping to give teenagers a vision of life beyond the ghetto, associate pastor Phill Carlos Archbold pages through the *New York Times* to discover free and inexpensive activities. When he finds them, he takes the youth group around the city, exposing them to opera, Broadway, drama and other cultural events.

●

The First Baptist Church in Los Angeles is an inner-city church four miles from downtown. Its membership is multicultural—Spanish, Korean, Filipino, Anglo, and African American. The church and its leadership reflect the changing community. The youth minister is white, and the youth group leaders are from Liberia, the Philippines, Brazil and Ohio.

On the surface, First Baptist's youth program is like most others—Sunday school classes, regular Bible studies and fellowship meetings, outings, summer camps. But there's more. Each week a Korean church member leads Christian Tae Kwon Do, teaching youth not only the martial art, but also self-discipline and respect. The church also sponsors El Centro, a community center for youth that reaches out to the gang-infested community with the positive alternatives of art, music and sports.

When it was having trouble with graffiti, the church initiated a mural project, inviting gang members to paint walls any way they wanted. One of the results was a stunning billboard promoting world peace.

●

Park Avenue United Methodist Church is a large, century-old urban church in Minneapolis. It used to be a suburban church. But the city grew and the population shifted. Faced with declining membership and revenue, the congregation made an intentional effort to reach out to the community.

Today, Park Avenue ministers both to its immediate community and to suburban members who commute to church activities. With this combination, the church has the financial resources to provide important ministries to its community. It operates a computer training center, a ministry to girls who have been sexually assaulted and an annual Soul Liberation Festival—a massive outdoor music outreach.

●

These congregations represent the thousands of churches involved in the most difficult and critical areas of youth ministry in the United States: ministry in the city. Their ministry is difficult because of the overwhelming needs and challenges they address. And their ministry is critical not only because of the lives at stake but also because the whole world is becoming increasingly urban.

The Growing Urban World

Most Americans now live in urban areas. The Census Bureau reports that 76 percent of Americans now live in metropolitan areas compared to only 56 percent of the population in 1950.[3] Government figures also reveal that 29 percent of families live in central cities, 47 percent live in adjacent suburbs, and 23 percent live in non-metropolitan areas.[4]

The teenage population shows similar trends, though more Americans with children live in the suburbs. The rural youth population continues to drop dramatically, while youth population in the cities and suburbs steadily increases. About 66 percent of teenagers live in metropolitan areas, with 28 percent actually living in cities. But when it comes to ethnic teenagers, the percentages jump dramatically. About 56 percent of black teenagers live in cities.[5] Also,

Diagram 1-1
The World's Urban Growth

The world's urban population growth has skyrocketed since the middle of the century. National Geographic reports the following examples of how even some of the most rural nations in the world are seeing rapid urban growth (as a percentage of the nation's total population):[22]

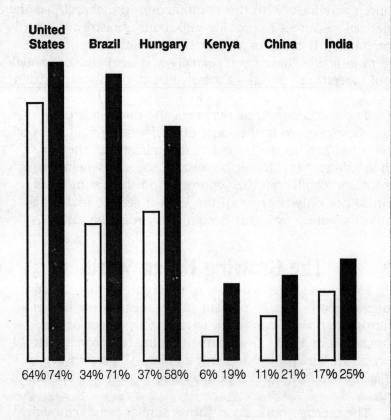

United
States Brazil Hungary Kenya China India

64% 74%   34% 71%   37% 58%   6% 19%   11% 21%   17% 25%

☐ 1950   ■ 1988

Diagram 1-2
Cities Around the World

If you were to name the 10 largest cities in the world, which would you name? If you're like most people, you'd probably name several U.S. cities plus a few others in developed countries.

However, many cities in developing countries are now larger than their counterparts in the developed world. Here are the 10 largest metropolitan areas in the world:[23]

	Projected 1990 Population (in millions)
1. Mexico City, Mexico	21.3
2. Sao Paulo, Brazil	18.1
3. Tokyo/Yokohama, Japan	17.2
4. New York/Northeastern New Jersey, U.S.A.	15.3
5. Calcutta, India	12.6
6. Shanghai, China	12.0
7. Greater Bombay, India	11.9
8. Greater Buenos Aires, Argentina	11.7
9. Seoul, Republic of Korea	11.5
10. Rio de Janeiro, Brazil	11.4

Only two other U.S. cities fall within the 30 largest cities in the world. The Los Angeles/Long Beach area ranks 11th. The Chicago/Northwestern Indiana area ranks 28th. But by the year 2000, experts predict that only two U.S. cities will make the top 30—the New York/Northeastern New Jersey area (sixth) and the Los Angeles/Long Beach area (18th).

53 percent of Hispanic teenagers live in cities.[6]

This urbanization trend doesn't affect the United States alone. In fact, urban areas in other parts of the world are growing even more rapidly. (See Diagram 1-1, "The World's Urban Growth.") At the beginning of this century, only 15 percent of the world's population lived in cities. Today the figure is near half, and it's expected to grow to 55 percent by the year 2000. At that time, at least 3.2 billion people will live in cities—as many people as the world's total population in 1965.[7]

Beyond the numbers, though, the need for urban youth

ministry takes on even more significance when you consider the important roles cities play in our society. Cities set the direction for fashions, trends and ideas in society. They are the centers for industry, commerce and trade. All major media are based in major cities. For example, all three major TV networks are based in New York City. In many ways, modern life revolves around city life—whether you live in Manhattan, New York; or Manhattan, Kansas.

As urban ministry expert Ray Bakke writes: "Urban culture is spreading out and colonizing the suburbs, small towns and rural areas. The city is less of a place and more of a process, taking its franchised outlets to the small towns, and its standard newspapers and TV broadcasts to the remotest rural village."[8] Youth worker David Miles of Flushing, New York, adds: "The urban world expresses to a greater extent the problems of the world in general. The whole world is moving toward urbanization. The problems that are expressed in an urban world are going to increasingly become the problems of our whole globe."

Growing Youth Needs

Adding to the urgency of urban youth ministry are the critical needs of urban teenagers. Sociologists, demographers and other observers point with growing alarm to the spiraling problems of urban teenagers—poverty, gang activity, drug abuse, illiteracy, teenage pregnancy and other social problems. While all communities—rural, suburban, urban—now experience these problems to some degree, they are exaggerated in urban areas. Consider these troubling statistics:

● About 19 percent of families living in the city live below the national poverty level. Among urban blacks, the percentage increases to 33 percent. And 32 percent of urban Hispanic families live in poverty.[9]

● Up to 2 million teenagers are homeless in America. Eighty percent of the homeless teenagers in New York City become involved in prostitution.[10]

● Forty percent of urban high school students drop out of school, compared with a national average of 29 percent. The rate rises to 50 percent among urban blacks, 80 percent among urban Hispanics and 85 percent among urban Native Americans.[11] Educators predict that more than half of all urban students will qualify for special education or other special programs by the 1990s.[12]

● Inner-city teenagers have an unemployment rate 40 percent higher than the national average.[13]

● In the past decade, drug-related arrests among young people have increased sharply in major cities. For example, there were 41 juvenile drug-related arrests in Los Angeles in 1980. The number climbed to 1,719 in 1987.[14]

● Urban teenagers are considered a high-risk group for contracting the deadly AIDS virus. U.S. Surgeon General C. Everett Koop says that Hispanics, who make up only 8 percent of the U.S. population, account for 24 percent of AIDS patients. Blacks (only 12 percent of the population) account for another 24 percent of the cases.[15]

● Homicide is now the second leading cause of death among black young people ages 15 to 24.[16] In 1985, 27,000 12- to 15-year-olds were handgun victims.[17]

● Eighty percent of public school children in the nation's 44 largest cities have incomes low enough to qualify for free or reduced-price school lunches.[18]

● Urban teachers report much higher levels of poor health and neglect among students. Half of urban teachers say child neglect is a serious problem (compared to 36 percent of other teachers), and more than 30 percent cite poor health as a serious problem (compared to 16 percent of other teachers).[19]

Urban youth workers deal with these and other issues daily. Diagram 1-3, "Urban Teenagers' Needs," shows Group Publishing's survey results of how urban youth workers rank issues their teenagers face.

A Search Institute study summarized its findings on the problems of urban youth by saying that "the condition of urban youth in the late 1980s calls for serious national attention. Among the most profound trends is the increasing rupture in three vital support systems for urban youth: family, school and work. As these support systems unravel, other threats to well-being emerge, including victimization in crimes of violence, incarceration and homicide."[20]

Ministry at the Crossroads

The two major trends discussed in this chapter—urbanization and growing urban youth needs—place urban youth workers at the crossroads of two critical trends in society. "The problems you have in an urban setting are distinctly youth-oriented problems—drugs, sex, not knowing how to deal with other people, not knowing how to hold a job," says youth worker David Miles of Flushing, New York. "For the church to ignore urban youth ministry is to ignore the people whom Jesus would have hung out with."

This reality presents a tremendous ministry opportunity and challenge. Never before have so many teenagers lived in such concentrated areas. As youth worker Wendell Fisher of Manhattan Bible Church in New York City says, "If we're going to turn our country around, we're going to have to reach the cities." Moreover, because the world is becoming more urbanized, the key to reaching the world in the next century will be in the cities.

The Church's Track Record

Some of the most creative and effective youth ministries in the country occur in certain urban churches. In the face of seemingly overwhelming odds, individual congregations are reaching urban teenagers, sharing the gospel and offering new skills and hope for the future. These congregations bridge economic, ethnic and educational gaps more successfully than churches in any other setting. And national and city leaders often turn to these pastors and youth leaders for ways to address critical urban problems—gang warfare, teenage pregnancy, drug abuse, homicide, to name a few.

On the other hand, the overall landscape of urban youth ministry is bleak. As a whole, city churches haven't effectively reached young people. Their programs struggle along with burned-out leadership, uncommitted teenagers and inadequate resources.

Urban youth ministry veteran James DiRaddo of Philadelphia says the church's urban ministry hasn't really been bad—"it's sort of been non-existent." He explains: "I don't think the church knows what to do with . . . the ever-changing urban scene. It poses kinds of circumstances where we can't go back to precedent. And we're not too good at being creative . . . We send people to Africa, but we don't know how to reach Africans who come over here."

The same principle holds true with reaching urban teenagers, DiRaddo says. "I don't think the church has been doing anything with urban youth. I don't think it speaks to their needs—I don't think it knows how."

DiRaddo notes that the problem of reaching the cities isn't limited to white congregations. "Even the ethnic churches haven't been too terribly successful," he says. For example, he mentions how many Asian congregations struggle to keep the young people interested in the church. A major barrier is that the church still has its roots in the "old world" while the young people are firmly planted in America.

Hispanic church consultant H.O. Espinoza of San Antonio, Texas, says the same lack of success plagues the Hispanic church. It sees the needs, he says, but "the Hispanic church doesn't know what to do in the urban environment. There is a high sense of guilt."

David Miles sees a similar issue in the traditional white churches. "I think urban youth ministry has been slow to

---

Diagram 1-3

Urban Teenagers' Needs

A Group Publishing survey asked urban youth workers to rank various issues they say urban teenagers face. Here are the top 12:[24]
1) Understanding and growing in their Christian faith
2) Dealing with negative peer pressure
3) Alcohol and drug abuse
4) Poor self-worth
5) Apathy
6) Knowing how to make and keep good friends
7) Lack of community because kids attend different schools
8) Lack of caring adults or mentors
9) Loss of interest in any Christian church
10) Abusive or dysfunctional families
11) Sense of hopelessness about the future
12) Relating to people of other ethnic backgrounds

catch on because it's so difficult," he says. "And nobody wants to do something that's really hard."

Keeping Perspective

While it's easy to criticize urban churches for not reaching young people, we need to remember how difficult it can be to reach these teenagers. Many urban youth issues baffle the experts—inside and outside the church. It shouldn't be surprising that, despite heroic, dedicated and skillful efforts, some urban churches simply won't successfully reach the city's young people.

First Baptist Church in Los Angeles made a major commitment to minister to urban teenagers through a recreation and arts center. The program gave teenagers positive recreation alternatives to the gangs and drugs that controlled the neighborhood streets. The center gave young people a place to play basketball, and it gave the opportunities to learn music, art and dance.

But despite good intentions, programs and supervision, the center itself became a gang hangout. "We had hoped to build an accepting environment of safety," youth minister Jim Hopkins says. "But they saw it as just another safe place to continue gang and drug activities." The results included graffiti, robberies and abuse of the facilities. As a result, the center had to close down and "clean house," Hopkins says. The church began working with the YMCA to develop a more structured and controlled program that would include more values education and drug education. While the program now reaches fewer young people, Hopkins hopes the center will now make a greater impact on the young people who are involved.

Urban churches can't be certain that *any* new program or approach will be successful—no matter how carefully it's planned and implemented. As youth worker Dave Carver of Rochester, New York, explains: "Unless churches recognize that working with unchurched urban kids is one of the toughest things to do and are willing to sink some major effort into it, they shouldn't try it . . . It takes a lot of energy."

Seeds of a New Vision for Urban Youth

In the midst of these tremendous challenges, seedlings of hope are blossoming into beautiful signs of God's presence in—and concern for—the city. In this book you will discover some of these blossoms to help you in your ministry.

The seeds of new vision come in many shapes. But, like the mustard seed, they each point toward the coming of God's kingdom:

Seeds of creativity. The most promising signs for the future of urban youth work are the many dedicated, caring, creative and thoughtful urban pastors, youth ministers and volunteers working in cities across the country. Their stories and ideas—the soul of this book—show without a doubt that they are today's "Nehemiahs," leading God's people back to rebuild the city.

Seeds of growing interest. National organizations and denominations appear to be taking interest in urban youth ministry. Little by little, they are recognizing and responding to the needs by hiring urban ministry consultants and including urban youth ministry in denominational executives' job descriptions.

Seeds of resources. National youth ministry publishers are beginning to address urban issues. In 1988, Judson Press released the first major youth ministry resource designed specifically for an urban ethnic group.[21] In 1989, at least two national youth ministry periodicals focused one of their issues on urban youth ministry (Youthworker and The Youth Leader). Other resources are probably not far away. Several national groups are exploring the possibilities and options.

Seeds of networking. National, regional and local networks have formed in urban youth ministry. Two national, interdenominational networks now exist—Urban Youth Ministries (formed in 1988) and the Coalition for Urban Youth Leadership (formed in 1985). In addition, formal and informal groups in various cities across the country have formed to offer support, resources and continuing education to urban youth workers and pastors.

The Church: Another Reluctant Prophet?

The seeds have been planted. But the question remains, will the church nurture those seeds and reach out to urban teenagers?

Or will the church be another reluctant prophet . . . like Jonah?

Remember Jonah? God called him to preach in Nineveh, "a great city" (Jonah 3:2). God had plans for that city, and he wanted Jonah to warn its people.

Jonah had other ideas. Ninevites were known for their evil ways, and they probably wouldn't take too kindly to his message. So instead of incurring their wrath, he went for a cruise in the opposite direction. The people in Tarshish (another mission field) needed to hear the word of the Lord too, Jonah must have thought to himself. And they were much less threatening.

But God didn't go along with Jonah's alternate plan, and he had a whale of a time trying to get the prophet to cooperate. Then when Jonah did finally preach in Nineveh, the people heard him and repented—everyone from the king down. The king even issued a decree declaring a fast and a fashion change to sackcloth. "Let everyone call urgently on God," he decreed. "Let them give up their evil ways and their violence. Who knows? God may yet relent and with compassion turn from his fierce anger so that we will not perish" (Jonah 3:8b-9).

When Jonah saw what had happened, he was anything but happy. He went out into the country to mope. He expressed his anger to God for not following through on his promise to destroy the city. The Lord said: "But Nineveh has more than a hundred and twenty thousand people who cannot tell their right hand from their left, and many cattle as well. Should I not be concerned about that great city?" (Jonah 4:11)

In some ways, the American church has been like Jonah. Our cities are permeated with poverty, hopelessness, crime, drug abuse, illiteracy, unreached teenagers and other tragedies. People have been called to take the gospel to the city, but they've gone just about anywhere they could to avoid the cities.

"There's too much crime."

"It's too dangerous."

"It doesn't fit my lifestyle."

"Suburbanites need the gospel too."

God doesn't deny what we say. He only responds, "Should I not be concerned about that great city?"

Reflection and Action

1. How does your church compare with the churches described at the beginning of this chapter? What are the similarities? differences?

2. Write your own church's youth ministry story in your personal journal, or share it with your volunteers. What's your community like? How does your church minister to urban teenagers?

3. How have you seen the urbanization trend taking place in your own city? How do you think it will affect your church? Check with your public library to locate recent research to indicate such trends in your own community.

4. Keep track of the TV shows you and your family watch during the next week. Then figure out how many of them take place in major cities. What does your discovery tell you about the influence of cities in the whole culture?

5. Think about the young people you minister to. How do they reflect the growing needs mentioned on page 24? List other needs you've seen in the urban teenagers you know.

6. Group Publishing asked urban youth workers to rank the issues they deal with most in working with teenagers. Before you look at how others answered, rank the issues yourself. With 1 as the greatest need and 12 as the least, rank the issues that you think urban teenagers face:

_____ Alcohol and drug abuse

_____ Apathy

_____ Dealing with negative peer pressure

_____ Knowing how to make and keep good friends

_____ Lack of caring adults or mentors

_____ Lack of community because kids attend different schools

_____ Loss of interest in any Christian church

_____ Poor self-worth
_____ Relating to people of other ethnic backgrounds
_____ Sense of hopelessness about the future
_____ Understanding and growing in their Christian faith
_____ Abusive or dysfunctional families

Now compare your list to the rankings given in Diagram 1-3, "Urban Teenagers' Needs" (page 27). How does your list differ? How would you explain any major differences or similarities? What surprises you?

7. Do you agree that urban youth ministry is at the junction of two critical trends in our society—urbanization and growing urban youth needs? Why or why not? What are the implications of this reality for your youth ministry?

8. James DiRaddo says: "I don't think the church has been doing anything with urban youth . . . I don't think it knows how." What's your gut reaction to his statement? Why do you agree or disagree with him? Think of examples to support your answer.

9. What "seeds of hope" have you seen in your own church, city or denomination for the future of urban youth ministry? Write an encouraging note to the people who planted or are nurturing those seeds.

Endnotes

[1]Marlene Morrison Pedigo, *New Church in the City* (Richmond, IN: Friends United Press, 1988), 5.

[2]Pedigo, *New Church in the City*, 6.

[3]Eugene C. Roehlkepartain (editor), *The Youth Ministry Resource Book* (Loveland, CO: Group Books, 1988), 21.

[4]U.S. Bureau of the Census, Current Population Reports, Series P-20, No. 424, *Household and Family Characteristics: March 1987* (U.S. Government Printing Office, Washington, DC, 1988), Table 2.

[5]Roehlkepartain, *The Youth Ministry Resource Book*, 24.

[6]*Household and Family Characteristics: March 1987*, 41.

[7]Harvie M. Conn, *A Clarified Vision for Urban Mission*, (Grand Rapids, MI: Zondervan Publishing House, 1987), 15.

[8]Ray Bakke with Jim Hart, *The Urban Christian* (Downers Grove, IL: InterVarsity Press, 1987), 31.

[9]U.S. Bureau of the Census, Current Population Reports: Consumer Income, Series P-60, No. 161, *Money Income and Poverty Status in the United States: 1987*, (U.S. Government Printing Office, Washington, DC, 1988), Table 18.

[10]Christina Kelly, "Street Kids," Sassy (February 1989), 34-37.

[11]Roehlkepartain, *The Youth Ministry Resource Book*, 101.

[12]Roehlkepartain, *The Youth Ministry Resource Book*, 99.

[13]Peter Benson et al., *Strategies for Promoting the Well-Being of Urban Youth*, (Minneapolis: Search Institute, 1986), 2.

[14]Jacob V. Lamar, "Kids Who Sell Crack," Time (May 9, 1988), 20-33.

[15]Jolene L. Roehlkepartain, "C. Everett Koop: Moralist and Scientist," The Christian Century (June 22-29, 1988), 598-599.

[16]Benson et al., *Strategies for Promoting the Well-Being of Urban Youth*, 3.

[17]George Hackett, "Kids: Deadly Force," Newsweek (January 11, 1988), 18.

[18]Benson et al., *Strategies for Promoting the Well-Being of Urban Youth*, 1.

[19]*An Imperiled Generation: Saving Urban Schools* (Princeton, NJ: The Carnegie Foundation for the Advancement of Teaching, 1988), 15.

[20]Benson et al., *Strategies for Promoting the Well-Being of Urban Youth*, 3.

[21]Donald Ng (editor), *Asian Pacific American Youth Ministry* (Valley Forge, PA: Judson Press, 1988).

[22]"Flight to the Cities," National Geographic (December 1988), 935.

[23]Raymond J. Bakke, "Are You Ready for an Urban World?" World Evangelization (September/October 1988), 12.

[24]Eugene C. Roehlkepartain, "Urban Youth Ministry," GROUP Magazine (October 1988), 72-76.

CHAPTER 2

Understanding the City

The gospel must penetrate the city if it is really to penetrate American society, for the city is the soul of the society . . . To understand the city is to understand the future. A world-class city is a microcosm of the world.
—*David Claerbaut*[1]

ities are too important to society and the future of the world to write them off as Jonah wanted to write off Nineveh. And urban teenagers have needs that cry out for attention from compassionate Christians. Instead of avoiding the city, Christians must learn about the city and how to minister effectively to it.

Unfortunately, many Christians see the city as an alien, negative world. Like Francis Schaeffer, they see the city as proof "that we live in a post-Christian world . . . There is death in the *polis. There is death in the city*."[2]

The negative attitudes and images many people have of

the city are significant barriers to urban youth ministry. These attitudes discourage youth ministers from hearing the call to the city. And, as Harvie M. Conn, professor of missions at Westminster Theological Seminary, writes, they "paralyze Christian initiative to reach cities for Christ, . . . they send Christian leaven and salt running for safety on suburban kitchen shelves."[3] (Diagram 2-1 summarizes Conn's analysis of myths about the city.)

Of course, not everyone sees the city in a negative light. While some people do see cities as unfriendly, unnatural, morally impoverished, unsafe and unfit for children, others see them as diverse, active, creative and exciting. (See Diagram 2-2, "Attitudes Toward the City.") In fact, Hispanic church consultant H.O. Espinoza says Hispanics "gravitate toward downtown . . . because that's the cultural center." He notes that "in Latin America the downtown area is the heart of the city."

This chapter seeks to present a balanced, realistic view of the city—its components, its people, its opportunities and its challenges.

What Is the City?

On the surface, defining "city" may seem simple: "It's a big place with lots of people, buildings and noise." People who live in Cannon Falls, Minnesota, shop in "the cities"— Minneapolis/St. Paul.

Yet beyond such obvious examples, no one seems to know exactly how to define the city. When does a conglomeration of people become a city, a suburb, a town, a village? In the Dallas/Ft. Worth metroplex, for example, when does the "city" area end and the "suburban" area begin? What qualifies a municipality as a "city"?

Diagram 2-3, "Making Sense of the Census," outlines the government's basic methods for defining a city. But as useful as the official definitions may be as a starting place, they don't really reveal much about the city. A more useful way to understand the city is to see it as a series of zones that distinguish the people and living conditions of different parts of a large community. (See Diagram 2-4, "Urban Areas.")

Diagram 2-1
Myths About the City

In his book *A Clarified Vision for Urban Mission: Dispelling the Urban Stereotypes*, Harvie M. Conn identifies and dispels stereotypes of the city. While each may contain a grain of truth, he says, it's only a half-truth.[29]

The rural/urban myth. This myth is summed up in the words of a missions executive: "God made the country and man made the suburb. But the devil made the city." People who accept this myth view the city as innately evil—something to escape from. In many ways, this myth reinforces all the other myths.

The depersonalization generalization. This myth associates "city" with "ghetto." People move to the city where they become just a number in a faceless mass. Conn writes, "Social networks are not destroyed by the city; new ones are created, not always connected strictly with family and kin."[30]

The crime generalization. The reality of crime in cities is undeniable. But, Conn says "the largely white suburbanites have a fear of city crime out of all proportion to the facts."[31] Crime is not limited to the center city. Conn notes that the crime rate of smaller cities and suburbs is climbing faster than in larger cities. In fact, the U.S. Bureau of Justice Statistics estimates that household crime victimization rates aren't that much different for different settings. Over a 20-year period, 80 percent of urban households are likely to be burglarized, compared to 70 percent of suburban households.[32]

The secularization generalization. This myth holds that faith dies in the city. Many people believe the city is a secular place, and religion cannot survive the onslaught of other attractions and competing values. Again, this myth has some truth. Yet cities are home to the largest and fastest-growing churches. Indeed, a Gallup survey found that 10 of the 15 largest cities in the country have unchurched rates well *below* the national average.[33]

The privatization generalization. This generalization sees sin as only personal. It doesn't see the social forces—the system—as a cause of any ills or sins. "People who don't work are lazy." "All that people buy with food stamps are champagne, cookies and frozen dinners."[34] However, many urban problems result from structural injustices such as instable neighborhoods and redlining (see page 44).

The monoclass generalization. To illustrate this generalization, picture in your mind the "typical" urban dweller. Who do you see?

If you're like most people, your image is of a poor, minority person. Through such stereotypes, Conn writes, "the city becomes another dirty word for one class, the poor." This image prevents the church from reaching out to meet the needs of the many different people in the city—the poor, the middle class, and the elite.[35]

Diagram 2-2

Attitudes Toward the City

More and more Americans say they want to live in cities. An analysis of Gallup surveys of residential preference by demographers Calvin Beale and Irma T. Elo shows the increase in the percentage of Americans who prefer living in cities in 1985 compared to 1976:[36]

Preferred Residence	1976	1985
Large cities (more than 100,000 residents)	13%	23%
Small cities (10,000 to 100,000 residents)	29%	29%
Town or village	20%	23%
Rural areas	38%	25%

Another study found that people who live in cities tend to love cities, while people who live elsewhere tend to hate them.

● Only 4 percent of rural and small-town residents said they'd prefer to live in a large city. In fact, most of these considered the city to be the *worst* place to live.

● Yet 61 percent of current large-city residents say the city is their top choice for a place to live.

When each group was asked to describe the characteristics of cities, the lists varied dramatically.[37] Take a look:

Urbanites' Perspectives	Suburbanites' Perspectives	Rural/Small-Town Residents' Perspectives
Pro-urban	Either pro- or anti-urban with ambivalence	Anti-urban
Cities as diverse, active, exciting, cultured, liberal, open, creative	Cities as unnatural and unsafe, yet exciting and sophisticated	Cities as unnatural, unfriendly, dangerous, not-for-kids, morally impoverished

Understanding the different zones is critical for urban youth workers, because each zone requires a different ministry approach. For example, a downtown church must discover ways to reach young people from great distances, since the business district has few, if any, residents. In contrast, a church in a transitional community must discover ways to reach the impoverished teenagers who hang out on the street corners around the church.

These are the different zones:[4]

Central business district. The central business district, or center core, consists of that central area of gleaming skyscrapers. It's the heart of the city's (and sometimes the region's or state's) cultural activities, commerce and government. Few people live in central business zones. This district is home to downtown churches that attract people from throughout the metropolitan area (see Chapter 4). Some cities, such as Los Angeles, actually have several central business districts.

The transition zone. Surrounding the business district is an area of dilapidated industry and poor housing. This zone is where you'll find non-working families who survive on welfare. It includes government housing projects that have become notorious for their poor living conditions,

---

Diagram 2-3
Making Sense of the Census

The simplest way to define the city is by measuring its size or population. The U.S. Bureau of the Census defines (somewhat tediously) cities using two basic categories:[38]

● Metropolitan Statistical Area (MSA): "A geographic area consisting of a population nucleus, together with adjacent communities which have a high degree of economic and social integration with that nucleus." An area qualifies as an MSA basically if: (1) its central city has a population of at least 50,000; or (2) it includes an urbanized area of at least 50,000 with a total metropolitan population of at least 100,000.

● Central city: The largest city in each MSA. For example, the city of Houston is the central city for a large MSA that includes dozens of suburbs.

Diagram 2-4
Urban Areas

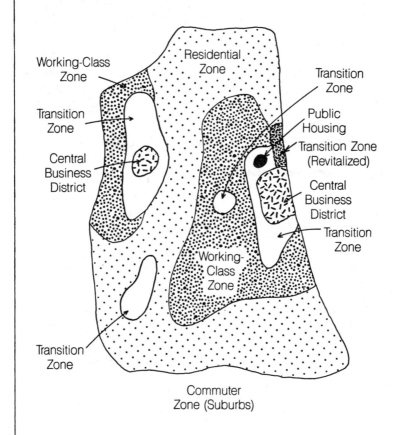

Working-Class Zone

Residential Zone

Transition Zone

Transition Zone

Public Housing

Central Business District

Transition Zone (Revitalized)

Central Business District

Transition Zone

Working-Class Zone

Transition Zone

Commuter Zone (Suburbs)

high crime and gang warfare. (See Diagram 2-5, "Government Housing Projects.")

The transition zone in some cities also contains a few revitalized sections that are being rebuilt by young, affluent professional families. These include places like the Longwood neighborhood of South Bronx, the Lafayette Park district of St. Louis and the Union Park area of Boston.

Diana Loomis is pastor of Lafayette Park United Methodist Church in a revitalized community in downtown St. Louis. She says about 70 percent of the neighborhood is baby boomers, and most are two-income families. "A lot of the people who moved into this area came back because they believe in the city and want to make it a better place for all kinds of people," she says.

These new residents like the old Victorian homes—

Diagram 2-5

Government Housing Projects

When they were envisioned and built, public housing projects seemed like an effective and compassionate way to provide adequate housing for underprivileged people. However, that dream has become a nightmare as housing projects become economic traps with overwhelming problems. "In cities across the country, buildings designed to shelter a mix of families too often imprison the poorest and most helpless," a Newsweek article reports. "Theirs is a dead-end world of strewn garbage, menacing stairwells and broken-down elevators. Homicide and rape are commonplace . . . Youth gangs run rampant and some janitors extort sex from young mothers."[39]

The article reported the following statistics about Chicago's housing projects, which federal officials call the worst in the United States:

● 145,000 people live in Chicago housing projects. Of these families, 97 percent are black, and 92 percent are headed by single women.

● The median annual income of housing-project families is $5,000. (Chicago's overall median income is $22,000.)

● Three-fourths of the residents live on welfare, and 75 percent of the residents are children.

● Rockwell Gardens on Chicago's West Side recorded eight violent crimes for every 100 people in 1987.

which they restore. And they like being close to downtown. She adds: "A lot of people are buying houses in the city because housing in the suburbs is so expensive . . . You get a lot more for your money in St. Louis."

Working-class zone. This zone is made up of the working poor in older homes. These residents are often people who have escaped the transition zone. Ethnic groups—blacks, old immigrants (Polish, Swedish) and new immigrants (Chinese, Filipino)—often populate these areas.

Residential zone. People in this zone tend to be in newer single-family dwellings and apartment buildings. They include wealthy, moderate-income and working-class families.

Commuter zone. This zone is the suburbs, made up of newer homes and middle- to upper-class residents. Though suburbs have their own shopping districts and governments, they remain economically dependent on the center city.

The City's Diversity

While cities each have the common characteristics suggested by this analysis, perhaps the best way to describe cities is to say that they're all different. They're filled with different populations, different businesses, different cultural attractions, different needs, different challenges. As Paul Tarro of Urban Youth Ministries in Kansas City, Missouri, says: "Every city is not a little Chicago or little Los Angeles . . . The environment in Minneapolis is different from Chicago."

Thus youth ministers must approach each city and each neighborhood as unique in order to minister effectively. "We need to realize that cities are not single, homogeneous units," urban ministry specialist Roger Greenway writes, "but are conglomerates of thousands of different groups, many of which require a specially designed missionary strategy."[5]

Urban youth workers agree that diversity is the key to urban youth ministry. And James DiRaddo believes that it is one reason churches haven't been effective in the urban setting. When asked to describe the city, he responds: "Which city are you talking about? What urban setting?" He says the church wants "nice things that are tightly packaged," and cities just don't come that way.

Let's look at some of the diverse characteristics of the city:

Ethnic Diversity

"There are 233 nations in the world, and in my one-mile-square block in the middle of Chicago, 60 of those nations (25 percent) are represented."[6] That's how Ray Bakke illustrates the city's ethnic diversity.

A disproportionate percentage of the country's ethnic minorities live in the city. Overall, 29 percent of U.S. families live in central cities. Yet, 58 percent of black families and 54 percent of Hispanic families now live in these cities. (See Diagram 2-6, "Ethnic Makeup of U.S. Cities.") As you can see, ethnic "minorities" are really ethnic "majorities" in some cities.

Consider these statistics:

● An article in GROUP Magazine reports that collectively "teenagers in Los Angeles high schools speak more than 100 languages. And the United States has more blacks than any country except Nigeria."[7]

● From 1910 to 1960, the African American population flip-flopped from 73 percent rural to 73 percent urban.[8] Today, 83 percent of black families live in metropolitan areas.[9]

● Los Angeles is the second largest "Mexican" city in

Diagram 2-6

Ethnic Makeup of U.S. Cities

The following chart shows the disproportionate percentage of the U.S. minority population that lives in central cities.[40]

Ethnic Background	Central Cities	Suburbs	Small Town/ Rural
All families	29%	47%	23%
White families	25%	50%	24%
Black families	58%	25%	18%
Hispanic families	54%	38%	8%

the world (4.5 million Hispanics), while Houston is the fastest-growing "Mexican" city.[10]

● Four-fifths of all Houston's schoolchildren are either Hispanic, African American or Asian.[11]

● Many urbanites are first-generation immigrants from other parts of the world. Among those cities with the highest percentage of new immigrants are: Los Angeles (22 percent); New York City (21 percent); and San Francisco (16 percent).[12]

Economic Diversity

"Urban" is not necessarily "poor." Harvie M. Conn says that, too often, people see a "monoclass" in the city made up of only ghettos. "The effect of this image is twofold," he writes. "It can close our eyes not only to the needs of shanty towns but also to the other groups that fill the city. And the same insensitivity that keeps us from planning churches for the slums impedes our vision for reaching the elite, the working class, the soldier and the politician. All disappear in a monoclass generalization that sees only the poor."[13]

A particularly dominant perception is that *all* blacks are poor. Dr. Giles A. Conwill writes that sociologists have rarely studied blacks across socioeconomic lines—as they nearly always do for whites. As a result, he says: "Class and identity are interwoven in the perception of many ethnic groups by outsiders—and this pertains especially to blacks. They are nearly always ascriptively designated as belonging to the lower socioeconomic class, notwithstanding the fact that blacks exist on all levels."[14]

Religious Diversity

Chicago's Rogers Park community has a United Methodist church, a Hare Krishna commune, an American Baptist congregation, a Unification church, a Roman Catholic parish, a Jewish synagogue, an Eckankar center, an Assyrian Orthodox church and an Eastern Yoga headquarters—all within easy walking distance.

That's not unusual for the city. David Miles sees the same diversity around his church in Queens, New York. "We have about eight different types of temples," he says. "In a four- or five-block radius, we have an Islamic mosque, Hindu temple, Sikh temple and Buddhist temple."

The urban world is rich with religious diversity. While it's true that most urban dwellers are unchurched, it's not for lack of options. The white, middle-class church may have left the city, but "the Holy Spirit did not leave," Ray Bakke writes. "The fastest-growing churches in the northern American cities are Black, and the Roman Catholics and the churches of many ethnic minorities are still strongly located in the cities."[15]

Understanding the City's Poverty

Cities have diverse populations. Not all urban people are poor. Yet the reality of urban poverty demands further exploration.

Cities are disproportionately poor compared to the national average. The U.S. Bureau of the Census reports: "In 1987, median family income was considerably higher in the suburban areas than in central cities."[16] Nationally, 14 percent of Americans live below the poverty line.[17] That figure rises to 19 percent in major cities (Metropolitan Statistical Areas) with more than 1 million people. The figures are even higher for ethnic minorities in these cities. About one-third of urban Hispanics and African Americans live in poverty.[18]

This poverty results from a complex series of social factors, which are constantly debated among urban experts. Without suggesting any definitive answers, let's briefly examine a few of the major factors behind urban poverty:

Suburban spread. After World War II, much of the middle class left the city for the more spacious, new and upscale life of the suburbs. That exodus drained much of the city's economic life, for it replaced stable, middle-income communities with unstable, low-income communities. John Shelby Spong describes the result:

> Super highways built with public money allowed suburban commuters to put larger and larger distances between themselves and the stresses of city life. As a result, the core cities were slowly reduced to near-bankruptcy,

becoming communities of the poor, of the elderly and of ethnic minorities at the bottom of the socioeconomic system.[19]

Lack of job opportunities. Some people look at the urban poor and say: "Why don't they all just get jobs? There are pages of job opportunities listed in the want ads." Unfortunately, it's not that easy. David Claerbaut notes three primary reasons why unemployment is such a problem in the inner city:[20]

● First, most jobs in today's post-industrial cities require education and skills that most poor people do not have.

● Second, many factories have moved to suburbs where land is cheaper. As a result, the inner-city poor can't get to the jobs, even if they are qualified. Also, many factories in the industrial cities have simply closed down, leaving no jobs in those communities.

● Finally, the jobs that are available to the poor most often pay minimum wage which, with most urban families, still leaves people below the poverty level. Plus, job-related expenses (travel, babysitting, and so forth) often make it uneconomical to take the job.

Redlining. Redlining is a banking practice that makes it impossible to get a mortgage loan in what is perceived as a deteriorating urban community. "When black people begin to move in," sociologist Tony Campolo writes, "the bankers look at the map and, as the name indicates, draw a line around that section of the city. That means they will no longer lend money for mortgages to people who want to buy property in that area."[21]

Redlining results in no money being invested in the community. Instead, "the money flows steadily out, with the neighborhood financial institutions sending money to larger downtown banks," Claerbaut explains. "In the meantime, nothing is built or developed, and the community deteriorates."[22]

Slum landlording. Slum landlords move into redlined areas and use cash to purchase large blocks of property at extremely deflated prices. They, in turn, rent out the buildings at inflated prices so they can recoup their investment quickly. They make no repairs to keep their overhead and taxes as low as possible. Often they don't provide utilities such as heat during the winter, making colds, influenza, pneumonia and frostbite common inner-city health problems.

With little legal protection in many cities, tenants have few avenues to combat the problem. And codes for building standards—if they exist—are often not enforced in low-income communities. When the building deteriorates so much that it collapses or is condemned, it is "torched"— "accidentally" burned to the ground. This relieves the landlord of maintenance expenses and enables him or her to collect fire insurance for the "loss."[23]

Tax structure. Large cities are notorious for bad streets, inadequate schools, underequipped hospitals and police departments, and poor city services in general. Why? Urban experts point to two primary factors:

● First, cities must rely on a smaller tax base because city residents, as a whole, don't have as much money. Put simply, urban residents can't afford better services.

● Second, because suburbs are economically dependent on the center city, city residents in effect pay for services that suburbanites use. As David Claerbaut writes: "Suburbanites drive in on public expressways and city streets that are paid for by city taxes, drink city water, flush city toilets and walk city pavements, but they pay taxes and acquire goods and services in a suburban municipality."[24]

Tony Campolo is even more to the point. He says cities cannot operate their schools and other services adequately because they put money into services that are used mainly by suburbanites—art museums, sports stadiums, airports.[25]

Getting to Know Your City

This chapter has emphasized that each city and each community is unique. That's what makes urban youth ministry so challenging. To minister effectively to urban teenagers, you need to get to know your *own* community—its history, its people, its institutions, its needs, its opportunities. Here are some simple steps you can take to update your perception of your ever-changing community.

Walk around the neighborhood. When Dave Carver moved to Buffalo, New York, from Pittsburgh, Pennsylvania, the first thing he did was walk around the neighborhood. This gave him a chance to get a feel for the community and get acquainted with its residents.

Walking around a community can answer lots of questions:

- What emotions does the community evoke? fear? excitement? curiosity?
- What are the businesses like?
- Who lives here?
- Is it a bustling or quiet community?
- What do the schools look like?
- Where do the teenagers "hang out"?

Visit other youth ministers and pastors. Ray Bakke writes: "It is sad to see churches competing with each other, or with other agencies, to reach the same groups . . . Because the city is so pluralistic, we need every single denomination, ministry-style and model . . . There is some ministry which a house church can do, and others which a cathedral can do."[26]

Visit other ministers in your community. Discover their perceptions of the neighborhood, its teenagers and their needs:

- What are the most important lessons they've learned in their ministries?
- What ministries are other churches providing?

Not only does such networking give you valuable insights into the community, but it also provides opportunities for cooperation and mutual support within the Christian community as you seek to reach and minister to young people.

Visit institutions. Schools, businesses, law enforcement agencies, social-service agencies and other local institutions have people who can tell you a great deal about the community.

- Imagine the insights you can gain about the neighborhood's teenagers from a perceptive teacher who spends several hours a day with them. Moreover, many urban youth workers have discovered that an excellent way to get to know urban teenagers is to volunteer as coaches or tutors to a school system that cannot afford to hire adequate staff.

● Real estate offices can provide information about community attractions, history and services.

● Political and community organizations can share their perceptions of the community's concerns and needs. They can describe current services for teenagers—as well as any voids your congregation may be able to fill.

Research the community. The library is a treasure of information about communities. With a little digging, you can discover valuable information for your ministry. This might include:

● The ethnic and economic makeup of your community
● The number of teenagers in the community
● The marital and employment status of families
● The community's educational level

Take your own interviews or surveys. Surveys and interviews can be ambitious projects for a church to undertake, but they yield valuable information. And they don't have to be detailed or scientific—your goal is to fine-tune your perceptions, not to write a research paper. Even three or four simple questions on a sheet of paper can help confirm or refute your assumptions.

You can survey or interview several different populations (both inside and outside the church):

● Teenagers—their needs, their worries, their attitudes about and expectations of the church.

● Parents—their concerns about their teenagers, their own struggles as parents, their perceptions of the neighborhood and its needs.

● Community organizations—their perceptions of teenagers and their needs, unmet needs in the community that your church might be able to address.

If you choose, you can take a more formal survey of the young people in your church and community. An excellent tool is *Determining Needs in Your Youth Ministry*, a 162-question survey kit complete with worksheets and tools for using the results.[27]

A Christian Attitude Toward the City

The city is a diverse and challenging context for youth ministry. Some things about the city are easy to celebrate and enjoy—cultural, educational and social opportunities. But at the same time, some things about the city are difficult to live with—drug abuse, crime, clashing values. How do urban youth workers maintain a healthy attitude toward the city?

Ray Bakke offers this challenge:

> We all can be timid Christians, when faced with modern conditions . . . The lonely commuter trapped in his car may feel more secure than he would feel walking home through a slum to a city address. But it is only by living in the city, with a theological vision for the city, that we can attempt to reach the city's people.[28]

Reflection and Action

1. On a sheet of paper, write all the words that come to mind when you think of the city. Then look at your list. What does your selection tell you about your attitude toward the city?

2. Go to your local library and find some basic statistics about your city. How large is the central city? the whole metropolitan area? What is the ethnic makeup of the city?

3. Get a map of your city and try to identify the different zones: central business districts, the transition zones (including areas that are being revitalized), the working-class zones, the residential zones and the commuter zones.

4. Look at the map you've drawn. What does it tell you about the people around your church? Are you planted solidly in one zone, or are you on the border between two zones?

5. Think about where your church members live:

● Do they all live in one zone, or do they come from several zones?

● What implications might this discovery have for your youth ministry?

6. Walk around the block in your community. Look for signs of the community's diversity:

● What are the ethnic backgrounds of the people you see?

● Is everyone from essentially the same economic class?

● What churches and other religious institutions do you see?

● What are some signs of diverse lifestyles?

7. What symptoms of urban poverty do you see in your own community? What factors would you add to the list on page 44, based on your experience?

8. Make a list of the other churches, institutions, agencies and organizations in your community that reach out to teenagers. Set yourself a schedule for visiting them.

9. If you know of individuals who are particularly in touch with teenagers' needs in your community, invite them to talk to your church board or your youth ministry volunteers about how your congregation can help meet those needs.

Endnotes

[1]David Claerbaut, *Urban Ministry* (Grand Rapids, MI: Zondervan Publishing House, 1983), 15-16.

[2]Francis Schaeffer, *Death in the City* (Downers Grove, IL: InterVarsity, 1969), 20, quoted in Harvie M. Conn, *A Clarified Vision for Urban Mission: Dispelling the Urban Stereotypes* (Grand Rapids, MI: Zondervan Publishing House, 1987), 26.

[3]Conn, *A Clarified Vision for Urban Mission: Dispelling the Urban Stereotypes*, 9.

[4]Based on classifications and descriptions in Claerbaut, *Urban Ministry*, 49-50.

[5]Roger S. Greenway, "Reaching the Unreached in the Cities," Urban Mission 2. (May 1985), 3, quoted in Conn, *A Clarified Vision for Urban Mission: Dispelling the Urban Stereotypes*, 194.

[6]Ray Bakke with Jim Hart, *The Urban Christian* (Downers Grove, IL: InterVarsity Press, 1987), 32.

[7]Jolene L. Roehlkepartain, "Ethnic Diversity: The Face of the Future," GROUP Magazine (March-April 1988), 64-69.

[8]Gaylord B. Noyce, *Survival and Mission for the City Church* (Philadelphia: The Westminster Press, 1975), 26.

[9]U.S. Bureau of the Census, Current Population Reports: Population Characteristics, Series P-20, No. 424, *Household and Family Characteristics: March 1987.* (U.S. Government Printing Office, Washington, DC, 1988), Table 2.

[10]Bakke with Hart, *The Urban Christian*, 33.

[11]Bakke with Hart, *The Urban Christian*, 33.

[12]U.S. Bureau of the Census statistics, reported in *The World Almanac and Book of Facts 1988* (New York: Pharos Books, 1987), 540.

[13]Conn, *A Clarified Vision for Urban Mission: Dispelling the Urban Stereotypes*, 192.

[14]Giles A. Conwill, "The Word Becomes Black Flesh: A Program for Reaching the American Black" in *Evangelizing Blacks*, edited by Glenn C. Smith (Wheaton, IL: Tyndale House Publishers, 1988), 61.

[15]Bakke with Hart, *The Urban Christian*, 56-57.

[16]U.S. Bureau of the Census, Current Population Reports: Consumer Income, Series P-60, No. 161, *Money Income and Poverty Status in the United States: 1987* (U.S. Government Printing Office, Washington, DC, 1988), 3.

[17]U.S. Bureau of the Census, Current Population Reports: Consumer Income, Series P-60, No. 160, *Poverty in the United States, 1986* (U.S. Government Printing Office, Washington, DC, 1988), 19.

[18]*Money, Income and Poverty Status in the United States: 1987*, Table 18.

[19]John Shelby Spong, "The Urban Church: Symbol and Reality," The Christian Century (September 12-19, 1984), 828-831.

[20]Claerbaut, *Urban Ministry*, 74.

[21]Anthony Campolo, "The Sociological Nature of the Urban Church," in *Metro-Ministry*, edited by David Frenchak and Sharrel Keyes (Elgin, IL: David C. Cook Publishing, 1979), 36.

[22]Claerbaut, *Urban Ministry*, 38.

[23]Claerbaut, *Urban Ministry*, 39.

[24]Claerbaut, *Urban Ministry*, 33.

[25]Campolo, "The Sociological Nature of the Urban Church," 37.

[26]Bakke with Hart, *The Urban Christian*, 117-128.

[27]Peter L. Benson and Dorothy L. Williams, *Determining Needs in Your Youth Ministry* (Loveland, CO: Group Books, 1987).

[28]Bakke with Hart, *The Urban Christian*, 85.

[29]These myths are the basis of Conn's whole book.

[30]Conn, *A Clarified Vision for Urban Mission: Dispelling the Urban Stereotypes*, 55.

[31]Conn, *A Clarified Vision for Urban Mission: Dispelling the Urban Stereotypes*, 72.

[32]U.S. Department of Justice, Bureau of Justice Statistics, *Report to the Nation on Crime and Justice* (U.S. Government Printing Office, Washington, DC, 1988), 29.

[33]Conn, *A Clarified Vision for Urban Mission: Dispelling the Urban Stereotypes*, 98-99.

[34]Conn, *A Clarified Vision for Urban Mission: Dispelling the Urban Stereotypes*, 129.

[35]Conn, *A Clarified Vision for Urban Mission: Dispelling the Urban Stereotypes*, 191-192.

[36]Cheryl Russell, "Bright Lights, Big City," American Demographics (August 1988), 13.

[37]David M. Hummon, "Urban Views: Popular Perspectives on City Life," Urban Life (April, 1986), 3-36.

[38]These categories are defined in most Census Bureau population reports.

[39]John McCormick, "Can Chicago Beat the Odds?" Newsweek (January 2, 1989), 24-26.

[40]U.S. Bureau of the Census, Current Population Reports: Population Characteristics, Series P-20, No. 424, *Household and Family Characteristics: March 1987* (U.S. Government Printing Office, Washington, DC, 1988), Table 2.

CHAPTER 3

The Many Faces of Urban Teenagers

When Dave Carver began ministering in the white, working-class community around First Presbyterian Church of Crafton Heights in Pittsburgh he often felt frustrated because "I wasn't working with black, ghetto kids, so I wasn't doing *real* urban youth ministry."

What Carver discovered, though, was that living in the city—not ethnic or economic background—is what makes teenagers "urban." "I have a lot more in common with the guy who's working in the ghetto," he says, "than with the guy who works with kids on the San Diego beach."

●

Sometimes people stereotype urban teenagers by their ethnic background, their economic status, their family make-up or their problems—drugs, gangs, dropouts, and so forth. Indeed, each of these factors can be significant. However, just because some urban teenagers *tend* to be or do things doesn't mean those qualities or problems are true for every urban teenager. Many urban teenagers *do* have problems with drug abuse. But so do suburban teenagers. Many urban teenagers *are* black. But not all of them. Diagram 3-1, "Myths and Realities About Urban Teenagers," illustrates some of the fallacies often associated with urban teenagers.

Like any other group of people, urban teenagers vary greatly depending on many factors: where they live, if they go to church, their family background, their family's economic status, and others. Oversimplified stereotypes of urban young people have at least two serious side-effects in youth ministry:

● First, the stereotypes overlook certain populations. For example, since the stereotype says urban teenagers are poor, the wealthier urban young people are often ignored by the church.

● Second, by placing all urban teenagers in a single category, churches can be unfair to those teenagers who overcome the challenges and avoid the negative behaviors. As youth worker Phill Carlos Archbold of First Church of the Brethren, Brooklyn, New York, says: "You hear of the bad kids. You don't hear of the good ones. You hear of the bad guys in school. You don't hear about the kids who are making it."

In an attempt to avoid these kinds of stereotypes, this chapter will look briefly at urban teenagers from several directions, emphasizing the diversity of their experiences. We will concentrate especially on the following areas:

● How city life affects teenagers

● How economic status affects teenagers in the city

● How ethnic background affects teenagers in the city

How City Life Affects Teenagers

What is it about urban teenagers that makes them urban? How does living in a large, diverse, densely populated community affect their attitudes, behaviors and perspectives? What makes urban teenagers unique?

Most urban youth workers believe living in the city has both positive and negative effects on teenagers. And they believe youth workers can build on the positives and help overcome some of the negatives. Let's look at some of these effects of city life and their implications for youth ministry.

City Life's Effect on Self-Esteem

Annette was nine when Marietta Ramsey of Bethel African Methodist Episcopal Church in Baltimore met her. Ramsey became like a mother to this girl, who by age 15 was in serious conflict with her family.

Annette was always in trouble. At one point, Annette's mother kicked her out of the house because of her disobedience. Through her teenage years, Annette lived in rebellion. She slept with different guys—not because she loved them, but because she didn't love herself.

"Yes, she was very attractive," says Ramsey. "Yes, her mother showered her with material things. But she really didn't like herself. So much of what she did was to prove that 'I am a lovable person.' She didn't feel any love from her mother. Other people did love her, but it didn't compensate for the absence of her mother's love."

Like most urban youth workers, Ramsey sees low self-esteem as the central need of urban kids. "Many of our kids," she says, "don't feel good about who they are. And, you know, when you don't feel good about who you are, you can get caught up in a whole other bag of things that are wrong."

Youth minister Harold Wright of Friendship Baptist Church in Vallejo, California, shares Ramsey's perspective. He says he spends most of his time focusing on self-esteem, and he deals with issues such as drugs, sexuality and identity out of this context.

Dave Carver says urban young people's basic need is for unconditional love. "Urban kids aren't looking so much to

Diagram 3-1

Myths and Realities About Urban Teenagers

Government statistics present interesting correctives to some of the myths about urban teenagers (ages 12 to 17). (This particular report did not include a statistical breakdown of other ethnic groups.)[41]

Myth: All urban teenagers are ethnic minorities.
Reality: Sixty percent of urban teenagers are white; 25 percent are African American; and 15 percent are Hispanic American. Of course, minorities do make up a greater percentage of the urban population than the general population:

Urban Teenagers

Hispanics   Blacks   Whites
(15%)   (25%)   (60%)

Teenagers in the U.S.

Hispanics Blacks   Whites
(8%)   (14%)   (78%)

Myth: Most urban teenagers come from single-parent families.
Reality: Many do. But 66 percent of teenagers in the nation's central cities come from two-parent families. One exception: Black teenagers are more likely to come from single-parent families than two-parent families. Here are the percentages of urban teenagers from single-parent families:
- All urban teenagers: 34 percent
- Black urban teenagers: 57 percent
- Hispanic urban teenagers: 33 percent
- White urban teenagers: 26 percent
Nationally, 21 percent of teenagers live in single-parent families.

be entertained by a youth program. That's a nice thing if they can have it—fun and everything. But I think they're looking for somebody who will tell them they're significant, for someone to tell them that their lives make a difference and that they're important."

Several factors contribute to low self-esteem among many urban teenagers:

Family problems. Many urban teenagers come from families that don't provide adequate affirmation and support. In some cases, problems result from dysfunctional family relationships because of drug or alcohol abuse. Other times, parents themselves—who may be unemployed and without hope—have such low esteem that they can't help their teenagers catch a vision for themselves. And finally, problems can result because parents are always away from home working and therefore take little time to nurture their teenager's esteem.

Carver tells about a girl named Melissa. She's really tough, he says. She regularly gets suspended for fighting. She has probably smoked since she was five. And her father is an alcoholic. One day Melissa came to Carver's house crying. She said to Carver: "Every day when I leave my house, my father tells me I'm no good. He tells me I'm not good for nothin', and I'd better not get pregnant. I'm no good."

"Her whole self-esteem," Carver remembers, "had been blasted because of the way her family is. And it's going to take some pretty powerful counseling to get her to the point where she's healthy."

Society's success ethic. Urban teenagers who live in poverty hear constant messages that implicitly condemn them for being "unsuccessful." Jay Macleod studied teenagers in public housing. He writes in *Ain't No Makin' It*: "When Clarendon Heights residents are asked for their address at a bank, store or office, their reply is often met with a quick glance of curiosity, pity, superiority, suspicion or fear. In an achievement-oriented society, residence in public housing is often an emblem of failure, shame and humiliation."[1]

Limited opportunities. When people manage to break out of inner-city poverty, they almost always leave the community. This "success exodus" leaves disadvantaged young people with another disadvantage: few successful role models in the community. Indeed, the most successful people, by outward appearances, are the drug dealers who have fancy clothes and fancy cars.

This lack of positive models can result in "a tendency not to see a lot of opportunity in life," says Bryan Stone, pastor of Liberation Community of the Church of the Nazarene in Ft. Worth, Texas. "One of the biggest challenges is to reaffirm their potential."

Like many other urban youth workers, Stone tries to introduce his black and Hispanic teenagers to as many "successful" positive role models as possible—in sports, business, entertainment, politics, church work.

Once Stone took the youth group to a Jesse Jackson political rally—not just to hear Jackson, but also to see all the other black candidates on the platform. Stone remembers the result of that trip: "We had a guy who saw all that, and

---

Diagram 3-2

Success in Sneakers

"In the inner city, you are what you wear on your feet."
—Brian Washington, a Harlem teenager

If that's true, the 18-year-old who said it is really somebody. He has 150 pairs of sneakers.

The Wall Street Journal reports that inner-city teenagers set off feet fashion flurries by their choices in sneakers. "What Paris is to haute couture, Harlem is to sneakers," the paper declared. "Fashion trends start here and in other inner cities and spread to suburbia and the rest of middle America."

This tennis shoe craze illustrates how urban teenagers seek status in the few things they can own. "To an inner-city kid, wearing a $120 pair of sneakers is a statement that his life ain't so bad," says a Washington, D.C., shoe salesperson. As a result, many teenagers in large cities buy two or three pairs each month—compared to two or three pairs each year elsewhere.

The fashion statement is having serious consequences, though. Police, school officials and social workers in major cities see teenagers turn to selling drugs to remain hip.[42]

he's now interested . . . in entering the political arena himself and making a difference in that way."

Misplaced Status Symbols

One of the results of low self-esteem is that urban teenagers look for external ways to feel important. And like most people in this society, the first place they look is money. "Today's urban youth live to make money," Marietta Ramsey says. "They live to wear designer clothes—the leathers, the suedes, the $100 tennis shoes. And this is where they get their good feelings from."

This emphasis on materialism appears in every economic group. Dave Carver, who worked with working-class whites, says: "They're acutely aware of the material things they don't have . . . So they try to get a couple of nice things—a skateboard, clothes—and put a lot of their esteem into those things."

Ironically, poor inner-city teenagers sometimes set fashion trends for the whole youth culture. See Diagram 3-2, "Success in Sneakers."

The City's Numerous Attractions

"Anything you want you can have in New York City." That statement by youth worker David Miles of Flushing, New York, captures a key benefit of city life. Cities offer dozens of options and attractions—museums, shops, music, restaurants, night life. Young people have opportunities to go to professional ball games, renowned museums and outstanding music concerts. With a subway token or a bus fare, they're free to explore the whole city.

Yet these options in the city can also lead to misplaced values and negative behaviors—drug abuse, gangs, sexual activity. "There are a lot of options for the young kids," Chicago youth worker Steve Pedigo says. "More so than ever before. That's true across society, but it's really true in the cities."

Teenagers' exposure to many negative influences is a significant concern of urban youth workers. "The urban world offers our young people so much," says Marietta Ramsey. But the social activities often involve drugs, sex and sometimes violence. So the church says: "No, you can't go to this club. And you can't do this. No, you can't do that." In the end, Ramsey says, "the church has taken away . . . all avenues for social development."

Ramsey, who is also a public school teacher, says that instead of just condemning and taking away negative influences, the church must offer positive alternatives. "If you're going to counteract their interests in the world, then you've got to offer them something . . . You really can't dictate where the kids go . . . so you have to offer alternatives."

In his booklet, *Winning and Keeping Teens in the Church*, Melvin E. Banks suggests a similar perspective: "Taking away one pleasure from youth without substituting another is very ineffective in changing behavior. If you ask young people to avoid the kind of parties that end up in smoking pot, drinking and sex, you ought to provide a different kind of activity which allows them to have genuine enjoyment. This points up the necessity of a complete program to meet all the needs of youth."[2]

Many urban youth ministries offer positive alternatives. For example, Lawndale Community Church in Chicago, offers a variety of after-school activities, including computer skills training and recreation. Other churches, such as Manhattan Bible Church, have fun, entertaining Friday night outreach programs that involve recreation, games, music and speakers. About 120 kids attend every week.

The Realities of City Life

Robert, 14, lives in a low-income neighborhood of Chicago. To buy new shoes, he worked for months selling newspapers. "You shoulda seen that boy's face the day he walked outta here in those shoes," his mother says. "He was nine feet off the ground." But Robert was crying when he returned home. Older boys had beaten him and taken his shoes.[3]

Urban teenagers are exposed to most of society's vices daily. "They learn at a very early age what life is all about," Phill Carlos Archbold says. "And they must deal with that." Many low-income young people live with their mother and a man, who may change every week or every day, Archbold says. Young people hear fights at night. They watch people using drugs in the stairwells of their tenement buildings. And they see couples having sex in the building doorways.

Youth worker Bruce Wall of Twelfth Baptist Church, Boston says inner-city teenagers "have to deal every single day in the school and on the street with life and death issues." He adds: "I have so many kids who spend so much time trying to survive that they do not prepare for life . . . It's unfair that they have to cope with so much reality at such a young age. They're taught how to shoot an Uzi when they're 8 or 9 years old."

The issues urban teenagers deal with are markedly different from the concerns of suburban teenagers. "The things most kids in the suburbs are worried about are what their parents will do to them if they have a bad grade or what to wear to impress someone at school," writes Tracy Hipps of Inner City Impact in Chicago. "But, added to that, the urban kids have to worry about wearing the wrong colors and being mistaken for a gang member. They wonder if they will make it home each day without anyone chasing them to beat them up."[4]

This exposure to so much so early builds a thick shell around urban teenagers. They can feel lonely and isolated. "The city can be so hard," says Phill Carlos Archbold. "I can live in a building and not know any neighbors. The church must reach out to these people who are hurting and needing a friend."

Wendell Fisher agrees. Urban teenagers, he says, "really need a lot of love and a lot of patience. It takes a long time to break through the hard shell they've built around themselves. These kids are very hard, you know, because they've seen a lot of hurt and they've had to learn to deal with it the best they could. So one way they deal with it is just to become tough and hard."

Fisher illustrates by telling about two kids in his youth group whose dads were murdered in the past year. "It's amazing just to see how much hardness these kids have developed to handle this kind of thing. It's like death is so commonplace here that it doesn't shake them as much. And, of course, they bottle it up inside of them and have to deal with it later."

David Miles tells about a mild-mannered group member who went to a different neighborhood. He was surrounded by a group of guys, one of whom was wearing an expensive sheepskin coat. When the big, burly guy asked, "What are you doing in our neighborhood?" this gentle teenager looked up and said, "If you even look at me wrong, I'm gonna be wearing your jacket." Miles says the teenager would never hurt anyone, but his survival instinct elicited a strong response.

Breaking through this tough shell becomes a significant challenge in urban youth ministry. Churches must create "safe space" where teenagers can let down their guards—if only for an hour—and share their feelings, fears, hopes, joys, struggles and faith.

At the same time, living in the city also can add to teenagers' ingenuity and creativity. Because they don't have ready-made attractions and recreation (baseball leagues, shopping malls and other suburban luxuries), they learn to create their own entertainment. Dave Carver tells about taking his youth group to a Christian rock concert. Halfway through, the sound system went out, and the concert came to a halt. As the crowd started becoming restless, some of the guys in Carver's group began asking, "What can we do that would be fun?" They came up with an idea that occupied the whole auditorium until the sound was fixed. They ran across the street to a drug store and purchased a bag of balloons. The whole auditorium joined in for a fun balloon-volleyball game.

Recreation in the City

Drive by McArthur Park on the corner of Alvarado Street and Wilshire Boulevard in Los Angeles some Saturday evening. You'll see 10,000 to 25,000 Hispanic young people milling around, meeting, talking and courting. That's because those evenings in the park are the center of social life for the city's Hispanic community, urban ministry specialist H.O. Espinoza says.

Urban teenagers don't "go out." They "hang out." "In an urban neighborhood, your kids are all over the place,"

Art Erickson says. "They're in parks. They're on street corners. And they're in schools."

Living so close together makes it easy to congregate outside. And that's part of the reason they do it. But another reason is that they have nowhere else to go:

● Their homes or apartments are crowded.

● There are few, if any, recreation facilities or parks nearby, and they may be unsafe because of gang activity. For example, Preston Robert Washington reports that there's only one movie theater in all of Harlem—a community with 175,515 households.[5]

● Financially-strapped urban schools cannot offer teenagers extracurricular activities. Even athletic programs are often cut because schools can't afford to hire coaches.

● There certainly are no malls to go to like suburban kids do.

As a result, the best way to get to know urban teenagers is often just to walk around the neighborhood in the late afternoon while they're socializing on the street corners.

"Psychological Overload" in City Life

By definition, cities are made up of lots of people living close together. In some areas, the numbers are staggering. For example, density is so high in the South Bronx that more than 1,500 people could walk from their apartments to church at St. Peter's-in-the-Bronx in less than three minutes.[6]

This kind of population density creates a different mind-set. Visitors to major cities are struck by the "crazy" things city people do in public. They walk along the street singing, talking, laughing or blasting a "boom box" with no regard for the people around them.

Why do they do that? Aren't they embarrassed? Probably not. In fact, they may not be aware that anyone's around. Because they have little or no personal "space," they must create that space themselves. So they learn to ignore people. They choose whom to talk to and whom to call a friend.

Because of the masses, Ray Bakke writes, urban people suffer from "psychological overload." They develop filters that "enable us to cope with noise, the constant bombardment of sales messages and thousands of casual daily relationships. People survive in the city by wearing mental blinkers: by filtering what they accept, and by opting out of relationships and situations."[7]

These "mental blinkers" are a key factor in reaching urban teenagers. These teenagers have learned to choose their relationships carefully. They tend to develop deep relationships with only a few people, David Miles notes. As a result, he says, "When you really touch their lives, you'll probably have a friend for life."

James DiRaddo tells about a youth worker in Philadelphia who doesn't plan traditional programs, but focuses all his energy on building relationships. He takes kids around the city in his car. They go out for pizza. They sit on the church steps and talk. And while his approach doesn't fit the expectations of most churches, DiRaddo says, this youth worker has had a significant impact on the kids' lives because he's taken the time to build relationships—when so few other adults take that time.

Diversity in City Life

While the city can affect teenagers in many negative ways, a major advantage to city life is that it fosters tolerance and acceptance for people who are different. By going to school with other ethnic groups and by associating with teenagers from other income brackets, young people learn to accept people who are different from themselves.

Because of this cosmopolitan mix, many urban youth workers believe prejudice is less of a problem in the city than in other settings. "These kids have been raised in multi-ethnic situations and multi-economic situations," Diana Loomis explains. "They have a very wide-open understanding, and they're very tolerant of differences in people. I think they have a real gift to bring to the church."

Of course, the opposite side of tolerance is prejudice, which is certainly a concern in many cities. The youth group at Sherman Street Christian Reformed Church in Grand Rapids, Michigan, had a "Bigger or Better" scavenger hunt. Teams were each given a cotton swab to start, and their job was to trade whatever item they had for something bigger or better that the youth group could use.

One group of black kids from the group managed to trade up for an old TV set. Police arrested the team as it walked down the street, assuming the kids had stolen the television. Too often, such racist assumptions are a daily part of city life for some teenagers.

Different Economic Groups in the City

Economic differences may have a greater impact on urban youth ministry than does any other single factor. The issues youth workers face in working with teenagers in government housing are markedly different from the issues they face if they're ministering to the working poor, the middle class or the wealthy.

Often the different economic groups live right next to each other. For example, Chicago's exclusive "Gold Coast" looms over the notorious Cabrini-Green government housing project. Similar stark contrasts can be seen in cities across the country. Therefore, it's important to look at the different income levels and the types of issues each face.

Non-Working Poor

The non-working poor are those who must live on welfare and who have only sporadic and unstable jobs. A study of the nation's 50 largest cities found that the number of residents below the poverty line is increasing, while the overall population is decreasing. The report estimates that 6.7 million of these cities' residents live in poverty. About 3.1 million of these people are black. Moreover, the report warned that these poor people are becoming more isolated and concentrated in low-income communities.[8]

The non-working poor also include homeless teenagers— up to 2 million nationwide, and 20,000 in New York City. Eighty percent of the homeless teenagers in New York City become prostitutes, and at least 7 percent of these are infected with the AIDS virus.[9]

This non-working poor population is caught in a cycle of poverty and hopelessness that demands the church's particular attention and compassion. Beyond the obvious lack of resources, living in such poverty has several negative side-effects:

● Family life is often unstable. A disproportionate number of the non-working poor are single mothers with children.

● They have little sense of ownership because they own little or nothing. Thus they tend to abuse rental property and don't know how to care for things.

● They have inadequate educational opportunities. Public schools in low-income communities are notoriously inadequate. And the dropout rate among these teenagers is unusually high.

● They feel hopeless, and they see few opportunities to improve their situation. "Pessimism and hopelessness corrode the spirit," David Claerbaut writes.[10]

● While they have a great deal of free time, these people have few opportunities for recreation and personal enrichment. Impoverished communities rarely have adequate recreational facilities. And homes are usually so crowded that they offer no privacy or opportunity for hobbies.

Working Poor

James DiRaddo grew up in a working-poor community. He describes these communities by saying they don't have much, but at least everyone works—usually in blue-collar industrial and service-industry jobs. Many new immigrants are part of this population.

Dave Carver says kids from this background have more hope than the non-working poor. "They have more investment in the system," he explains. "They think, maybe the system can work for them . . . They have the ability to think of things that can be better for them personally."

However, they're not like middle-class suburbanites, even though they may sometimes pretend to be. "We go to conferences with suburban kids, and it's real obvious which kids are the urban kids," Carver explains. They try to dress like the other kids, but you can see the differences. For example, he explains, "My kids were almost always the ones who smoked."

Carver also tells about taking his kids back to the suburb where he grew up. "The kids couldn't believe these people had lawns and their own bedrooms in the house," he recalls.

In other ways, these teenagers are much like their peers from non-working families. Many come from single-parent families, and most have little opportunity for continuing education. Carver estimates that only 15 percent of the adults in his Pittsburgh community have post-high school degrees.

Middle Class

While many middle-class people have moved to suburbs, not all have. Established, stable communities within cities include middle-class families of all ethnic groups. Young professionals who have moved into revitalized communities are also part of this population, though some are part of the elite.

Middle-class teenagers in the city are much like middle-class teenagers everywhere. They live comfortably, and they have high aspirations for themselves. However, the city does affect them in several ways:

● They're exposed to different ethnic and economic groups. Thus their perspective is more cosmopolitan and global than their suburban peers. "These kids look past differences more than adults do," says Rob Grotheer of First United Methodist Church in Houston.

● Unlike people from low-income levels, middle-income teenagers sometimes have trouble building social networks, particularly in larger cities. They don't have yards to relax in or malls where they can "hang out." And parks are usually dangerous for teenagers, particularly in the evenings. As a story in New York Woman reported: "If there's anything that makes life in New York different for teenagers, it's the lack of obvious places to hang out—places where they can have privacy without spending money."[11]

● They're spread out all over the city. The urban middle class tends not to live in confined neighborhoods. And when they do, their kids often go to different private and accelerated public schools. They have few opportunities to build relationships with their peers.

United Methodist pastor Diana Loomis says her middle-class kids attend St. Louis' magnet (or accelerated) schools across the city. So even though they may all live in the same community, they may have difficulty finding friends. As a result, she says, "the church becomes essentially a common ground for a lot of these kids."

The Urban Elite

The elite are the people who make cities the nation's centers of power, commerce, fashion, law, politics and industry. Though many live in suburbs, others live in exclusive historic homes, condominiums and penthouses in the city.

Teenagers in an elite urban world made headlines in 1986 when an upscale New York teenager strangled his girlfriend while having sex with her in Central Park. The incident brought to light a "Manhattan circle of rich and privileged young people for whom life is private schools, fancy apartments, foreign vacations and underage drinking."[12]

This elite urban teenage population is often overlooked in discussions of urban youth ministry. Government statistics show that 17 percent of families in the large cities have annual incomes above $50,000, and 6 percent have incomes above $75,000.[13]

Ironically, the problems of these wealthy urban teenagers most resemble the problems of the poorest urban teenagers:

● Both tend to come from broken homes and have absentee parents.

● Both develop streetwise shells that hide emotional struggles.

● Both have easy access to drugs, alcohol and sex.

Three primary factors intersect to make the problems in this population particularly troubling:[14]

● Their parents give them large amounts of spending money. San Francisco psychologist John Levy says these wealthy teenagers suffer from "affluenza," which results from family wealth that insulates them from challenges, risks and consequences. Thus they're bored, feel guilty, have low self-esteem and are unmotivated.

● They have easy access to the city's glamorous night life. "A pseudo-sophistication develops among the children of the rich," says psychiatrist Charles William Wahl of the UCLA School of Medicine. "They are very soignée. And often that obscures some of the basic uncertainty and insecurity that middle-class kids aren't afraid to show."

● They come from broken families. Not only is divorce high among the elite, but many jet-setting parents are never home. "When parents spend 90 percent of their time making more money than they can possibly spend and 5 percent of their time with the family, those values are passed on to the kids," says Bernice Berk, a psychologist at a private Manhattan school.

Few urban churches appear to reach the teenagers in these families. Paul Tarro speculates that one problem is that youth workers, who certainly aren't wealthy, feel intimidated by the young people's money.

Different Ethnic Groups in the City

In many ways, urban youth workers are like foreign missionaries. They work with people who come from around the world. They often need to be bilingual, speaking English, along with Spanish or Chinese or Korean. Youth workers learn about the different cultures' values and priorities in order to minister effectively.

While ethnic minorities are often thought of as one group by Anglos, they're each quite unique. Indeed, you'll find distinct cultural, historical, familial, social and religious patterns within each ethnic category. For example, the category "Asian Pacific Americans" includes Americans with roots in China, Japan, India, Singapore, the Philippines, Vietnam, Korea, Thailand and other nations in that part of the world. Each of these countries has a distinct heritage which affects immigrants to the United States.

It would be impossible to discuss the unique characteristics of each ethnic group adequately.[15] Instead, let's examine some specific concerns in major urban minority groups—concerns that impact ministry to those teenagers.

Black African Americans

Black urban teenagers have been the focus of a great deal of research and concern in recent years. Search Institute summarized much of the research: "Despite increases in opportunity inspired by the Civil Rights Movement of the 1960s, that progress has now slowed to a crawl, and most black youth are not thriving. On the contrary, they are said to be being shaped by our culture into a permanent underclass."[16]

David Claerbaut notes that African Americans are the only minority group that did not come to this continent by choice.[17] Their history has been one of humiliation, oppression and prejudice. Claerbaut notes: "To expect any group to endure 350 years of assault and be anywhere but at the lower end of the social and economic structure is unrealistic. That blacks have even survived is testimony to their fortitude and character strength. They have not only survived, but have developed a culture in language, food, drama, sports and music that is abundant in diversity and impact."[18]

It should be noted that not all research about black teenagers is negative. Analysis of surveys of high school seniors found that blacks had lower usage rates of cigarettes, alcohol, marijuana and cocaine than whites.[19]

Also, recent economic gains by African Americans have made the black middle class larger than the black lower class. According to a Rand Corporation report, the middle class has grown to 56 percent of the total African American population. The report concluded, "The growth and size of the black middle class has been so spectacular that as a group it outnumbers the black poor."[20]

Yet concerns persist based on other trends. Experts point to deterioration of support systems like family, school and work as a primary factor behind the growing concerns about poor black teenagers. And at the base of all of these problems is the overriding issue of poverty.

Family. Urban youth workers trace many of the problems in black teenagers to a dysfunctional home environment. After discussing low self-esteem, misplaced values and lack of morals among the teenagers she works with, Marietta Ramsey says: "A large part of the problem goes back to the home. If parents were to do some things a little bit differently, a lot of these needs could be met."

Thus reaching the black family becomes a critical key to reaching black teenagers. "The church must minister to the entire family," youth ministry expert Buster Soaries writes. "Young people are products of their environment. The church must be prepared to minister to and treat damaged families as it attempts to save black communities."[21]

Harold Wright says the black church should "be consistently in a compassionate position of teaching families." He says families want training in parenting and adolescent issues.

Education. Urban schools are notoriously inadequate. As Gene I. Maeroff writes:

> *No white suburb in America would long tolerate the low academic achievement taken for granted in urban high schools attended largely by blacks and Hispanics. In big city after big city, minority students by the tens of thousands leave school each year—some as dropouts, some as graduates—utterly unprepared to participate in and contribute to a democratic society . . . My visits to urban high schools across the country showed them to be large, impersonal places in which students lack a sense of belonging and see no connection between what they are asked to do in the classroom and the world that awaits them outside the school.*[22]

The poor education black urban teenagers receive has serious long-term consequences. They're less likely to be able to find work, and the jobs they do find pay low salaries.

The low educational opportunities of many urban black teenagers make a tutoring ministry critical in helping these young people, Bruce Wall of Twelfth Baptist Church, Boston believes. "Any inner-city ministry must have a tutorial program," he says. We'll discuss these types of programs in more detail in Chapter 10.

Unemployment. Urban teenagers have unemployment rates 1.4 times higher than the national rate. And black teenagers are three times as likely to be unemployed as whites.[23]

Unemployment traps black teenagers in poverty with few opportunities to escape. The problem is compounded by the unusually high dropout rate among urban blacks. As a result, churches in urban black communities may need to offer job-training and dropout prevention programs to give these young people opportunities, hope and a vision for their future.

Responses

Search Institute's research suggests the following responses to these urban teenagers' needs:

- Prevention-oriented intervention
- Social skills training
- Self-esteem building
- Hope-building
- Spirituality[24]

One of the particular challenges for the African American community is to redefine itself in post-segregation times. Buster Soaries notes that "black children born in America since approximately 1970 were born in a different America than any previous generation." He continues, "These children are the first generation of descendants of slaves for whom it is illegal and punishable to treat them differently from any other people because of the color of the skin."[25]

As a result of these changes, Soaries believes the black church must become more evangelistic in order to reach teenagers. "In the more oppressive past," he writes, "the black church never needed to be actively evangelistic. The limited social options of blacks made the church a magnet that naturally attracted generation after generation."[26]

However, he says, the church has lost much of its influence in the black community, which now hears its messages and values from the media and other sources. He says the church must first get teenagers' attention, minister to the whole family, develop and rebuild neighborhoods, and "mobilize for spiritual renewal as it did for civil rights."

Hispanic Americans

Hispanics, or "Latinos," constitute the fastest-growing ethnic group in the United States. By some estimates, their growth will rise by 60 percent by the year 2000.[27] They come from places such as South America, Central America, Mexico, Puerto Rico and Cuba. They bring with them their own language, their own heritage and culture, and their strong roots in Catholicism. An estimated 85 percent of the Hispanic population in the United States is Catholic.[28]

Urban Hispanic teenagers face a number of challenges, many of which involve culture clashes between old and new cultures. Let's look at some of the specific needs:

Identity. "One of the basic traumas for Hispanic youth is the trauma of finding their identity," H.O. Espinoza explains. "Our urban youth are a very unique youth. They have a blend of the urban mentality and attitudes, the Anglo mentality and attitudes, as well as a mixture of several other races."

The challenge of living in two cultures, American and Latino, is exacerbated at home where many parents expect young people to speak Spanish and to maintain Hispanic culture. "One of the things we hear most from our young people," Espinoza says, "is 'I have to be two persons in order to have peace and in order to be with my family. I have to be one person inside the house where Spanish is spoken, where the music is Hispanic and all the culture is Hispanic. And I have to behave like a Mexican or an El Salvadoran or what have you. And then the minute I'm out the door of the house, I'm another person. I have to become another person to have friends.' And it is another language, another culture, another music."

Maria Torres-Rivera, Hispanic youth coordinator for the Archdiocese of Philadelphia, sees the same problem. "Very few kids know who they are. They don't feel like they fit anywhere," she says.

Language. The Spanish language is the most important unifying factor in Latino culture in the United States. Four-fifths of Hispanics live in homes where Spanish is spoken some or most of the time. And 75 percent of Mexican Americans say they hope they'll maintain their bilingualism.[29]

The importance of Spanish to the culture becomes a critical tension for Hispanic teenagers (just as it has become a tension in society as is evident in the debates over bilingual education and making English the official language in several states). Parents want to speak Spanish at home. But teenagers who have become enculturated in the United

States prefer speaking English. Their parents want to attend church in Spanish, Espinoza says, but the teenagers want to attend an English-speaking church.

Another result of this tension is that they don't speak either language well, Torres-Rivera says. Instead they turn to "Spanglish," a free-form blend of the two languages. Unlike broken-English efforts of earlier immigrant groups, Spanglish has become widely accepted across the country.

Some advertisers have even ventured into Spanglish to reach that market, not always successfully, though. According to Time magazine, "A Braniff airlines ad that sought to tell Spanish-speaking audiences that they could settle back *en* (in) luxuriant *cuero* (leather) seats, for example, inadvertently said they could fly without clothes (*encuero*)."[30]

Espinoza says churches have tried all kinds of experiments to reach Hispanics who are caught between two languages:

● Some just have services in English.

● Some have most of their programs in English, but offer a couple of Spanish-speaking classes.

● Some are bilingual, speaking and singing both languages at once during worship.

When he goes to speak in a Hispanic church, Espinoza says he has to ask what language they want him to speak. Often they ask him to speak a mixture of both English and Spanish.

Dropouts. Hispanic teenagers have the highest dropout rate of any ethnic group in the country. Half of all Latinos drop out of high school before graduation.[31]

The same school problems that contribute to the low educational opportunities for black teenagers also affect Hispanics. However, Hispanic teenagers also deal with a cultural difference, since Hispanic culture traditionally has not placed much emphasis on education. One Hispanic educator writes: "If you drop out to father a child or to buy a car, you're a big man. But when I came home with my Ph.D., my friends acted like they didn't know me."[32]

The education problem also grows out of the expectation that teenagers will contribute to the family's well-being, which usually means dropping out of school. Bryan Stone, who works primarily with Hispanics in Ft. Worth, Texas, describes some of the pressures on teenagers: "They carry a heavy responsibility to provide for the family. They may even drop out of school so they can provide for the family . . . They're the major source of revenue."

Responses

Hispanic American young people's specific needs require specific responses. Here are some ways to minister to those needs:

● Be aware of the culture. Get to know the teenagers and their cultural traditions, beliefs and values.

● Build self-esteem. Encourage young people to see themselves as unique and worthwhile in the context of their own cultural heritage.

● Provide tutoring and educational support. Encourage students to continue their education. Give them the support skills and vision to overcome the pressures to quit school.

● Learn the languages. Since Hispanic culture is a bilingual culture, ministers are severely handicapped if they don't know both Spanish and English. Teaching English to new immigrants can also be an important ministry.

● Involve families in the ministry. Because Hispanic culture is family-oriented, ministry will be ineffective if it doesn't support and include the whole family.

Asian Pacific Americans

Asian Pacific Americans fit few of the stereotypes of minorities in the United States. They don't have unusual problems with poverty. They're high achievers in school and business. If they start in a low-income community, most move out within a generation or two to a middle-class community.

Yet Asian Pacific American teenagers in the city face their own set of challenges. In an essay in *Asian Pacific American Youth Ministry*, Rodger Y. Nishioka identifies the following challenges and pressures for Asian American teenagers:[33]

Personal identity. Perhaps the greatest struggle for these young people involves being part of a minority racial culture that shares the same values as the predominant white culture. Nishioka writes: "They struggle with what it means to be an Asian Pacific American versus simply buying into the white culture completely."

These tensions often arise in relations between parents (who hold the values of the old country) and teenagers (who are becoming Americanized). Melanie Monteclaro of North Shore Baptist Church in Chicago, illustrates the tension by describing how Filipino parents tend to be more conservative than their Americanized teenagers about dating. High school kids often want to go on dates, but many Filipino parents won't let their children date until after they've graduated from high school.

Academic pressure. Asian Pacific Americans are noted for their academic achievement. And rightly so. But as a result, these teenagers face high academic pressure from family, school and society. "Too often," Nishioka writes, "they are labeled 'model' students and more is expected from them."

Jerald Choy of First Chinese Baptist Church in San Francisco agrees, "There's a lot of pressure on the kids to do well in school, to get into the right colleges." He says most of his English-speaking kids do well. About 95 percent of English-speaking group members go to college, and 70 percent go away to college at larger, more prestigious state schools.

This pressure to excel also shows up in the young people's career choices. Monteclaro says: "Parents really want them to get an education for a good career. Filipino youth ask themselves, 'Do I decide because my parents want it or because I want it?' "

Family pressure. Family is a supreme value in Asian culture. People work for the family's good, not for their own advancement. While that support and nurture is central to their self-understanding, its flip side has the potential of becoming an albatross if a teenager fails in some way. As Nishioka writes, "Family pressure not to bring shame and to make ancestors proud is strong and sometimes overbearing."

Racism and prejudice. Despite the city's pluralism, Asian Pacific American teenagers must still live with prejudice. Nishioka writes, "Whether it is in the form of 'slant-eye' jokes, name calling, or in a rejection letter from a major university because there are already 'too many' Asian Pacific American students, they must cope with racism."

Responses

What are some appropriate ways to address the needs of Asian Pacific American teenagers? Here are some suggestions:

● Affirm their identity and culture. The church can play an important role in helping young people celebrate their own culture and history.

● Work with families. Asian Pacific Americans have strong ties to families. By working with parents, youth ministers will have a greater influence on teenagers. Also, by cooperating with parents, youth workers can avoid conflicts that may arise because of cultural clashes.

● Offer vocational guidance. Because of pressure from families and schools, Asian Pacific American young people need support and guidance from the church in making vocational decisions. Youth workers can challenge them to make career choices based on a sense of calling and personal interest, as opposed to outside pressure.

Native Americans

More than half of all Native Americans live in urban areas. Some moved to the city voluntarily; most were forcibly moved beginning in the 1950s under a government policy of "termination." "More often than not," says Phil Tingley, "the people who signed up were moved to the city, put in dilapidated army barracks and given no training." The Kiowa tribe member who lives in San Francisco adds: "The BIA (U.S. Bureau of Indian Affairs) paid their rent for a month and left them there. Many didn't even speak English."[34]

Many of the same problems that have beset Native Americans on reservations have followed them to the city—poverty, poor health, suicide and alcoholism. Yet Native Americans have a rich and diverse heritage that has been hidden by stereotypes. Dr. Leonard P. Rascher identifies three common stereotypes:[35]

The "vanishing American" concept. Many people believe that few Native Americans exist anymore. In fact, today there are close to 1.5 million Native Americans in the country—more than half of whom live in cities.[36]

The "all Indians are alike" concept. While Native Americans do share some characteristics, Rascher notes that there are significant tribal differences and distinctions. "We need to recognize," he writes, "that Native Americans belong to separate and often independent nations of people with very specific and oftentimes unrelated concerns."[37]

The "Indians are just like other American minorities" concept. Native Americans have special status with the U.S. government. Moreover, they have strong ties to their tribal lands.

Rascher also identifies several key contemporary issues that are important to address in ministry with Native Americans. Two apply directly to teenagers:

Identity. Urban Native American young people struggle with what it means to be a Native American in the city. A report to Congress said: "The Indian youth is alienated from himself and others. He is not effectively identified with his Indian heritage, nor can he identify with the hostile, white world facing him."[38]

Urbanization. Moving from reservations to cities rarely eases the problems of the reservations. Rascher writes, "Often they find that the problems they tried to leave behind are not only still with them, but have grown to crisis proportions."[39] In the cities they find poor education, poor housing, few jobs, a lack of health care and alienation from their cultural and religious roots.

Responses

While few urban churches have reached out to Native American teenagers, there are several ways the church can minister to these young people:

● Understand their culture, history and current needs. It's impossible to understand current needs without first understanding the cultural and historical context of the Native American community. Young people also need opportunities to search for what it means to be a Christian Native American in the city.

● Avoid stereotypes. Youth workers need a clear understanding of the many differences between tribes, generations and settings.

● Communicate according to their thought patterns. Rascher writes: "Learn to communicate with illustrations, diagrams and storytelling. Teach by demonstration, not by explanation. Use appropriate gestures and other non-verbal techniques."[40]

Understanding the Differences

Throughout this chapter are disclaimers: "most;" "in many cases;" "often;" "sometimes;" "tend to." That's intentional. Because any time you begin describing people, you risk painting with too broad of a stroke, thus reinforcing destructive stereotypes. Urban youth ministers must remember that each city, neighborhood, church and teenager is different.

How can you keep them all straight? How can you remember all the differences between Hispanic and black and poor and rich urban teenagers?

You can't. And you don't have to.

What urban youth workers find they *do* have to do is to keep these differences in the backs of their minds all the time. They can help one understand dynamics, conflicts and ways to celebrate diversity.

Most urban youth workers say not to focus on these differences. Rather, focus on the teenagers. Build relationships with teenagers regardless of their income or their color. Then you'll start understanding them better than any book or workshop or video or article could ever teach you.

Reflection and Action

1. Make a list of the kids you work with. Do they fit the image you have of "urban youth"? Why or why not? What are the differences?

2. Go through the section that lists ways the city affects teenagers (page 54). Do you think these factors are mostly positive or negative? What other influences should be included in the list?

3. Do you think city life has more of a positive or negative influence on teenagers? What implications does your view have for your ministry?

4. Check with neighborhood organizations or your library for statistics on teenagers in your area. Compare your local statistics to the images of urban teenagers you saw in this chapter. What are the similarities and differences? How do your local statistics affect the way you minister to young people?

5. If you have a multi-ethnic group, divide the group into teams by ethnic background. Have each team list the challenges their ethnic group faces living in a city. Then have each team share its list with the whole group so everyone can learn more about each other.

6. Find out about your teenagers' family and economic backgrounds. What do they tell you about those teenagers and their needs?

Endnotes

[1]Jay Macleod, *Ain't No Makin' It: Leveled Aspirations in a Low-Income Neighborhood* (Boulder, CO: Westview Press, 1987), 4.

[2]Melvin E. Banks, *Winning and Keeping Teens in the Church* (Chicago: Urban Ministries, 1970), 6.

[3]Phyllis Thompson, "Case Study: The Urban Family," Missions USA, (November/December 1985), 75-83.

[4]Tracy Hipps, "Jr. High Ministry: A Look at the Inner City," (An unpublished paper, April 1987), 2. Used by permission of the author.

[5]Preston Robert Washington, *God's Transforming Spirit: Black Church Renewal* (Valley Forge, PA: Judson Press, 1988), 96-97.

[6]Bonny Vaught, "A South Bronx Ministry: Symbol and Reality," The Christian Century, (June 22-29, 1983), 616-618.

[7]Ray Bakke with Jim Hart, *The Urban Christian* (Downers Grove, IL: InterVarsity Press, 1987), 41-42.

[8]"Urban Poor: More Blacks, More Concentrated," Eternity, (May 1987), 22.

[9]Christina Kelly, "Street Kids," Sassy, (February 1989), 34-37.

[10]David Claerbaut, *Urban Ministry* (Grand Rapids, MI: Zondervan Publishing House, 1983), 56.

[11]Alexandria Auder et al., "Wishing and Hoping," New York Woman, (March-April 1987), 80-87.

[12]Samuel G. Freedman, "Glitter, Vice of 'Affluenza' Blamed in Teenager's Death," Louisville (Kentucky) Courier-Journal, (September 14, 1986), A1, A24.

[13]U.S. Bureau of the Census, Current Population Reports: Consumer Income Series P-60, No. 161, *Money Income and Poverty Status in the United States: 1987* (U.S. Government Printing Office, Washington, DC, 1988), Table 14.

[14]Freedman, "Glitter, Vice of 'Affluenza' Blamed in Teenager's Death," A1, A24.

[15]The resource listing on page 245 suggests other resources to explore for more information.

[16]Dorothy L. Williams, "Two Stories About Black Adolescents," Source newsletter, (May 1988), 1.

[17]Claerbaut, Urban Ministry, 151.

[18]Claerbaut, Urban Ministry, 154.

[19]Williams, "Two Stories About Black Adolescents," 2.

[20]David Gelman with Karen Springen, "Black and White in America," Newsweek, (March 7, 1988), 18-25.

[21]Buster Soaries, "Putting First Things First," Christianity Today, (September 19, 1986), 24-26.

[22]Gene I. Maeroff, "Withered Hopes, Stillborn Dreams: The Dismal Panorama of Urban Schools," Phi Delta Kappan, (May 1988), 633-638.

[23]"Inner City Youth: Problems and Strategies," Source newsletter, (December 1987), 1.

[24]Strategies for Promoting the Well-Being of Urban Youth, (Minneapolis, MN: Search Institute, 1987), 21.

[25]Buster Soaries, "Church Based Youth Ministry in the Black Community," (an unpublished paper distributed at GROUP Magazine's 1989 Youth Ministry University), 4. Used by permission of the author.

[26]Buster Soaries, "Putting First Things First," 24-26.

[27]Celebrating Differences: Approaches to Hispanic Youth Development, (a position paper developed by Quest International and its Hispanic Advisory Committee, Columbus, OH, 1987), 2.

[28]Celebrating Differences, 6.

[29]Celebrating Differences, 6.

[30]Janice Castro, "Spanglish Spoken Here," Time, (July 11, 1988), 53.

[31]Eugene C. Roehlkepartain (editor) The Youth Ministry Resource Book (Loveland, CO: Group Books, 1987), 101.

[32]Quoted in Celebrating Differences, 7.

[33]Rodger Y. Nishioka, "Developmental Characteristics of Youth," in Asian Pacific American Youth Ministry, edited by Donald Ng (Valley Forge, PA: Judson Press, 1988), 46-47.

[34]Cheryl Sullivan, "Indians in the City," Christian Science Monitor, (June 26, 1986), 16-17.

[35]Leonard P. Rascher, "Ministry Among Urban Indians," in Metro-Ministry, edited by David Frenchak and Sharrell Keyes (Elgin, IL: David C. Cook Publishing, 1979), 175-178.

[36]Cheryl Sullivan, "Indians in the City," Christian Science Monitor, (June 26, 1986), 16-17.

[37]Rascher, "Ministry Among Urban Indians," 177.

[38]Quoted in Rascher, "Ministry Among Urban Indians," 179.

[39]Rascher, "Ministry Among Urban Indians," 180.

[40]Rascher, "Ministry Among Urban Indians," 186.

[41]Based on U.S. Bureau of the Census, Current Population Reports, Series P-20, No. 424, Household and Family Characteristics: March 1987, (U.S. Government Printing Office, Washington, DC), 1988.

[42]Joseph Pereira, "The Well-Heeled: Pricey Sneakers Worn in Inner City Help Set Nation's Fashion Trend," Wall Street Journal, (December 1, 1988), A1, A6.

CHAPTER 4

Snapshots of Urban Churches

Picture in your mind a typical urban church. What's the building like? How many members does it have? What's the congregation's ethnic makeup? What type of music is being sung? Where do the members live?

You're probably right.

Whatever images you have in your mind undoubtedly match some urban churches—no matter what those images are.

Urban churches are large. They're also small.

They're in storefronts. They're in cathedrals.

They're black, white, Hispanic, Asian, Native American,

integrated.

The music is gospel. Or contemporary Christian. Or classical.

Members live in the neighborhood. Or they commute from the suburbs.

●

One thing you discover when you ask about the urban church is that each person's image of it is different. Urban churches are as diverse as the cities they seek to reach. They reflect both the problems and the opportunities of city life.

Different types of urban churches face different challenges and opportunities in reaching urban young people. To understand these differences, let's look at snapshots of several different urban churches. By necessity, the pictures are snapshots, not studio portraits. Many urban churches may resemble several different images, and the pictures don't capture all the nuances of a particular type of church. Nevertheless, taken together, they compose a useful family portrait.

It's important, however, to emphasize that no single type of church or ministry is "the" model for the city. Each urban congregation must develop its ministry based on its own situation and calling. It would be nearly impossible, for example, for a church in a downtown business district to be a neighborhood church—it has few neighbors. Yet downtown churches can meet needs that might be impossible for a neighborhood church to meet. As Ray Bakke writes:

> *Ministry and models need to be as vast, diverse and as open to change as the church itself: the whole gospel to the whole city. Because the city is so pluralistic, we need every single denomination, ministry-style and model. One is not better than the other, any more than a bus is better than a car. It depends on the task to be done.*[1]

Neighborhood Churches

In 1961, theologian Gibson Winter predicted that "the attempt to perpetuate the local parish or congregation as a basic unit of the Christian church is doomed to failure."[2] Like many religion pundits, he believed the neighborhood church had little to offer a nation infatuated with fast cars and smooth freeways. If people could go anywhere for work, recreation and shopping, they'd do the same for church. So if churches wanted to survive in the city, these people said, they would have to reach beyond their neighborhoods to the whole metropolitan area.

However, while many churches today do draw members from throughout a metropolitan area, many other urban congregations continue to build their membership and ministry within their own neighborhoods. By focusing on their own community, these churches are in a unique position to address specific needs and to build relationships in the community that are almost impossible for downtown or metropolitan churches.

Manhattan Bible Church in New York City is one example of a successful neighborhood church. The congregation started in 1971 as a house church on Manhattan's northwest side. The church grew quickly as the pastor, Tom Hahairas, intentionally reached out to the immediate community. Before long, the church bought a garage and turned it into a church building. Then when the congregation outgrew that facility, it bought a nearby skating rink (which used to be owned by the Mafia) and turned it into the church building.

Today, the 1,000-member congregation has essentially the same demographics as the community—primarily Hispanic and black, with a few whites and Greeks. Most members would be classified as low-income.

Not only does the congregation worship in the community, it also ministers to the community. Among its ministries are a Christian school (with about 300 elementary students), a soup kitchen (which serves about 300 people every day) and a drug-rehabilitation center the church operates in upstate New York.

The youth group also reaches out to the community, providing positive alternatives and discipleship to the neighborhood teenagers. Each Friday evening the youth group sponsors a "Friday Night Live" program which includes recreation and an evangelistic message for the non-Christian young people. The church also offers a variety of programming for young people who become involved in the church.

Neighborhood churches can vary considerably, depending on their community. Four general types deserve mention:

Inner-city churches. These congregations are located in and serve impoverished communities. While some of these churches receive outside help to sustain their ministries, others rely only on the low-income congregation for financial support. As a result, these churches rarely can support a full-time pastor, much less a youth worker.

Revitalized-community churches. Across the spectrum from inner-city churches are neighborhood churches in revitalized urban communities. These congregations attract a diverse membership, including the young, upwardly mobile urbanites.

Lafayette Park United Methodist Church in St. Louis is an example of these churches. It's in the heart of a national historic district that's being redeveloped. The area, which had been virtually abandoned, now attracts a variety of people. As a result, pastor Diana Loomis says, the church reflects its diverse community, which includes many ethnic and economic groups—from people who live in public housing to people who have restored Victorian-age homes for their families.

Ethnic churches. These congregations are defined not by economics, but by ethnic background. They're like First Presbyterian Church of Crafton Heights in Pittsburgh. The neighborhood is a blue-collar, Polish community with some fourth-generation families, says former youth minister Dave Carver. These congregations often have deep roots in their community and their ethnic heritage—be it Polish, Irish, Swedish, Russian or German. Thus changing communities can be particularly traumatic on these congregations, since long-time members move away, and new residents are not comfortable with the "Old World" traditions.

Storefront churches. These congregations are often outside the mainstream of Christianity. Many are independent, with few connections to national organizations or other congregations. Yet they're a significant piece of the urban church landscape.

In their book *The Expanded Mission of "Old First" Churches*, Ray Bakke and Samuel K. Roberts describe storefront churches as: "a rather unique urban response to the sense of marginality many people may feel in mainline denominations and churches. These congregations are led by a strong charismatic figure. They rent space in commercial buildings in their primary stages of development in route to more permanent quarters."[3]

●

While neighborhood churches are as diverse as the communities they represent, they do share two basic traits:

Mirroring the community. Membership in neighborhood churches usually reflects the neighborhood's economic and ethnic makeup. Thus, if a church is in a mostly black neighborhood, the church's membership and leadership are mostly black. If the neighborhood includes a variety of ethnic groups, so does the church. And if the community is impoverished, the church's membership is also.

This characteristic of the neighborhood church has significant implications. First, it gives the congregation a specific focus for ministry and outreach. Neighborhood churches don't try to reach and serve all of Chicago, New York, Boston or San Francisco; they reach out to Rogers Park or the Bronx, Dorchester or Chinatown.

These churches also struggle with the neighborhood's needs. If the neighborhood shifts between ethnic groups, the church experiences a similar shift—with both its opportunities and its struggles. If a nearby factory lays off workers or closes, the church will likely suffer decreased giving since many members are directly affected.

Committing to the neighborhood. First Church of the Brethren in Brooklyn, New York, used to be in an Italian neighborhood and had an Italian membership. When the neighborhood changed to predominantly Hispanic, the church moved. But then the new neighborhood also changed.

At that point, associate pastor Phill Carlos Archbold says, the church made a firm commitment to grow where it was planted. Archbold says the church decided: "We will remain where we are and open our doors to the community . . . The scripture says to go into all the world. Well, we don't have to go into the world. The world is at our doorsteps, and we take care of them as they come."

Neighborhood churches commit themselves to their communities for numerous reasons—both practical and theological. Perhaps the strongest reason is their sense that God has placed them in their community, with all its struggles, problems and challenges, for a purpose. They answer the question "Who is my neighbor?" by reaching out to people on their own blocks.

Mission Churches

In many ways, Ft. Worth's Liberation Community of the Church of the Nazarene is an inner-city neighborhood church. Its members come from the low-income community, and membership is about 70 percent black and 30 percent Hispanic.

However, Liberation Community is somewhat different. Its pastor, Bryan Stone, came into the community in 1985 to form a mission church. Because of the denomination's commitment to the church, Liberation Community receives financial support from numerous Nazarene churches across the country, which see the congregation as part of their own ministry.

In addition to the traits of neighborhood churches, mission churches have two important characteristics:

Mission zeal. Young mission congregations have a zeal for ministry that matches their pioneering spirit. As would be expected, their programming generally emphasizes outreach and missions.

Fewer lay leaders. Particularly in early years, mission congregations rely heavily on outside leaders to run the church. Members usually have little previous experience in the church. Building lay leadership becomes an important priority for the congregation's long-term health.

Downtown Churches

With more than 13,000 members, First United Methodist Church in Houston is its denomination's largest church. Its sanctuary and six-story education building are surrounded by the skyscrapers that define downtown Houston's skyline.

Each Sunday the church holds two overflowing worship

services in its sanctuary built for 2,000. People drive for as long as an hour from across the Houston metropolis to attend. The second service is broadcast live on television.

People come to the church because it offers attractive and diverse programming. Its music program includes a fine arts series that sponsors guest artists and special programs. For example, the choir performed Handel's *Messiah* with the Houston Symphony Orchestra during the 1988 Christmas season.

In addition to various programs to meet special needs and interests in the congregation, the church is also actively involved in working with Houston's social service agencies and other ministries to help disadvantaged people in the city, country and around the world.

To a large extent, the youth program reflects the congregation. It has about 350 members, with 70 to 80 involved in the Sunday morning activities, according to youth minister Rob Grotheer. And because people travel so far to church, most regular youth activities take place on Sunday.

After church, about 40 young people change clothes and go out to eat as the "Out to Lunch Bunch." Then the afternoon is filled with activities such as intensive Bible study, service projects and recreation. That's followed by a regular fellowship meeting, a free supper, youth choir practice and the evening worship service.

Because the church draws people from such a large area, the youth group also holds four Bible studies during the week—one in each of the city's quadrants. Fifteen to 20 young people attend each of these weeknight meetings.

First United Methodist is a fairly typical (though unusually large) downtown church. These congregations rely on freeways, outstanding preaching, and polished, diverse programs to draw people to church from across the city and suburbs. Few, if any, church members live in the church building's neighborhood. In fact, the church's only neighbors may be offices, shops and other institutions that close up on weekends.

Gaylord Noyce characterizes the downtown church as a "scattered congregation."[4] The churches maintain their identity by attracting suburbanites through exceptional programming and preaching. Some of the nation's best-known preachers fill these pulpits. By continuing to draw middle-class people, downtown churches overcome the perennial money problem in low-income areas.

Downtown churches serve an important function for their cities. They can become focal points for interchurch activities and efforts, cosponsoring major music, lecture and evangelistic events with other churches. They can also serve as guardians of the church's artistic expression. Thus they become, according to Noyce, a "regional center of many other churches or chapels."[5]

The same principle holds true for youth ministry. The youth program must be exceptional in order to entice suburbanites to drive past a dozen nearby churches in order to participate downtown.

Grotheer says that "youth are involved at First United Methodist partly because their family is involved here." They also come because of the variety of programming the church offers. No one is expected to participate in all the youth activities. Instead, young people may choose those programs that particularly interest them.

But beyond these factors, he says, the youth leaders know how difficult it is to build community in a large group from many different schools and communities. As a result, the program emphasizes small groups. Each group includes five or six young people and a volunteer, adult counselor. This approach gives teenagers contact with at least one adult and prevents anyone from being lost in the large group.

The necessary emphasis on quality has made some people look to downtown churches as models to emulate in the urban areas. However, the very quality that helps them succeed may also result in their eventual decline. C. Kirk Hadaway writes in *The Urban Challenge*:

> *Downtown churches may be less dependent on their environments than are neighborhood churches, but they are only able to maintain this independence by remaining exceptional. For example, an inner-city church of 12,000 members cannot afford to have a poor preacher. If it did, a large number of its constituents would not feel the*

drive to the inner city was worthwhile . . . Who wants to
drive ten or more miles to an ordinary church when there
are vital, active, growing ones nearby?[6]

Another challenge for downtown churches is that they
are an unusual mix of city life and suburban culture.
Though they're located in the heart of the city, their members are mostly suburbanites. Thus, the youth group members attend suburban or parochial schools, have suburban
values and deal with suburban problems. Youth ministries in
these churches, therefore, have fewer connections with the
issues and struggles of the city.

Metropolitan Churches

With 1,500 members, First Baptist Congregational
Church is one of Chicago's most prominent black congregations. Its pastor, Arthur D. Griffin, is well-educated and in-
fluential not only in the church but also in city politics. The
church attracts prominent black business leaders from across
Chicago for dynamic worship—complete with orchestra,
four choirs and the city's second largest pipe organ.

At the same time, the church also reaches out to its
own neighborhood that includes the Henry Horner Housing
Project. Youth minister Michael Walton estimates that 25
percent of the kids in his program are from the neighborhood; the other 75 percent commute in for worship, weekly
meetings and special events.

Like First Baptist Congregational Church, metropolitan
churches are something of a cross between a neighborhood
church and a downtown church. As a result, they have
unique ministry opportunities. They can rely on suburban
and middle-class members to support their ministries, while
also maintaining ties with the local community. Thus the
church becomes a vital link through which concerned,
middle-class Christians can work in a deteriorating community.

The importance of this link for youth ministry is vividly
evident at Park Avenue United Methodist Church in Minneapolis. Each summer the youth program kicks into high
gear with about 40 different programs that reach inner-city
young people. However, those programs would be impossi-

ble without the financial and leadership support from the active members who commute to the church from other communities.

Metropolitan churches have several common characteristics:

Commitment to the neighborhood. Unlike downtown churches, metropolitan churches have a strong commitment to their immediate community. In cases where the community is impoverished (as is usually the case), this commitment means not only reaching out to bring community residents into the church, but also taking the church's ministries out to the community.

Attractive programs. Like downtown churches, metropolitan churches must maintain strong programs in order to attract people from across the city. First Baptist Congregational Church sponsors a monthly Friday Midnight Special that draws 200 to 300 young people from across Chicago for five hours of quality Christian drama and music.

Strong leadership. Metropolitan churches essentially have two congregations—people from the neighborhood and people from wealthier parts of the city. Art Erickson of Park Avenue says that his church's leadership is the unifying factor between the two groups in his youth program.

Immigrant Churches

Each year, cities become home to thousands of immigrants from all over the world—Europe, Asia, Central America, South America, Africa. These people bring with them their language, customs and symbols of faith.

First Korean United Methodist Church in Chicago exemplifies how some urban churches cater specifically to these new residents. It provides a familiar, supportive community for people who have been transplanted into a strange culture. Not only does its worship and church life reflect the homeland's culture, but the church provides cross-cultural services for new residents—job placement, translation and language training. Because its focus is on a particular, small immigrant group, the church attracts Koreans from throughout the greater Chicago area, not just the immediate neighborhood.

Diagram 4-1

The Black Church Tradition

Black churches make up a major proportion of urban churches. In Chicago, for example, about half of the city's 2,000 churches are traditional black churches. Thus it's inaccurate to characterize or judge the urban church based only on the experiences of traditionally white congregations. Indeed, while other churches are lamenting "white flight" from the cities, urban black congregations—particularly in America's northern cities—are growing rapidly.[13] Such a perspective leads Tony Campolo to write: "The church has not left the inner city—only the white Anglo-Saxon Protestant church has left . . . What remains in the city storefronts is a vital, biblical Christianity, not middle-class WASP religion."[14]

While it's simplistic to lump all African American churches together into a monolithic group, most black churches do share common links that grow out of their shared culture and history of oppression by whites. Most black denominations were formed in response to white Christian racism before the Civil War. The church became the central force in developing black community, identity and solidarity. And because blacks had no entries into secular politics after the war, the church became the place where the black political consciousness developed. As a result, "the church is the single-most prominent and important institution in the black community."[15]

Urban youth ministry expert Buster Soaries writes that until 1970, "everything significant to Black America, including education, civil rights and social services, had been the responsibility of the church to either sponsor or support . . . It was all we had. We generally did not have social clubs, vacations, schools, political parties and other societal options exclusive from the church."[16]

It's important to understand the unique characteristics that developed in black churches because of African American history. They include:

● A unique worship style. Emotive, prophetic and biblical preaching, as well as a strong emphasis on music characterize worship in black churches.

● A sense of community. With few other institutions open and accepting, black community life often centers around the church (though this influence decreases in urban areas).

● No spiritual-political dichotomy. Black churches tend to be active in political affairs, believing that the gospel message has important implications for society, and that political concerns are vital to the church's mission.

Immigrant congregations may also form around an existing Anglo congregation, using its facilities and being supported by it financially. North Shore Baptist Church in Chicago is one example. Church life centers around various ethnic congregations—Japanese, Chinese, Hispanic and Anglo. (In the past, Filipino members also formed a separate group, but they have joined with the Anglo congregation.) Each ethnic group worships separately in different languages, but each also has a voice in the whole church's operations. Several times each year the various congregations join together for festive, multicultural worship and fellowship experiences.

These congregations serve an important role in the city by building a bridge by which new immigrants can become accustomed to American culture. Yet their task becomes complicated as their members become second- and third-generation Americans. Immigrants find themselves having to become bilingual, particularly in children's ministry and youth ministry. Parents often speak their native tongue, while young people pick up English at school.

Churches in Transition

> *Grace Episcopal Church in Elizabeth, New Jersey, . . . was once the second largest parish in the diocese, with more than 500 in the Sunday school class alone. As the affluent relocated to other parts of the city and beyond, the parish dwindled. Its lifeblood was drained as the first European immigrants, then blacks and, finally, Hispanics moved into the neighborhood. In 1981, unable to maintain even a semblance of an Anglo enclave, the parish was abandoned when the priest and the last parishioner died.*[7]

Similar stories could be written about hundreds of urban churches across the United States. These churches were once neighborhood churches. But when white, middle-class people moved to the suburbs, and minority, low-income residents moved into the community, the churches failed to keep pace.

These churches have found themselves caught in the push and pull of transition—one of the unavoidable qualities of city life. Some became multi-ethnic congregations that reflected the neighborhood. Some maintained their old identity and sought to become like downtown churches, relying on membership from outside the community. Others sold their property to ethnic congregations and built new facilities in the suburbs. The rest simply died. (Diagram 4-2, "Stages of Transition," outlines the stages churches go through in transitional communities.)

Though many churches went through transition in the '60s and '70s, the issue is still alive. For example, out of 175 United Churches of Christ in Chicago, 30 were in transitional or pre-transitional communities in 1980.[8]

While it's easy to criticize these churches for not reaching out to their communities, it's also important to remember that transition is difficult and painful. In his book *Urban Churches in Transition*, Walter E. Ziegenhals writes that churches in transitional neighborhoods are confronted with complex problems. These include:

● Aging and declining membership

● Diminishing financial base

● Insufficient or inadequate leadership

● Racial, ethnic, cultural and class fears

● Inability to understand the interaction between the community's fate and the church's future

● Estrangement from new neighbors

● Difficulty in defining its mission[9]

Each of these problems has implications for youth ministry. As the congregation ages, young people begin feeling out of place in the congregation. Moreover, church leaders lose their vision for youth ministry. As resources diminish, the youth ministry budget is one of the first cut. If the leaders try to include minority young people in the church's ministry, the dominant group may react in fear of what "those kids" will do to their building. And finally, if the church has difficulty defining its mission, it is unlikely to put time or commitment into youth ministry.

James DiRaddo once worked with a Swedish congregation in New York City that became completely isolated from its immediate community as it became surrounded by blacks. But instead of reaching out to the neighborhood children and teenagers, the church retreated, defending its

Diagram 4-2

Stages of Transition

In his studies of urban churches in transitional communities, Dr. Carl Dudley, professor of church and community at McCormick Theological Seminary in Chicago, has discovered that these churches go through the following phases of transition.[17] With work and vision, the process can sometimes be arrested at some point along the line. But, all too often, the church simply dies.

1. Expansion of the base. When churches feel the community beginning to change—signaled by the fact that prominent church members leave the community—churches immediately try to become metropolitan or move to a new location. The churches often spend their valuable resources in an attempt to become more attractive. Some churches succeed, but most of the time, the pastor leaves, funds are drained and the church collapses.

2. Formation of a covenant community. The members admit the changes in the community, bond together and become more committed to "our church." In the process, the church may cut its ties with other groups and the denomination, believing "We can do it ourselves, thank you."

3. Accommodation. Accommodation begins when the church runs out of money. The church's leadership becomes willing to work with anyone, and the congregation sees itself as "pastor to the changing community." They often begin renting out the church facility to anyone who needs it, and often they invite an ethnic congregation to use the church facility—at a different hour. Yet the older congregation often feels uncomfortable with the arrangement.

4. Leaving. Seeing little hope remaining for returning to the church's "glory days," the old congregation leaves. It may be a sudden exit—selling the building and disbanding. Or it may be a gradual decline as the church goes into a low-energy state of depression until all its members have either left or died.

---

traditions and memories as its youth ministry fizzled. "There were 10 times more children there on the streets," DiRaddo says, "but the church had no strategy and no interest in working to reach them."

While churches in transitional communities face significant struggles, they also have a unique opportunity to model the rich diversity of Christ's body. Chapter 9 shows ways to celebrate and foster diversity in your youth group.

Parachurch Ministries

Many local and national parachurch ministries (most notably Young Life and Youth for Christ) make a conscious effort to reach urban young people outside the organized church structure. In fact, much of the literature about urban ministry gives the distinct impression that *all* successful urban youth work is parachurch youth ministry—or at least based on the parachurch model.[10] In 1987, Young Life's Urban Ministries Division sponsored 78 clubs, had 73 full-time staff, and reported an average weekly attendance at club meetings of more than 2,500.[11]

Inner City Impact is a fairly typical and successful parachurch ministry in Chicago. The ministry was begun by a pastor who was frustrated because unchurched teenagers wouldn't come to church because it was called church. So he started an evangelistic ministry that seeks to reach unchurched young people.

The Inner City Impact program is like many other parachurch programs. It centers around evangelistic outreaches, weekly Bible studies and building relationships with teenagers. The goal, says junior high coordinator Tracy Hipps, is "reaching out to these kids where they are" to introduce them to the gospel of Jesus Christ and to help them grow into mature Christians. For most urban teenagers who get involved in the program, it's the only Christian community they know. Hipps estimates that only about 25 to 30 percent of the kids in the program attend a local church.

The parachurch model is particularly successful with urban youth for at least five reasons:

● It meets young people on their own turf. Youth workers try to work in schools and recreation centers, and they hold meetings in homes or community centers in the young people's neighborhoods.

● It builds relationships. Parachurch ministries pour their energies into having staff people build relationships with urban young people. These Christian adults give teenagers the love and affirmation they may never receive at home or with their peers.

● It offers attractive programming, using a ministry vehicle such as a recreation room or gymnasium and Bible studies that relate directly to the teenagers' lives.

● It relies on strong young adult leadership, often from local colleges, who are attractive role models for urban kids. Camps and retreats are a central programming element.

● It has an outside source of funding that can provide quality programming without the worries of raising funds in impoverished neighborhoods. Inner City Impact uses a missionary model for funding. Staff members are supported by congregations and individuals around the country. Periodically these "urban missionaries" visit supporting congregations to tell about the ministry and to raise new support.

Parachurch ministries also have their drawbacks, particularly when not connected to a local congregation. Art Erickson worked on the Young Life staff for 10 years before moving into the local church. He became frustrated focusing on high school students because he was not able to work long enough with the young people to make a significant difference. By the time the young people had reached high school, they had already developed destructive habits that were difficult to break. Then when they graduated, they had no connection with an intergenerational church. So too often they simply stopped attending any religious activities.

What the Church Can Offer Urban Youth

Each church has its limitations. But each also has great potential for reaching urban young people. Let's look at some more images of urban churches. But this time, let's look at the church from the teenagers' viewpoint. Perhaps from this perspective we can begin to find ways to introduce young people to the church and its message of hope.

Like most symbols, each of the images is an inadequate definition of the church, and none of the images should be taken literally. But perhaps the ideas behind them open options for churches wanting to break out of traditional patterns in order to make a difference in teenagers' lives.

A gang. With family life in disarray and few other support systems available, young people yearn for love and acceptance—benefits that gangs appear to provide at a high price.

Churches can offer a similar attraction without the high price. At its heart, the church's message is one of love and acceptance. Churches that offer love to urban young people find themselves attracting kids to *the* Lord who might otherwise turn to the Vice Lords.

Home turf. Turf is important to urban young people. They need a place where they feel some sense of ownership and pride—where they feel important. These young people live in a world that tells them they're inconsequential.

But the church knows better. Each young person is a child of God with a stake in God's turf—God's kingdom. Every young person can make a valuable contribution to God's world. When the church becomes the young person's turf, he or she no longer feels the need to seek status and self-worth through destructive gangs.

A street corner. With few recreational facilities available and no room for private space in crowded apartments, urban young people spend their free time on street corners. There they talk, laugh, argue, ask questions, discuss issues and share problems together.

Churches can be like street corners to urban youth. They can provide the space and the listening ear that allows teenagers to relax, ask their questions, build relationships and discover who they are and who they are becoming.

A street light. Wilderness camping can be a frightening experience for urban youth. They're afraid to do anything outside after the sun goes down. Why? Because it's so dark. In cities, street lights illuminate the nights, providing a sense of safety to local residents.

The church can be like a street light for urban youth. It can become a safe place young people can retreat to in a sometimes hostile world. At church, young people can let their guards down, if only for a while. They learn to trust others, to become vulnerable and to let others touch their lives.

A neighborhood committee. If you want to change something in the city, you don't go to city hall. More likely, you turn to a neighborhood committee. Community organizers have learned that one of the most effective ways to influence city policy is to form local organizations that promote neighborhood issues.

The church can be like a neighborhood committee for young people whose concerns might not otherwise be heard in the seats of power. Decisions in city hall, the state legislature and the nation's capital all directly affect the well-being of urban youth. Cuts in education funding could mean they won't go to college or they won't have a qualified teacher in high school. Changes in social programs can affect whether they can afford the bus fare to ride to school. A city hall decision to build a stadium in a poor community could mean that teenagers and their families will be left on the streets with no affordable housing.

Churches that are concerned with the total well-being of urban youth must discover ways to become modern-day "Josephs" and "Daniels" who gain access to people in power and use their influence to help young people in need. As Daniel Buttry writes:

> *A church with a vision for mission that is reaching out evangelistically with any degree of sensitivity and wisdom will encounter the social structures, dynamics and relationships that crush people. The problems of racism, unemployment, poor education, poverty and shattered families all have a bearing on the well-being of the individuals we reach for Christ.*[12]

A television. The church can be like a television for urban youth, a window on the world for young people who never experience or see life beyond their own neighborhoods. The church can model a better life for teenagers caught in a trap of hopelessness.

Many young people in his Brooklyn community have never experienced healthy family life or interaction, Phill Carlos Archbold says. When young people eat meals with his family, they experience for the first time what it's like for a whole family to sit, pray and eat together. Through this simple "ministry of modeling," these young people see healthy family life patterns and relationships. "Many times we don't say anything," Archbold says. "We just live it."

Similarly, Bryan Stone says urban youth tend not to see a lot of opportunity to improve their lives. The church can affirm them and show them that they can rise beyond their current circumstances. He helps them do this by introducing them to healthy mentors—African American and Hispanic ministers, business leaders, athletes, politicians and other successful people who have improved their life situations. By interacting with these "heroes," young people catch a vision for how they, too, may be able to rise above their current situations.

Reflection and Action

1. Read through the descriptions of the different types of urban churches. Which description do you think best fits your congregation? What elements of the description ring most true to you? Which elements seem not to fit your church? Write a paragraph describing your church.

2. Do you think your congregation is fulfilling its calling through its current ministry model? Why or why not? If so, how is it fulfilling its call? If not, what would need to change to make your church fulfill its call?

3. Karen Battle says, "I really think the church hasn't even begun to address urban ministry with any zeal." Do you agree with her? Why or why not? Where have you seen signs that the church is, indeed, ministering effectively in the city?

4. Go back through the list of images in the section on what the church can offer urban youth. Which images do you think are most important? Which are most difficult? Which fall beyond the scope of the church's ministry? What other images would you add?

5. Which images of the church fit the ministries your church provides? Which other images would you like to offer to urban youth?

Endnotes

[1] Ray Bakke with Jim Hart, *The Urban Christian* (Downers Grove, IL: InterVarsity Press, 1987), 128.

[2] Quoted in Gaylord B. Noyce, *Survival and Mission for the City Church* (Philadelphia, PA: Westminster Press, 1975), 91-92.

[3] Raymond J. Bakke and Samuel K. Roberts, *The Expanded Mission of "Old First" Churches* (Valley Forge, PA: Judson Press, 1986), 111.

[4] Noyce, *Survival and Mission for the City Church*, 17.

[5] Noyce, *Survival and Mission for the City Church*, 41.

[6] C. Kirk Hadaway, "The Church in the Urban Setting" in *The Urban Challenge*, edited by Larry L. Rose and C. Kirk Hadaway (Nashville, TN: Broadman Press, 1982), 88, 95.

[7] Glenn Chalmers, "A Ministry of Hope in the Inner City," The Christian Ministry, (January-February, 1988), 18-19.

[8] Walter E. Ziegenhals, *Urban Churches in Transition* (New York: Pilgrim Press, 1978), 16.

[9] Ziegenhals, *Urban Churches in Transition*, 15.

[10] David Claerbaut, *Urban Ministry* (Grand Rapids, MI: Zondervan Publishing House, 1983), 123.

[11] Reaching Out 1987 (annual publication of Young Life), 38.

[12] Daniel Buttry, *Bringing Your Church Back to Life: Beyond Survival Mentality* (Valley Forge, PA: Judson Press, 1988), 82.

[13] Bakke with Hart, *The Urban Christian*, 56-57.

[14] Anthony Campolo, "The Sociological Nature of the Urban Church," in *Metro-Ministry*, edited by David Frenchak and Sharrel Keyes (Elgin, IL: David C. Cook Publishing, 1979), 28.

[15] Preston Robert Washington, *God's Transforming Spirit: Black Church Renewal* (Valley Forge, PA: Judson Press, 1988), 19.

[16] Buster Soaries, "Church Based Youth Ministry in the Black Community," (An unpublished paper presented at GROUP Magazine's 1989 Youth Ministry University), 2-3. Used by permission of author.

[17] Carl Dudley, "Churches in Changing Communities," in *Metro-Ministry*, 84-88.

CHAPTER 5

Barriers to Urban Youth Ministry

Everyone you ask about urban youth ministry agrees on at least one thing: Urban youth ministry is, above all else, difficult. If you consider all the churches that either struggle along in youth ministry or let it die completely, the odds seem to be against success.

Earlier chapters have already addressed different factors within the city that make urban youth ministry challenging—the stresses of city life, the needs of people in poverty, the complex problems of urban teenagers. In this chapter, though, let's focus on the problems in churches themselves.

Why have urban churches often failed to reach teenagers?

Let's examine that question and some of the responses to it before turning to ways to minister effectively to urban young people. There are four overarching barriers:

- Churches lack motivation.
- Teenagers don't feel comfortable.
- Common youth ministry models don't apply.
- Few quality resources are available.

Churches Lack Motivation

For several years, the Evangelical Association for the Promotion of Education has sought to build partnerships with inner-city Philadelphia congregations. Program director John Carlson says the organization makes this offer to congregations that have no youth outreach in their community: Let us work with you to reach kids in nearby government housing. Let us be your youth department. You don't have to pay us anything; just let us work with you.

You'd think the offer is too good to be true. But many churches turn it down. Reasons vary, but Carlson says a major reason is that the churches simply don't have a vision for ministry to teenagers in the community. Many urban churches aren't prepared for a youth ministry. Let's look at some of the barriers within these churches that prevent them from having an effective outreach to young people.

Lack of Concern

Many urban churches fail to reach teenagers simply because they don't address those teenagers' needs. Young people who need love and acceptance, for example, won't participate in an impersonal youth group no matter how polished the program is.

Pastor Wayne Gordon began his ministry in the Lawndale area of Chicago by starting a Fellowship of Christian Athletes group for teenagers. He encouraged the young people to attend church on Sunday, and he recommended several congregations to them. But they never went. They didn't feel comfortable, and none of the congregations made any intentional efforts to meet teenagers' needs. As a result, Gordon says, "Kids were becoming Christians, but they didn't go to church."

Because he believed strongly in the local church, Gordon decided to lead a Bible study on the church. He hoped that by studying scriptures, the teenagers would discover how important it was to be a part of a congregation. Instead, the young people decided they wanted to start their own church. The result is Lawndale Community Church, which now has an intergenerational membership as well as a strong youth program.

Lack of Vision

Many urban churches simply don't have a mind-set for young people. Their leadership and core members are aging. And, in many cases, no one in the church (including the pastor) understands the importance of youth ministry or even Christian education. As a result, says Michael Walton of First Baptist Congregational Church in Chicago, "Most youth ministries are just babysitting services."

A Search Institute study of urban youth ministry included interviews of denominational executives in five major black denominations. Their perceptions support Walton's contention. These leaders believe a major hindrance to youth ministry in their denominations is "the low priority accorded it by the membership of many congregations." The Search Institute report continues: "In their form of worship, in their decision-making, in their activities, congregations are oriented toward adults. Youth are included if they want to be, but generally only as observers or passive participators. They are not given any special focus nor hold any decision-making power."[1]

The same report also noted that no major black denomination has a full-time person on the national staff whose sole responsibility is youth ministry. Youth work in these denominations is, for the most part, limited to traditional Christian education programs—primarily Sunday school. As a result, urban black congregations often lack leadership, training and resources for youth ministry.

John Carlson sees a lack of vision for community youth ministry as a major obstacle to urban youth ministry, particularly in the inner city. He says that most urban churches—

Diagram 5-1
Youth Ministry in Black Denominations

A major factor making it difficult for black congregations to run strong youth programs is the lack of support and interest in youth ministry at the denominational level. Search Institute's research into youth ministry in five major black denominations found that ''youth ministry programs conducted by Black churches are relatively rare.'' The study found:

- None of the denominations have someone on the central staff whose only responsibility is youth ministry.
- The denominations have little or no budget for youth ministry.
- Virtually the only youth-oriented printed resources from the denominations are traditional Sunday school materials.
- There is no training for youth ministry conducted within the denomination.
- None of the denominations produce a youth ministry professional journal.
- The denominations' seminaries offer only one course in youth ministry, if any.[12]

---

both black and white—are middle-class churches. Like neighborhood churches, they're often located in residential communities, but they don't open their doors to any of their neighbors. Instead, their members commute to the church from other communities. "It's rare for an urban church to have a neighborhood ministry at all," he says. "People tend to think primarily of the kids who come to their church already and want them taken care of. Typically, inner-city churches—just like suburban churches—do not minister to the neighborhood."

Lack of Pastoral Support

In many urban churches, the pastor dominates church life. In Anglo churches, this dominance may result as a fearful response to changes in the community—a way to "manage" the change. In African American churches, this dominance reflects the tradition that "the power comes from the pulpit down, as it did with prophets of old," says Clay Evans of Chicago's Fellowship Baptist Church.[2]

A similar pattern often develops in white urban churches, according to urban ministry experts Ray Bakke and Samuel K. Roberts. When pastors begin feeling inadequate and overwhelmed by their task, "many overcompensate for their feelings . . . by resorting to cynicism or coercive, authoritarian schemes."[3] This response helps them feel that they're in control of their situation.

Whether or not this theological perspective is appropriate, it hampers youth ministry—unless the pastor strongly supports youth ministry. According to Michael Walton, this pastoral dominance is *the* major barrier to youth work in urban black churches. Walton tells of one 2,000-member church where the pastor actually believes he can personally meet the needs of every parishioner. Such a narrow vision eliminates the opportunity for important shared and specialized ministries such as youth ministry.

An African Methodist Episcopal Church in California encountered a similar problem. The church was building a successful youth program with the pastor's support. But then the pastor left and a new pastor with less vision for youth ministry came. The youth program quickly dwindled and died, highlighting the pastor's impact on youth ministry.

The issue of pastoral dominance is certainly not unique to the black church experience. Maria Torres-Rivera has encountered similar problems in her work as Hispanic youth coordinator for the Catholic Archdiocese of Philadelphia. Of the 300 parishes in the diocese, she says only a handful have paid youth workers. She adds that a lack of support from parish priests is a major factor in the low number of effective youth programs. "If I don't have full support of the priest in the parish," she says, "it's like pulling teeth to get anything done."

Adding to the problem, few Hispanic churches have developed specialized ministries, says urban church consultant H.O. Espinoza of San Antonio, Texas. "It's very rare for a Spanish church to have a pastor and then a youth minister or a Christian education director . . . We haven't gotten to that point yet. We haven't developed that type of ministry."

Of course, a pastor who strongly supports youth ministry can be a great asset. James DiRaddo tells about one ur-

ban youth minister who was almost fired because he was
bringing neighborhood kids into the church who weren't
"our kids." The struggle with the church board continued
for about two years. He only kept his position because the
senior pastor told the church board, "If he goes, I go."

Low or No Budget

Few urban youth workers discuss the challenges of
youth ministry without mentioning the need for funds and
other resources. "In the urban setting," Shawn Kafader of St.
Peter's United Church of Christ in Chicago said, "budget is
the key to the game." DiRaddo adds, "Urban churches can't
afford to sustain themselves, let alone put money into a
youth ministry."

The lack of money for youth ministry results from a
number of different factors. In impoverished inner-city
neighborhoods, church members are simply too poor to
support a youth program. Thus most of these churches use
all their resources for congregation-wide ministries and
building maintenance. John Carlson says, for example, that
churches near government housing can't fathom reaching
out to neighborhood teenagers "simply because they're
struggling themselves, and public housing people have such
big needs."

Other congregations find themselves caught with low
membership and high utility bills for large, old facilities.
When the neighborhood switched from being white to ethnic, long-time members (and contributors) headed for the
suburbs. "Because of 'white flight,' " Ron Scates explains,
"many of your urban churches have been crippled . . . They
really don't have the resources to do dynamic youth ministry." Instead, explains this youth minister from First Presbyterian Church in San Antonio, they have to spend their
limited budgets on heating bills, roof repairs and mortgages.

Low (or non-existent) youth ministry budgets have three
significant side-effects:

● First, most urban churches can't afford to hire
trained youth workers (many don't even have salaried senior
pastors).

● Second, urban churches can't afford to buy youth

ministry resources. Because they can afford only inexpensive Sunday school curricula, they don't have access to program materials for youth group meetings. And they certainly can't afford the amenities of suburban youth groups such as snacks, videos, game boards and special events.

● Finally, because urban churches can't afford youth ministry resources, few publishers or denominations produce them. Instead, urban youth workers must learn to adapt materials designed for suburban congregations.

Teenagers Don't Feel Comfortable

The second major barrier to urban youth ministry is that teenagers don't feel welcome in the churches. The structure, expectations, traditions and style of many urban churches say to teenagers, "No Teenagers Welcome." While similar barriers occur in all settings, they're particularly acute in urban areas because so many young people have no previous religious experience.

Because of history, traditions and cultural expectations, James DiRaddo explains "the church stands as a very imposing figure in the community, representing a whole lot of things with which the people in the streets simply aren't comfortable. They come feeling self-conscious." Whether intentionally or unintentionally, urban churches put up many different "No Teenagers Welcome" signs. Let's look at some of them:

"No Trespassing"

When unchurched teenagers begin coming to an urban church, some members often become highly protective of their traditions and facilities. As a result, they convey to teenagers a paternalistic attitude that "you're lucky to be here," says Dave Carver. Such patterns, however subconscious, make young people feel that the church is someone else's, not theirs. And they won't stay.

Ron Scates says he had to deal with this issue when he first came to his church. The church had made a commitment to reaching young people, but concerns arose when they started coming. Walls were scuffed, and a few things were broken.

When members approached him about the problem, Scates told them: "Buildings are going to get worn. Things are going to get scuffed." Then he would compare wear and tear on a building to a worn Bible. A dog-eared Bible is probably a well-used Bible. In the same way, a building with a little wear and tear is probably a well-used building.

Other churches don't resolve the tension so amicably. DiRaddo once worked with a Manhattan church that opened a drop-in center in the church basement for neighborhood teenagers. But when church board members noticed the scuffs on the walls, a few cracked windows and backed-up toilets, the church shut down the center because "those kids cause too much damage."

"No Suit, No Cash, No Service"

Wayne Gordon says his church canvassed the community to discover why so many people didn't attend church. The canvassers found three primary reasons:

1. People didn't have nice clothes to wear.
2. People didn't have any money to put in the offering plate.
3. People were angry with God.

Since that discovery, the church has never collected an offering, and it emphasizes that there is no dress code—spoken or unspoken.

But other churches aren't so quick to respond. Like the churches criticized in James 2:1-4, too many congregations put wealthier people in positions of power, leaving the less fortunate in the back pews. Since many urban teenagers are impoverished, they're effectively left out of the church.

Phill Carlos Archbold says many urban churches fail to reach young people because "the person who's wearing jeans would have no place in those churches. He or she would feel uncomfortable." He adds, "I think if our Lord came by, he would feel uncomfortable too."

Youth programs also run the risk of turning away urban teenagers with subtle financial pressures. Events with high registration fees (and no scholarships), unspoken fashion "requirements" and other expectations can be prohibitive barriers to urban families that may have difficulty paying utility bills. "If a church expects them to pay, then they won't come," DiRaddo asserts.

If churches want to include low-income teenagers in their special events, then scholarships and subsidized programs are essential. First Chinese Baptist Church in San Francisco, for example, pays all programming and staff costs for its annual summer camp. And while most of the young people can pay their room and board, youth minister Jerald Choy says the church offers "camperships" to those who can't.

"Whites Only"

It's often said that 11 a.m. to noon on Sunday morning is the most segregated hour of the week. Research bears witness to this sad truth. A survey of high school seniors found that teenagers have more interracial contact at school, at part-time jobs, on athletic teams and even in their neighborhoods than they do at church. Only 9 percent of those surveyed said they often get to know people of other races at church.[4]

Such racist sentiments are rarely blatant, and they're difficult to admit. However, many traditionally white, middle-class congregations can unconsciously turn away low-income, minority teenagers because of subtle racism and class prejudice. If they're going to reach out to ethnically diverse urban teenagers, urban congregations must directly address such sensitive and volatile issues. While many people may choose to worship within their own ethnic traditions, churches from all backgrounds must be sure they welcome all who seek to worship the one true God.

Ron Scates, who works with an ethnically diverse youth group in San Antonio, says he doesn't see blatant racism in his group. But he does worry that racial jokes, though told in jest, may be symptoms of latent racism. Teenagers who are great friends with each other sometimes joke around during church activities. When planning for a retreat, kids teased each other by saying, "Be sure to bring the watermelon for Tyrone."

"I worry sometimes," Scates admits. "I wonder what's

underlying our jokes."

Subtle racism is evident when teenagers from an ethnic group are expected to "stay with your own kind" at church, James DiRaddo says. Such ostracism can take place regardless of whether these teenagers share interests with the other handful of teenagers from their background. As a result, these minority teenagers become isolated and excluded from the core of the youth group and its leadership.

One urban church experienced this problem because the youth group is dominated by close-knit Filipinos. A teenager from another minority group felt shut out of the other kids' conversations and socializing, and his ideas during youth group meetings were always dismissed or overruled by the majority. Fortunately, this young person persisted in vocalizing the problem. The group members were forced to deal with their attitudes toward another ethnic group.

"One Way"

Traditions have rich meaning and history for long-time church members. But they seldom mean anything to urban teenagers, most of whom come from unchurched backgrounds. What's more, the importance some churches place on these traditions implies to young people that there's only one way to worship or study scripture or pray or sing in the church. And if young people aren't comfortable with that "one way," they'll leave.

Worship services are the most common area where tradition clashes with youth culture. As Scates says, "Our worship service is very alive, but it's very alive in the Presbyterian tradition . . . I think that's a turnoff for some of our kids."

Trying to change traditions can be extremely difficult. As James DiRaddo observes: "Many white churches would love to have a black choir come over and sing on Sunday morning. And they'll tolerate it—even enjoy it—and say, 'Wasn't that neat? The blacks have such rhythm' . . . But if you try to introduce that music into the church, even in an urban setting, folks will defend their right to maintain their traditions to the point where they alienate a vast number of people."

Different urban congregations have tried to address such issues in different ways. Some, like First Baptist Chinese Church in San Francisco, offer different worship services with different styles. The San Francisco church has one traditional service in Chinese, a traditional service in English and a more contemporary service in English. A different minister leads each service, adding to the variety.

In order to reach teenagers (indeed, any new people), congregations must constantly evaluate their traditions and make choices about them, argues Daniel Buttry in *Bringing Your Church Back to Life: Beyond the Survival Mentality.* He suggests the following options:[5]

● Some traditions may need to die because they've outlived their usefulness.

● Others may need to be reinvigorated and reinterpreted so that young people learn to accept the tradition as their own and celebrate its rich meaning.

● Other traditions must be created afresh to be meaningful symbols of Christian truth for this generation.

"Do Not Disturb"

When black teenagers go to movies, they often cheer, boo and talk back to the screen. They get up and move around. They interact with each other during the movie.

Then they come to church, where they're expected to sit silently for one to four hours without moving more than to stand, sit or kneel. And they can only talk when they're reading or singing songs and litanies they can hardly understand.

No wonder they feel uncomfortable!

The traditional church atmosphere is foreign to urban teenagers, DiRaddo says. "We're uptight. We need to accept the fact that this segment of society has a style of life with which they are comfortable"—even if the church is not.

Common Youth Ministry Models Don't Apply

The third major barrier is that most traditional youth ministry models are inappropriate in the city. Most training, writing and programming in youth ministry assume a white, suburban, middle-class context. Most professional youth workers come from suburban or rural settings, then they attend suburban colleges and seminaries where they learn step-by-step plans for implementing a youth ministry. And when they arrive in an urban church, they find that the needs and assumptions are vastly different—nothing they learned and practiced works. Art Erickson of Park Avenue United Methodist Church in Minneapolis says they "either leave or eventually begin to put some pieces together."

Daniel Buttry contends that urban churches need ministers who are committed to the city. Too often, he writes, "urban churches have been steppingstones for career advancement." He notes that denominational executives sometimes contribute to the problem when they "steer the inexperienced seminary graduates into the most difficult and decaying churches."[6]

Urban youth ministers find that traditional youth ministry approaches simply don't work in the city. "You can't run a traditional youth ministry and reach urban kids," Ron Scates asserts. He says you have to "understand their turf" and you have to see your ministry as "cross-cultural mission work."

The program options for urban churches are innumerable, and what works will vary from city to city—even from neighborhood to neighborhood and church to church. What urban workers need, Ray Bakke insists, are diagnostic tools to help them understand and meet the needs of the community—not ready-made models that either won't fit or will become outmoded as the urban environment changes.[7]

Urban youth workers find that several aspects of traditional youth ministries must be adapted or changed to be effective in the city. Individually, these issues may seem trivial. But taken together, they become significant concerns that need to be addressed before a church can reach urban teenagers.

Emphasis on Programs

Many traditional youth ministries have programming at their heart. But while programs are certainly an important key to effective urban youth work, leaders have found that they're much less important than relationships. "You don't win urban kids through programs," says pastor Steve Pedigo of the Chicago Fellowship of Friends. "You win them through relationships. You could have the worst program in the world, but because you have good relationships, the kids are going to be there."

Emphasizing programs in the city isn't effective for at least two reasons:

Too many other attractions. It's nearly impossible to compete with the "attractive" options urban youth have available. Urban churches that try to attract young people to exciting programs sometimes find themselves trying to out-do the city's slick and splashy attractions. But unless the congregation has a great deal of money and unusual talent, the efforts usually fail.

"Kids compare what you do to everything they see from Hollywood. And everything you do is not going to match Hollywood," Wendell Fisher says. For example, this youth minister at Manhattan Bible Church in New York City says no church skit or music performance will ever compare to the latest comedy or the polished look of music videos.

Loose commitment to programs. City people don't commit to programs and institutions. They commit to people. Erickson notes, for example, that church membership may be important to suburbanites or rural residents, where religious events are central ingredients in community life. But in the city where people are unchurched, church membership means nothing.

Scheduling

Many urban churches still rely almost exclusively on Sunday school and maybe weekly fellowship to reach teenagers. However, many urban youth workers find that these traditional times are ineffective. Unchurched teenagers often won't go to the trouble to get up early on Sundays.

John Carlson has seen another schedule barrier that prevents young people from attending black congregations. These churches generally have long services and other programs that can last all day on Sundays. Unchurched teenagers who have never participated in church are overwhelmed at that kind of schedule. So they don't come.

By breaking from traditional models, these urban youth workers have created their own custom-designed programs that fit the urban setting and meet young people's needs:

● The youth group at Chicago's First Baptist Congregational Church meets Monday night. It's the only unscheduled night for most urban teenagers, and it's easy to publicize events during Sunday morning activities.

● Manhattan Bible Church offers a Friday night program to provide a positive alternative to the destructive options that unoccupied teenagers might otherwise choose.

Narrow Focus on "Spiritual" Needs

Youth programs in suburban and middle-class settings generally assume that families take care of young people's basic physical needs. Such an assumption misses important ministry opportunities in the city.

Suburban congregations often follow Jesus' admonition to feed the hungry and clothe the naked (Matthew 25) by going on mission trips. Urban congregations must meet those needs in their own youth groups and congregations. As Preston Robert Washington writes about a housing project his church undertook in Harlem: "Our church was not confronted by problems of groups struggling to survive in some distant mission field. The issue of ministry was right next door, a stone's throw away from our church."[8]

Sometimes urban churches discover these ministry opportunities almost by accident. One summer, Dorchester Temple Baptist Church in Boston included breakfast and lunch in its vacation Bible school program. The leader noticed that some children were eating more ravenously than an average growing child would eat. After watching longer, the leader discovered that the children were going hungry, and one girl even showed signs of serious malnutrition. The church responded by serving breakfast at Sunday school, as well as meals during many youth programs.[9]

Of course, no congregation can meet every need. But churches that are concerned about every aspect of those teenagers' lives discover ways they *can* meet specific needs— whether they're spiritual, physical, emotional, social or intellectual.

Chapter 10 focuses on ways churches can address some of the critical needs of urban teenagers—needs that most other churches don't address.

Few Quality Resources Are Available

A major frustration for urban youth workers is the lack of resources that speak to the needs of urban teenagers. Though a few resources are available, most urban youth workers are not aware of them.[10]

"I pick up any magazine, any youth resource, and it's all—100 percent—geared to white kids," Wayne Gordon complains. "Many of the things that are out in youth ministry aren't applicable to the city."

Given the numerous books, magazines and videos currently available for youth ministry, such a claim may seem outlandish. But urban youth workers find most current youth ministry materials inadequate. They point to several problems:

Resources Are All White

Scanning most youth ministry resources quickly confirms this problem. Most, if not all, illustrations and photographs depict white teenagers and leaders. Such first impressions make minority leaders and young people feel that the resources are "not for us."

Beyond the illustrations, the content is usually geared specifically to white teenagers and their needs. For example, Gordon recalls one Bible study that uses sunburn as an analogy for a lesson. Gordon says, "Right away that analogy says it doesn't apply to me, so probably this truth doesn't apply to me." It might have been an effective image with a white youth group, but it was useless for his black teenagers. Before he can use any curriculum or programming resources, he says he has to "read it with a black mind-set."

Michael Walton sees a similar issue at stake. "We need to see black kids doing good things," he says. He challenges Christian publishers to present a positive image of blacks.

Middle-Class Values and Realities Are Assumed

Most resources assume values, attitudes and realities that simply don't exist in inner-city areas. "We have a suburban gospel in America," Gordon contends, "and it's a distorted gospel in many, many ways." As a result, he says, "There's nothing for these kids."

One of the reasons the materials don't fit urban teenagers is that they make numerous assumptions. Art Erickson lists the following:

- Teenagers have already developed basic life skills.
- Teenagers have basic education and study skills.
- Teenagers come from relatively stable families.
- Teenagers have life goals and a vision for the future.

Erickson says urban youth workers can't make *any* of these assumptions. For example, he says most of the young people he works with come from single-parent families. Also, his kids rarely have a vision of a better life. Thus you have to begin at a level of basic needs and values that connect with the young people. And there's little available to help youth workers do this.

Wendell Fisher also points out that many youth ministry resources and programs rely on role plays, skits, stories and other situations that "kids can relate to." But the situations are foreign to urban teenagers' lives. Urban teenagers don't have cars. Their dating patterns are different. Their family situations are different. As a result, Fisher says, "Things I used in my suburban youth group are duds here."

Fisher also says he would like to show Christian films and videos on a regular basis at his weekly Friday evening program, which attracts unchurched teenagers. But it's difficult. "There are just so few films geared to inner-city kids," he says. Christian films almost always show middle-class suburban people in suburban settings dealing with suburban issues.

Urban Issues Are Not Addressed

Ed Chandler, state youth director for the Church of God in New York City, once showed a popular Christian video about sex to a group of urban teenagers. The video has had a great impact in churches across the country. But the urban teenagers laughed at it. It didn't connect with their reality, Chandler learned. The video addressed such issues as "Should Christians date?" and "How far should I go?" Urban teenagers live in an ethos where being sexually active is normal and expected. In one way or another, they all had to answer those basic questions for themselves years earlier.

Because urban teenagers are exposed to so much in the city, many of the issues addressed in youth ministry resources seem trite and simplistic to these teenagers. Improving family communication is a nice idea, but what if you don't know your father and you're abused by your mother? Theological debates about AIDS may be needed. But they seem irrelevant when several friends—even church members— have died from the disease.

On the other hand, urban teenagers need help in dealing with issues that are overlooked in other settings. Because of constant contact with other ethnic groups, urban teenagers must learn to overcome their prejudices against other races and find unity in Christ. They live with violence at home, at school and in the community. They face pressure to join gangs, sell drugs and have sex. These are issues and decisions that a Christian perspective should influence, but youth workers find themselves without resources to address them.

Bryan Stone, pastor of Liberation Community in Ft. Worth, Texas, says a related problem is that few youth ministry resources address other social issues that are important to urban teenagers. "Kids in our area are more sensitive to social issues," he says. "I don't mean abortion or nuclear war, but the way society is structured . . . They're more concerned perhaps with justice as a social issue." And, he says, while it may be difficult for suburban youth workers to get kids interested in social issues, "if you're part of the group who's being disadvantaged or exploited by these problems, you're definitely going to take more of an interest than someone who's unaffected."

Adequate Education Is Assumed

"Have group members read the handout and answer the questions." "Ask a young person to read Isaiah 52." "Call on three volunteers to read the parts in the Christmas skit."

Youth ministry resources often revolve around reading. And because urban teenagers often have lower-quality education and higher illiteracy, they tend not to understand the materials designed for their better-educated peers.

Wayne Gordon believes most youth ministry materials are too difficult for urban teenagers to use and understand. He believes materials must be written at a fourth- or fifth-grade reading level for urban high schoolers to understand them at all.

Paul Tarro, executive director of Urban Youth Ministries, says this problem also involves shifting the emphasis away from reading because many urban people are non-book people. They're verbal people who have difficulty using and learning from written resources. This reality, he says, puts publishers in a Catch-22 position: Urban teenagers need resources, but they will have trouble using them. He believes the best way to reach urban youth is through trained youth workers who can translate print into the verbal communication that young people can understand.

A Church Background Is Assumed

Almost all available curricula for junior and senior highers assumes a church background and at least basic biblical knowledge. But since most urban teenagers come from unchurched backgrounds, urban youth leaders can't use the resources. Tracy Hipps of Inner City Impact in Chicago explains the problem:

> *Traditions in rural, middle-class and suburban neighborhoods have been set where they have knowledge of the church, the stories of the Bible, the language of the Christian community and just general knowledge of the Word. But most youth in the inner city do not attend church. They have little if any knowledge of what a daily relationship with Christ means. The stories and concepts are foreign to most of them . . . So in dealing with them, you have to start from the beginning and the basics.* [11]

Are the Barriers Insurmountable?

Ministry in any setting with any age group is challenging. Yet the needs and issues are concentrated and multiplied when you minister to teenagers in the city. As a result, urban youth ministry can seem overwhelming—even impossible.

At the same time, many youth workers have discovered ways to overcome the barriers—not all at once, but one by one with carefully planned strategies and priorities. The next section presents some specific strategies to overcome the barriers.

Reflection and Action

1. On a scale of 1 to 5 (1=not a barrier; 5=a great barrier), how significant is each barrier in your congregation?

a. The congregation isn't motivated for
youth ministry.   1 2 3 4 5
b. Teenagers don't feel comfortable.   1 2 3 4 5
c. Church uses inappropriate youth
ministry models.   1 2 3 4 5
d. The church doesn't have quality re-
sources.   1 2 3 4 5
e. Pastoral dominance interferes.   1 2 3 4 5

2. Think about ways you can begin overcoming the greatest barriers.

3. Scan the list of reasons why urban churches often fail to reach teenagers. Do you agree with the list? What would you add or take away?

4. Think about your own congregation. What are some "No Teenagers Welcome" signs you hang on your church's doors (either those in the chapter or others you can think of)? Use the following spaces to list some of these:

5. How can you begin to take down those signs?

6. What new signs would you like to put up to make young people feel welcome?

Endnotes

[1]*Strategies for Promoting the Well-Being of Urban Youth* (Minneapolis: Search Institute, 1987), 29.

[2]Quoted in Hiawatha Bray, "A Separate Altar: Distinctives of the Black Church," Christianity Today, (Sept. 19, 1986), 21-23.

[3]Raymond J. Bakke and Samuel K. Roberts, *The Expanded Mission of "Old First" Churches* (Valley Forge, PA: Judson Press, 1986), 105.

[4]Cited in Jolene L. Roehlkepartain, "Ethnic Diversity: The Face of the Future," (GROUP Magazine, March/April 1988), 64-69.

[5]Adapted from Daniel Buttry, *Bringing Your Church Back to Life: Beyond the Survival Mentality* (Valley Forge, PA: Judson Press, 1988), Chapter 8. (This book presents an excellent framework for overcoming the intransience of traditions to give a congregation new life.)

[6]Buttry, *Bringing Your Church Back to Life: Beyond the Survival Mentality*, 88.

[7]One excellent tool is *Determining Needs in Your Youth Ministry* (Loveland, CO: Group Books, 1987). The book is a complete 162-question survey kit to determine teenagers' worries, values, views of themselves, views of the church and so forth.

[8]Preston Robert Washington, *God's Transforming Spirit: Black Church Renewal* (Valley Forge, PA: 1988), 100.

[9]Buttry, *Bringing Your Church Back to Life: Beyond the Survival Mentality*, 81-82.

[10]I could find only two publishers that regularly provide resources for urban youth ministry: Urban Ministries Inc. and Open Door Ministries. See the resource listing on page 245 for more information.

[11]Tracy Hipps, "Junior High Ministry: A Look at the Inner City," (An unpublished paper, April 1987), 3. Used by permission of the author.

[12]*Strategies for Promoting the Well-Being of Urban Youth*, 25-27.

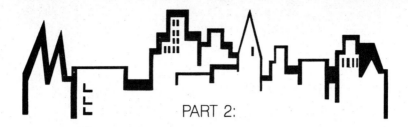

PART 2:

Building an Urban Youth Ministry

CHAPTER 6

Designing Your Youth Ministry

Effective urban youth ministry can take place in the most unlikely churches.

When the Evangelical Association for the Promotion of Education (EAPE) began working with Lombard Central Presbyterian Church in west Philadelphia, it didn't look promising. Though the church seemed rather healthy, its membership was old, most people commuted to church, and it was struggling financially.

"I figured this would be difficult, right?" remembers EAPE program director John Carlson.

. It wasn't. The church immediately became excited about reaching its neighborhood. Members volunteered to help with the kids, and the church and pastor actively supported the outreach. The church's first day camp had to turn kids away when it reached capacity at 100 young people.

●

There's no magic formula for urban youth ministry. What works in one church in one city won't necessarily work in another church in another city. Therefore, it's important to custom design your youth program for *your* church in *your* community.

In an article titled "The Practice of Urban Ministry: Christian Social Ministries," C. Anne Davis suggests a four-step process for designing urban ministries. The steps are:[1]

● Identify resources.
● Identify needs.
● Construct an action plan.
● Implement and evaluate.

Davis' approach provides a helpful structure for designing an urban youth ministry program—whether you're designing a whole youth ministry or a specific outreach such as a tutoring program or a pregnancy-prevention program. This chapter begins by examining Davis' approach. Then it concludes by focusing on how to get two important types of support for your youth ministry: financial and congregational.

Identify Resources

What resources does your church have for youth ministry? Your first reaction may be: "None. We can hardly pay our heating bills—much less fund an exciting youth program." But most congregations do, in fact, have the primary resources for youth ministry: spiritual resources, people resources and facility resources.

Davis believes it's essential to identify resources before identifying *needs*. If you begin by looking at needs in the cities, needs are so great that you'll feel compelled to respond to all of them. As a result, you'll become overwhelmed. In contrast Davis writes: "If the motivation for helping grows out of the Christian's relationship with God, however, he or she must keep on helping, regardless of the actions of the person who has the need. Christians cannot stop trying to help, because the God to whom they belong does not stop."[2]

Spiritual resources. Urban youth ministry is, above all
else, *ministry*. It involves listening to what God wants your
church to be for young people. It involves listening to how
God calls you, your congregation and individuals within
your congregation to serve the young people in your community.

Thus, it's important for your congregation to pray for
direction and to engage in Bible study while looking inward
for resources. LaSalle Street Church in Chicago developed its
innovative and widely acclaimed ministry to its community
after an in-depth Bible study about poverty.

People resources. Who within your congregation feels
called to minister to young people? Who has gifts of listening? compassion? reaching out? understanding? patience?

Urban youth workers invariably mention these personal-
ity traits when they're describing the kinds of people who
make effective urban youth workers. Skills such as playing a
guitar, speaking with charisma, planning creative programs
and coaching basketball are much less important.

Urban youth ministry veteran James DiRaddo says
churches need to ask: "Who do we have here who's willing
to get it started? . . . If you find someone who really loves
kids and who really wants to spend time with them, it
won't be long before kids are coming and hanging around.
I've seen some pretty poor programs and pretty great gangs
of kids. And it just boils down to the fact that someone really loves them and cares about them."

Discovering people resources can be the key to innovative programs. Daniel Jeonj, a Korean immigrant with a
black belt in Tae Kwon Do, began a Christian Tae Kwon Do
program at his church that taught inner-city young people
the martial art, emphasizing respect and self-discipline. He
combined the instruction with a weekly Bible study
designed to build character and self-confidence in the young
people.

Facility resources. Space is one thing many urban
churches have plenty of. Often they feel burdened with
oversized facilities that sit empty every day but Sunday.
Could that space become a tool for reaching young people?

Shaffer Memorial United Methodist Church in Cleveland,

Ohio, found itself in this position. "Our limited budget was not an obstacle but an opening to address the community's problems," writes pastor Ralph Fotia. "We had a large empty building with a well-constructed, well-equipped educational unit which we could make available to the community."[3]

So the church opened its doors to the community, providing a Saturday school in place of Sunday school for young people. Neighborhood kids with few other positive recreational outlets packed the program. Caring teachers provided quality lessons and relationships with the young people. The church also invited non-profit organizations to use the space for minimal rent. This arrangement not only helped with the bills, but it also brought badly needed services into the community.

Identify Needs

What needs do young people in your community have? What's missing in their lives? What negative influences need to be countered? What would improve their quality of life and their prospects for the future?

Needs can vary both in urgency and scope. If teenagers have no recreational facility, perhaps they need a safe place to play and socialize. If gangs are a force in the community, perhaps teenagers need a positive alternative. If the young people are scattered across the metropolitan area, maybe they need more fellowship opportunities.

In some cities and neighborhoods, many needs will be obvious. They make the headlines—gang killings, teenage pregnancy, substance abuse. However, these issues may actually be symptoms of deeper needs—low self-esteem, lack of community, family distress. Thus, it's important to study teenagers' needs within your own community and not assume you already know the needs.

There are dozens of ways to discover unmet needs in your community. Many of them were described in Chapter 2. They include talking with teenagers, visiting other pastors and youth workers, visiting teachers and school officials, talking with parents, taking surveys and checking for published information about your community's kids. Each can give valuable insights. Often a combination of two or three methods gives the most well-rounded picture. Also, informal discussions with teenagers, parents and community leaders after a survey can help you interpret the survey results.

The needs in Cass Community Church's Detroit community were clear. On average, one young person was being shot each day in the city. Thirty-four were killed in the first 10 months of 1987—the highest youth homicide rate in the nation.

The problem was close to the youth group too, says former pastor Bill Wylie-Kellermann. One former group member was imprisoned for life for killing an ice cream truck driver. Another group member shot himself during a game of Russian roulette with other group members. Both the low-income and middle-income kids were experiencing violence in school. And everyone felt helpless.

The community was calling out for the church's ministry. And the church responded with a special youth-led, youth-initiated program on discipleship and urban violence. It involved intense spiritual disciplines combined with training in non-violence techniques. (This program is described in detail in Chapter 10.)

When identifying needs, be sure to involve the community in the process. Otherwise, your ministry may fail because only you *think* something's a need or because people resist an outsider's interference. Youth workers can follow Jesus' model when he restored the blind man's sight. The man, who was obviously blind, came to Jesus asking for his help. But before doing anything, Jesus asked, "What do *you* want me to do for you?" (Mark 10:51).

Another factor to consider is to be careful to identify *unmet* needs. If someone else—another church or a social service agency—is already addressing the issue effectively, there's no reason to duplicate efforts. Resources are too limited and needs are too great for different ministries and agencies to duplicate services unnecessarily. As urban ministry expert Ray Bakke writes: "Before spending your limited money, it is wise to see the big picture. It is sad to see churches competing with each other, or with other agencies, to reach the same groups."[4]

Construct an Action Plan

An action plan brings together the resources and the needs into specific ministries. For example, Manhattan Bible Church in New York discovered that young people in its community particularly needed positive relationships with adult role models. The church, which has plenty of volunteers, enlisted people whose only responsibility in the youth program is to build relationships with young people. They're called FOCUS leaders, an acronym for:

Friend
Outreach
Caring
Understanding
Serving

Author C. Anne Davis suggests that an action plan should:

● include in the planning process the people being helped;

● include in the leadership the people being helped;

● enhance the worth and dignity of everyone involved; and

● be well-rounded, addressing the physical, spiritual, emotional and social needs of the people involved.[5]

Action plans can take many different forms. Some plans may involve starting or reshaping the church's whole youth ministry. Or they may focus on beginning a specialized ministry. They may be as simple as having two adult volunteers tutor students one evening each week. Or they may be as complicated as organizing and staffing a drug rehabilitation program as a church outreach. (Chapters 7 through 10 outline the specifics of various potential ministries.)

One effective model for urban church youth ministry has been developed by Buster Soaries. The model is designed to provide a whole-person ministry for young people. Soaries believes a balanced urban youth ministry should include the following emphases:[6]

● Spiritual growth (Bible study, personal faith development)

● Academic excellence (tutoring, career planning)

● Family support (parent workshops, counseling)

● Cultural enrichment (drama, museums, music)

● Ethnic heritage awareness (black history, denomina-
tional history)
   ● Economic opportunity (banking, money management)
   ● Civic awareness (political awareness)
   ● Recreational activities (athletics, special outings)
   ● Special needs (crisis ministries, referrals, follow-up)
   The structure, which is being piloted at Shiloh Baptist
Church in Trenton, New Jersey, is called JAM (Jesus And
Me). It includes a dozen specific programs that meet specific
needs. These include:
   ● JAM Session, a weekly evangelistic youth meeting
   ● JAM Special, unique seminars and field trips on
topics such as black history and politics
   ● JAM Band, a music group that performs gospel and
contemporary Christian music at JAM sessions
   ● JAM Fun, organized recreational activities for teenagers who participate in other church activities
   In addition to the programs, the model includes several
support structures that provide services to the various programs. These include a counseling committee, a public relations committee and a committee that keeps track of
political issues that affect neighborhood teenagers so that
the church can play an advocacy role for the community.

Implementing and Evaluating

Once a program is in place, you've got to run it. While
actual implementation may seem like the easy part after all
the preparation, it's often the most difficult and discourag-
ing. No matter how well a program is planned and publi-
cized, there's always the chance that no one will come,
particularly in the city. And there's no guarantee that the
program actually will meet the needs.
   Lafayette Park United Methodist Church is in a revitalized community in St. Louis. They discovered an expressed
need for a parent support group. So, pastor Diana Loomis
says, the church started one. But "people then had to make
the decision: 'Do I go out one more night and be away
from my child? Or do I spend the time at home with my
child?' " Loomis says. Parents chose the latter option, and

the support group never worked. So the church had to try to find other ways to meet the need while also accounting for members' hectic schedules.

Another reason some programs are difficult to implement is that urban teenagers have had so many negative experiences with people who want to "help them." These people fly into town, do some kind of ministry "for these poor kids," and then quickly leave.

"Inner-city adolescents often have few, if any, adults who show a genuine interest in their life as they live and experience it," David Claerbaut writes. "A serious, non-patronizing approach to them, by a concerned adult, is potentially very effective . . . There is a tremendous desire to determine whether a person 'is for real.' The tests may be frequent and repetitious. But, once the tests are passed, there is real potential for growth and relationship . . . Once a youth feels he is genuinely associated with an adult he respects and who cares about him, all facets of being are opened up."[7]

Phill Carlos Archbold illustrates this testing by telling about a Sunday morning program he initiated. Beforehand, he visited all the group members in their homes, inviting them to the first meeting. They all assured him they'd be there.

The first Sunday, no one showed up. Everyone had excuses.

The next Sunday, the same thing happened.

And the next.

But Archbold kept inviting the kids. He wouldn't give up. After several weeks, the young people started responding to his invitations by saying, "You're really serious about this, aren't you?" And they started coming. "They test your strength. They test your energy," Archbold explains. "It's not really tricks. It's just that they want to make sure you're for real and that you really love them." Because it can take time for a program to catch on, leaders and planners need support and encouragement from the church staff and congregation.

Program implementation should be accompanied by evaluation. Many churches neglect program evaluation, leaving them without systematic opportunities for fine-tuning and improvement. Involve many different people in the evaluation—teenagers, church staff, church lay leaders, parents, community leaders—anyone who might have valuable insights into your ministry and its direction. Also, an evaluation can take many forms, both formal and informal. Formal evaluation might involve surveys and suggestion cards. Informal evaluation might include small groups sharing their thoughts and ideas.

Buster Soaries suggests evaluating the youth ministry by matching programs with objectives using the chart illustrated in Diagram 6-1, "Diagnosing a Youth Ministry." Write the programs you offer across the top. Then list your objectives or emphases for ministry in the left column. For example, Soaries lists spiritual growth, academic excellence and cultural enrichment as major emphases for urban youth ministries (see page 132).

Then check which programs meet which objectives. For example, the JAM Excel academic program at Shiloh Baptist Church may meet the objectives for academic excellence, personal development and economic opportunity.

Once you've plotted all your programs on the chart, you can begin to see which objectives are being met, which ones are being neglected, and which ones are being overemphasized. This information then becomes an important guide for beginning new ministries. If, for example, most of your church programs deal with "economic opportunity," it would be inappropriate to add another program with a similar emphasis, however good it may promise to be.

Whatever evaluation method you choose, this step can be a critical link in ensuring that your program effectively uses your congregation's resources to meet young people's needs.

Funding for Urban Youth Ministry

Finding funds for youth ministry is a perennial problem in many urban churches. The problem is particularly difficult for churches in low-income communities where neither the church nor its members can afford much.

Diagram 6-1
Diagnosing a Youth Ministry

Programs

	1.	2.	3.	4.	5.
1.					
2.					
3.					
4.					
5.					
6.					
7.					

Objectives

There are several ways, however, to cope with the funding problem:

Freebies. With a little digging, most urban youth workers can discover numerous free opportunities for groups working with underprivileged young people.

Archbold says he "scans the New York Times page-by-page to look for free things." He says major foundations often donate tickets to worthy causes. As a result, he frequently takes kids to Broadway shows, Carnegie Hall and other cultural events. (The box offices keep these tickets, waiting for worthy groups to ask for them.) Other youth workers get free or discounted tickets to professional ball games, the zoo and community events.

The city's resources. Many cities sponsor free events for the city—concerts or drama in the park, art festivals, free nights at the museum. Church youth groups can take advantage of these as fun, educational group-building experiences. The city itself offers many free outings for creative youth groups. Dave Carver says his group can often walk to city parks and swimming pools for special programs, saving the cost of transportation. During the winter, Carver says, the church can rent an indoor community pool for very little money, providing a great setting for a fun social occasion.

Many times kids just want to get out of their own neighborhood with the group. Wendell Fisher sometimes takes his group on the Staten Island Ferry to enjoy the ride and scenery together. Chapter 7 includes some creative ways youth workers have taken advantage of the city's subways and other "attractions" for programming.

Other churches. If approached, many wealthier suburban congregations will financially support your urban youth program as a part of their ministry. "Inner-city churches and missions must be adopted by suburban congregations in order to connect resources with needs," writes Michael J. Christensen. "Urban ministries can only survive if they are supported by those on the outside who know the needs and want to help."[8] His ministry—Golden Gate Community located in the impoverished Haight Ashbury district of San Francisco—would not survive, he says, without the support it receives from churches across the country that consider his ministry *their* ministry too.

City and community organizations. Friendship Baptist Church in Vallejo, California, wants to open a youth center in the community. Youth worker Harold Wright says no such facility exists in the community, so other churches as well as the city government are sharing the costs of rehabilitating an old house. By sharing the expense, the church can provide a ministry that might not otherwise be possible.

If your church has a large facility but doesn't have funds for programs, cooperate with other organizations. You supply the facility; they provide the programming resources.

Grants. Many national and local businesses, foundations and denominations have funds specifically earmarked for community development, youth programs or other similar concerns. Oftentimes, churches can ask for and receive these funds to support their special projects and programs.

Park Avenue United Methodist Church has been particularly effective in this regard. It funds a major summer camp program, a computer training program and an annual Soul Liberation Festival largely with monies donated by businesses and foundations. Each year, youth worker Art Erickson asks local businesses to support his programs. Erickson believes the programs' proven track records are the keys to his success in getting money. "We're really producing people who are living productive lives in an almost impossible situation," he says. "Businesses are eager to contribute."

Receiving grant money is not automatic, however. The church usually must write a grant request and then be held accountable. James DiRaddo says some businesses become frustrated with short-lived and ineffective programs. He says the high turnover rate of urban youth workers can be particularly damaging to grant requests.

Even with this problem, though, DiRaddo adds that the main reason people don't get support from foundations is that they don't know how to ask for it. Diagram 6-2, "Writing Grant Proposals," outlines some of the basic elements of preparing a grant proposal. Of course, each business or foundation is different, so it's important to find out specifics about an organization before applying for a grant.

Diagram 6-2
Writing Grant Proposals

In an extensive article titled "Program Planning and Proposal Writing," Norton J. Kiritz, executive director of the Grantsmanship Center in Los Angeles, suggests the following format for writing a proposal:[9]

Proposal summary. The summary is the first thing people at a funding source will read, so it's a critical element on the first page of your proposal. "It should be clear, concise and specific," Kiritz writes. "It should describe who you are, the scope of your project and the projected cost." In some cases, your summary may be the only thing that's read in an initial screening, so take time with it.

A proposal should also include each of the following elements:

1. Introduction. A proposal introduction tells about your organization, church or ministry. The goal is to build credibility as an organization since grants are given based on your reputation or connections, as well as the program content. This information should be tailored to appeal to the specific funding source.

An introduction should include:

● How your ministry got started (including anything unique about your beginnings)

● How long you've been around

● Your ministry's most significant accomplishments (If your ministry is new, include accomplishments of the people involved in the ministry.)

● Your organization's goals

● Information about support you've received from other organizations or individuals (including endorsement letters, if possible)

2. Problem Statement or Assessment of Needs. This section focuses on the specific needs you want to address through your program. Kiritz urges people to be specific and focused. "Narrow down your definition of the problem . . . to something you can hope to accomplish within a reasonable amount of time and with a reasonable amount of additional resources," he writes.

It's also important in this section to document the problem. Use key statistics, but don't overload the proposal with charts. Interview key people in the community and include their perceptions. Then make logical connections between your ministry's background and the problems you want to address.

3. Program Objectives. This section describes "a specific, measurable outcome of your program" that you hope to achieve. Kiritz writes that the objectives answer the following question: "If I support your project for a year, or for two years, and come back at

continued

that time and say, 'I want to see what you have done—what you have accomplished,' what can you tell me?''

For example, if you want funding for a tutoring program, you might set an objective of reducing the number of dropouts in your community by a certain percentage. The objectives must be realistic, or a funding agency will be led to think that you aren't familiar enough with the field.

4. Methods. This section tells how you're going to fulfill your objectives. What programs will you initiate? This section should also explain why you chose particular methods, which requires that you know a good bit about programs that are addressing similar problems in your community and elsewhere. Be sure you address the issues you raise in the problem section.

5. Evaluation. In this section, explain how you plan to evaluate your proposed program to determine its effectiveness. Evaluation should grow naturally out of your objectives. ''If you have difficulty in determining what criteria to use in evaluating your program,'' Kiritz writes, ''better take another look at your objectives. They probably aren't very specific.'' To avoid the dangers of a subjective evaluation of your own program, it's sometimes helpful to work with another organization in your community to provide a more objective appraisal.

6. Future funding. This section answers the question, ''How will you continue your program when the grant runs out?'' If your proposal is a one-time request (such as funding for equipment), this section may be irrelevant, but it's vital to ongoing programs. Agencies want to know that you have a specific funding plan so you can continue your program when the grant is completed. This plan may involve a commitment for continued funding from other agencies. Or it may rely on the program becoming self-sufficient when the grant money runs out.

7. Budget. Each agency will require slightly different budget outlines. Most of the time, Kiritz suggests, agencies want the following information:

● Personnel. This category includes wages and salaries, fringe benefits, and consultants and contract services. Kiritz says this section often takes 80 percent of the budget for most social service programs.

● Non-Personnel. You'll include in this category space costs, equipment rental, lease or purchase, consumable supplies, travel, telephones and other costs.

Congregational Support

"Moral support" from the church is probably even more critical to urban youth ministry than financial support. Without the congregation's backing, urban youth ministries almost always fail.

Congregational support can be particularly difficult to cultivate for several reasons:

● First, church members may expect the youth program only to "take care of our own." If outreach into the community is perceived as neglecting the church kids, the congregation could begin challenging the program.

● Second, congregations may react negatively to having streetwise kids in the church building. They may look and act differently from the "church kids." And they may not show as much respect for church property. The result is overprotectiveness and suspicion from the congregation.

● Finally, if church members don't know the kids, they're unlikely to support the youth program when conflicts arise.

How can urban youth workers help build bridges to the congregation? Here are a few suggestions:

Build relationships. The most important key is to get the adults and the kids to know each other, Dave Carver says. "We tried to get the kids and adults to meet each other," he explains. "And when that happened, it was easy. If Mrs. McGillicuty is choosing between . . . those rowdy kids and our dear old church, well, there's no contest. But if Mrs. McGillicuty is choosing between Ricky and Carrie and that messy old room on the third floor, then there's also no contest." (Diagram 6-3, "Dealing With Negative Behaviors," focuses on how to maintain relationships while also maintaining your integrity.)

Carver notes that worship is the most difficult area in which to build bridges because of all the tradition involved. So it's best to establish a common relationship in other aspects of church life. His church sponsored intergenerational retreats, spaghetti dinners with the help of the women of the church and a hoagie sale with help from retired women. Carver says they use "any excuse we can think of to try to get them together."

Diagram 6-3
Dealing With Negative Behaviors

Youth workers who minister to unchurched urban teenagers often deal with kids who do things they disapprove of—smoking, drinking, drug use, sex outside marriage. While youth workers can hope to influence kids to change behavior, urban teenagers will usually do what they choose to do.

Dave Carver has encountered this situation many times in his work in Pittsburgh. "It's hard for me to watch a kid do something that I think is hurting the kid." Yet even when he disagrees with what teenagers do, "I love them because of the image they have in them. If this one smokes or that one drinks or this one sleeps around, I don't have to accept that behavior, but I need to accept that kid," Carver says.

So where do you draw the line? Carver defines the limits and lets his kids know them:

● No smoking in his house or car (though they can smoke in his presence)

● No drinking

● No excessive swearing

"Being honest with the kids allows them to respect you," Carver says. "The kids knew what I believed . . . but we also tried to make it pretty clear that they were choices the kids had to make."

He would often tell the kids: "God gave us all the right to be stupid . . . If you want to be stupid, that's your God-given right. But you're not allowed to be stupid in here."

Make kids visible. The youth group at North Shore Baptist Church in Chicago is actively involved in congregational life, says youth leader Melanie Monteclaro. "Youth ministry is not just a separate arm . . . Kids want to be involved in the whole church rather than just being in the youth group." So they present reports to the church, serve on committees, help with cleanup, greet on Sundays, perform special music—almost anything. In this way, the church says to group members: "You're the church, too. We're not just ministering to you; you have a vital part in ministering to us too."

Maintain credibility. A final key to keeping congregational support is to be sure the young people respect the congregation's wishes too. Dave Carver says he explained to his group members that the older church members needed their space just like the youth group needed its space. If they want the congregation to respect the youth room, then they needed to respect the church parlor, sanctuary and other special areas. (See Diagram 6-4, "Responding to Vandalism," for more about how to deal with this issue.)

Patience for the Long Haul

Building programs for urban teenagers is often a slow, tedious process. Then, just when you think everything is going well, something negative happens. And you're ready to give up. But God's Spirit intervenes—usually through another person.

Jim Hopkins, youth minister at First Baptist Church in Los Angeles, tells how his church's community youth center appeared to be doing so well. Kids were using it, and it was widely hailed for being a positive influence in a gang-infested neighborhood.

Despite the program's success, it was also beginning to have trouble—graffiti, break-ins, vandalism. Then one night

---

Diagram 6-4

Responding to Vandalism

An article by Rich Van Pelt in GROUP Magazine suggests several things you can do if your church is vandalized by teenagers:

● Remember who holds the "deed." Van Pelt writes, "Sometimes we see the church building as the center of worship rather than the worship center." While we shouldn't condone vandalism, it is important to keep ministry priorities straight.

● Respond with love and hope. Use the opportunity to show Christ's love to the teenagers. A youth worker in Nashville, Tennessee, invited an unchurched kid who had previously vandalized the church to attend a youth group overnight event. The kid became an active part of the youth group because of the experience.

● Offer creative alternatives. Work with the juvenile justice system to discover creative and healthy ways to deal with the problem. This may involve restitution, repair and community service, depending on the judge and the legal code in your state.[10]

three guys and three girls who had been involved in the youth program broke into the church gym and vandalized property. Hopkins says he was frustrated and furious. Maybe he had been coddling the kids too much. It was time to get tough. He decided to prosecute the kids, hoping they'd go to jail. It would be a lesson that you don't mess with the church.

Hopkins reported all this to the church council meeting that week. It upset the whole council. Then after the meeting, a woman came up to the youth minister and asked: "Could we have the names of the kids who broke in? We'd like to pray for them. We can't give up on them yet."

That's what urban youth ministry is all about.

Action and Reflection

1. Make a list of the resources your congregation has. Include spiritual resources, people resources and facility resources. What do you have that seems ideally suited to youth ministry?

2. Lead a Bible study on helping adults and teenagers discover their spiritual gifts. Who in the congregation is God calling to work with young people?

3. Tour your church facility. Is all the space being well used throughout the week? Keep notes on what rooms or other facilities might be available for particular youth programs.

4. Discover needs in your community. Look back at Chapter 2 where you'll find suggestions for getting to know your community. Work with young people and church leaders to discover ways to bring resources and needs together into a vision and plan for youth ministry.

5. Take time to evaluate your current programs. Ask yourself tough questions:
- Is the program really effective in reaching teenagers?
- Is this the most effective way to minister to teenagers?
- How might the program be changed to be more appropriate?
- Should the program be dropped in order to free up resources for other ministries that fit your congregation and community better?

6. Look at your youth ministry budget. What does it tell you about your church's commitment to youth ministry? Is it adequate to sustain the type of ministries you think you need?

7. Look through your local newspaper for free opportunities for your youth group.

8. Call major civic, cultural and sports organizations in your city. Investigate the possibilities for free or discounted tickets for your youth group. Explain your needs and tell about your ministries.

9. Tour your neighborhood to find free recreation opportunities that might be available for your youth group.

10. Evaluate the level of moral support you feel from your congregation. Talk with the pastor or another individual to discover where potential conflicts lie.

11. Arrange opportunities for your youth group to interact with people of other ages in the congregation. Give young people opportunities to be visible in congregation-wide events.

Endnotes

[1]C. Anne Davis, "The Practice of Urban Ministry: Christian Social Ministries," Review and Expositor, (Fall 1983), 523-528.

[2]C. Anne Davis, "The Practice of Urban Ministry: Christian Social Ministries," 523-528.

[3]Ralph Fotia, "Inner-City Ministry in a Small Church," The Christian Ministry, (September/October 1988), 11-12.

[4]Ray Bakke with Jim Hart, The Urban Christian (Downers Grove, IL: InterVarsity Press, 1987), 117.

[5]C. Anne Davis, "The Practice of Urban Ministry: Christian Social Ministries," 523-528.

[6]Buster Soaries, "Church Based Youth Ministry in the Black Community," (An unpublished paper presented at GROUP Magazine's 1989 Youth Ministry University), 8-10. Used by permission of the author.

[7]David Claerbaut, Urban Ministry (Grand Rapids, MI: Zondervan Publishing House, 1983), 122.

[8]Michael J. Christensen, City Streets, City People: A Call for Compassion (Nashville, TN: Abingdon Press, 1988), 84.

[9]Norton J. Kiritz, "Program Planning and Proposal Writing," a reprint from The Grantsmanship Center News. Copies of the complete article are available from The Grantsmanship Center, 1015 W. Olympic Blvd., Los Angeles, CA 90015.

[10]Rich Van Pelt, "Vandalism!" GROUP Magazine, (November/December 1988), 30-32.

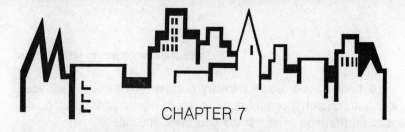

CHAPTER 7

Youth Programs for the City

Most churches take Monday off. Sunday's the big day, and the church staff needs rest.

But Monday night is the busiest night of the week for Michael Walton, youth minister at First Baptist Congregational Church in Chicago. That's the night for Son City, the church's weekly youth group meeting. As many as 70 teenagers from across the Chicagoland area come for an evening of recreation, fellowship and study.

Like other urban youth ministries, Walton's church has discovered that a traditional Sunday night meeting isn't always effective. And while urban youth programs may contain the same elements as other youth programs (fellowship, Bible study, recreation), the emphasis shifts to meet the unique needs of *urban* teenagers.

This chapter describes ways different urban youth ministers have designed their programs to meet their teenag-

ers' needs. The chapter includes the following:
- Keys to effective programming
- Different program formats (meetings, retreats, special events, and so forth)
- A potpourri of program ideas that have worked in different cities

Chapters 8 through 10 deal with specific elements of programming—Bible study, celebrating diversity and meeting critical needs.

Keys to Effective Programming
While there are no perfect formulas for effective programming, there are some basic principles that undergird the specific programs you develop. These principles tell young people that they're important and welcome in the church.

Ministry Orientation
It's obvious that church programs should enhance the church's *ministry*. Too often youth programs in the city are started just "to get the kids off the streets."

Buster Soaries points out serious problems with this attitude. First, he says, you rarely take the kids off the street; they bring the street in with them. Second, unless a program grows out of ministry priorities, it won't keep the youth ministry balanced. Thus, these programs consume valuable resources and energy that could be used to advance the church's ministry.

Openness and Acceptance
It's difficult to be open to teenagers who say and do things you disagree with. And that often happens in the city. Yet, in order for ministry to take place, the church must accept these teenagers and be open to their concerns. "These kids are very genuine and honest about where they are," says Tracy Hipps of Inner City Impact in Chicago. "And you've got to accept them just the way they are."

This openness and acceptance characterizes the "Teen Rap" sessions at Bethel African Methodist Episcopal Church in Baltimore, Maryland. The program takes place once a month on Friday evening. The young people choose a topic to discuss. Parents and adults can come if they want, but they can't say anything. In fact, for a while even youth leader Marietta Ramsey couldn't talk. Now she can talk, but only to clarify scripture passages.

The result of this approach is that teenagers have a place where they can talk about their real and tough concerns in a trusting and supportive environment. "Some of them are very honest," Ramsey says. "There are sessions in which kids really lay their stuff out—put their feelings on the line."

Ramsey recalls one teenage girl telling about the pressure she was feeling from her boyfriend to have sex. She knew it was wrong, but she also knew she had to do it to keep her relationship with her boyfriend. The group helped by supporting her and encouraging her to make the right decision.

This openness and acceptance is also important because urban teenagers are constantly criticized, and their self-esteem is generally low. They may hear from a parent that they're "no good," and they hear news reports about all the "problems" they have. The church needs to be a place where they are affirmed and lifted up.

As Michael Walton says: "When you talk to these young people, don't criticize them all the time. I know they do goofy things, but remember when you were a kid, okay? Remember the ups and downs you had to go through."

Emphasis on Relationships

The Church of the Open Door in Miami often has difficulty getting kids to come to meetings because "there are so many other things to do," says youth leader Freddie Watkins. Yet she says sometimes it's beneficial to have only one or two kids because she can build strong relationships with them.

Large groups such as Manhattan Bible Church find many adult volunteers so they can form small groups during meetings. These groups then become the context for building relationships that wouldn't be possible in larger groups.

This emphasis on building relationships holds true whether you serve in a neighborhood church or a metropolitan church. Deborah Ban, a pastor at Calvary Baptist Church in Denver, Colorado, says the relationships are vital to her group. "Because our kids come from all over the city and have no connecting life, the youth group at the church needs to be a place where they feel comfortable and welcome . . . They come because they feel they have a group of friends here who are very different from their friends at school."

Caution with Games

David Miles says the key to planning games in a city church is to never make the young people the brunt of any practical jokes. He says that urban teenagers will never loosen up enough for some of the crazy antics that are common in suburban youth groups. Unlike many of their suburban neighbors, urban teenagers have developed a hard shell around them to protect them on the streets. They don't show weakness or vulnerability because of their fear of becoming a target for aggression. It's very difficult for them to take off this shell, even for a couple of hours every week.

Miles learned this the hard way. Once he put a pie in the face of a group member—someone he thought he had a great relationship with. He says the young person was furious with him and left the room feeling humiliated. It took several weeks to repair the relationship.

Basic Youth Group Programs

While the emphasis in urban youth ministry is on building relationships, sharing the gospel, and helping young people grow in their faith, these goals take place in the context of a variety of programs. As urban youth workers serve in a community, they discover what types of programs work—and what types don't. Here are some of the different kinds of programs that are often useful in the city:

Regular Meetings

Like other youth groups, urban youth groups need a regular time for Bible study and building relationships. Most churches (but not all) sponsor weekly programs that involve recreation, Bible study and fellowship.

These regular meetings meet some important needs of urban teenagers. Marlene Pedigo writes about the youth meetings at the Chicago Fellowship of Friends. She tells of the frustration of seeing teenagers continue to turn to negative peer groups for their friendships. "Something other than drugs and organized gangs needed to fill their need for a sense of security and belonging," she writes. "Through our Youthquake program, we provide a sense of community and support for young people . . . Youthquake becomes a place where teens can find positive peer support."[1]

One of the challenges of regular meetings is to balance the needs of kids from unchurched backgrounds with the needs of young people who've grown up in the church. Neighborhood teenagers who may not have a Christian commitment won't be attracted to in-depth Bible study. Yet the long-time group members need more depth for their own growth.

To meet both needs, some urban churches provide two different programs. For example, First Baptist Church in Flushing, New York, holds a regular group meeting which attracts both churched and unchurched teenagers. Then the church also has small discipleship groups that meet other times for in-depth Bible study and spiritual growth.

A similar approach is taken by Lawndale Community Church in Chicago. Every Monday night, the church opens its gymnasium and recreation facilities. For an hour the kids can play whatever is available—basketball, board games, racquetball, and so forth. Ten adults work during this time, building relationships with the kids and supervising activities. Then the whole group plays community-building games together. Finally, the group has a simple, 15-minute devotion time that's designed, pastor Wayne Gordon says, to "scratch people where they itch."

After this basic meeting, kids who want to study scripture in more depth can stay for a discipleship study called "Roots." This program involves a 10-week commitment to Bible study, including some homework.

Regular meetings not only vary in content and focus,

they also take place at different times based on needs. Let's look at some of the options:

Sunday afternoon. First United Methodist Church in Houston draws kids from across the metropolis for its Sunday morning activities. Then teenagers are invited to stay the whole afternoon and participate in a wide range of activities such as recreation, service projects, intensive Bible study, youth choir and a free supper.

Monday night. As we saw in the introduction to this chapter, First Baptist Congregational Church sponsors a Monday night meeting. Youth minister Michael Walton says Monday works best for his group because it's an off-night in the city. There are few conflicts. Also, it's easy to promote Monday night activities on Sunday.

Friday night. While Friday nights often don't work in the suburbs because kids have high school activities and other options, many urban teenagers don't have many positive options that evening. For example, Miles says all the high school ball games are in the afternoons since schools don't want to risk having evening games. A Friday night meeting gives kids a positive alternative to the city's negative weekend activities.

All-day Saturday. Some urban churches that draw members from around the metropolitan area find that weekly meetings are too much trouble for people to drive to. Instead, they sponsor a monthly, all-day Saturday meeting. Christ Church in Manhattan, New York, takes this approach, and finds that it attracts more unchurched teenagers whose families aren't used to regular church activities.

Saturday night. First Chinese Baptist Church in San Francisco had terrible luck getting the Chinese-speaking teenagers to attend Sunday school on Sunday mornings. So, youth worker Jerald Choy says the church switched the Chinese-speaking program to Saturday night.

But while this time has been successful for the Chinese-speaking teenagers (who live mainly in the immediate Chinatown community), the church has to maintain an English-speaking youth group on Sundays, since these young people drive in to church with their families from all over San Francisco.

Athletics and Recreation

Ever since churches and parachurch groups have begun trying to reach urban teenagers, recreation and athletics have been major outreach tools. When he became a pastor in Chicago, Ray Bakke wasted no time organizing the Inner City Athletic Mission. He teamed up with Christian football players and challenged the gangs drinking alcohol on the beach to play football. "We drew up lines on the beach, beat the stuffing out of them and then invited them to a barbecue," Bakke writes. "We really roughed them up and we became known as the 'butcher priests'! It was interesting evangelism . . ."[2]

Other urban youth workers usually take more conventional approaches, providing young people with the recreation facilities that are usually lacking in the community. This approach is generally successful. "Basketball is the most popular sport in the inner city," Michael Walton says. "I can go out and minister on a basketball court real easy because there will always be kids there. The only time you might not find somebody there is when you have a foot of snow outside."

Lawndale Community Church has a heavy emphasis on athletics in its youth program—hardly surprising since the church itself grew out of a Fellowship of Christian Athletes (FCA) group. "Athletics is such a huge part of the black community," Wayne Gordon says. "It's been a natural for us." In 1976, Gordon purchased a weight machine for his FCA group. "That was one of the first draws because the school I coached at didn't have one."

While the church emphasizes athletics, it doesn't emphasize competition. Rather, the games are considered a natural, fun way to build relationships with the teenagers.

Another church with a major sports program is Riverside Church in New York City. According to a report in Sports Illustrated, the program started when a government housing project was built right next to the church in the 1960s. The church decided to reach into the community. Ernie Lorch, a church member who was a former college basketball player, took the lead. "One day I went over to the Grant Projects with 12 jerseys, rounded up a dozen of

the toughest kids and brought them all back to the church."
That's how the league began.

The Riverside program involves about 300 players each
year—both guys and girls. It's broken into four age groups,
beginning with 11-year-olds and going through high school
seniors.

Lorch's strategy shows why his athletic program is an
important ministry. He uses the kids' love for the game to
help the teenagers begin to see some good in themselves.
Many of the teenagers have been written off by society, and
the program gives them self-respect by challenging them
and expecting something of them. "If you can earn a kid's
respect, make him respect himself and at the same time
show him you care, it's so easy to turn a kid around," Lorch
says.

In order to participate in the basketball program, Lorch
insists that the players attend school. If kids fulfill that basic
requirement, Lorch will support them in any way he can—
particularly tutoring—so they have a chance at college
basketball scholarships.[3] This blend of academics with
sports is credited with keeping urban teenagers in school
longer, and giving them opportunities that otherwise might
never have been possible.

Lorch's success rate is high. Several kids from his basketball league have actually ended up in the pros. But, more
importantly, the program gives these teenagers a vision that
they can do something with their lives.

(See Diagram 7-1, "Protecting the Recreation Program,"
for information on potential problems in these programs.)

Special Events

Athletic programs aren't the only events that draw urban teenagers into the church. Some urban congregations
have found that special music and drama programs have a
particular appeal to city neighborhoods. By providing quality entertainment, churches gain credibility in the community and access to people.

There are many different ways churches can reach into
their community through special programs. To see some of
the options, let's look at two churches that have taken dif-

Diagram 7-1

Protecting the Recreation Program

Many congregations begin recreation ministries to provide a positive, safe environment for a community that doesn't have any recreation facilities. But too often, the outreach backfires because rules and expectations aren't clear. "We had hoped to build an accepting environment of safety, but they saw it as just a safe haven to continue gang activity," says Jim Hopkins of First Baptist Church in Los Angeles.

Once the church discovered the problems, it temporarily closed the facility. When it reopened, it established clear guidelines and expectations:

● The staff more closely monitors the doors to the street. The doors open at 4:30 p.m. and close soon afterward.

● Only people who want to participate in the activities can come in. If they get tired of an activity, they must leave. This prevents the problem of having kids hanging around in the entrance.

● Participants must respect basic behavior guidelines established for the facility.

Hopkins says that the new rules have reduced the number of kids who participate—at least in the short term. But he believes the program now has a greater impact on the kids who come.

---

ferent approaches:

Midnight Special. Periodically through the year, 200 to 300 teenagers converge on First Baptist Congregational Church in Chicago for five hours of music and drama. The Friday night program begins at 7 p.m. and runs until midnight.

Youth pastor Michael Walton says the attractive program offers kids something they rarely have in the city—a well-produced program of drama, music and guest speakers. Walton says the program is particularly effective because many urban teenagers have never seen live drama. They come to these productions and are overwhelmed. Kids leave saying: "These people got music. They got spotlights. They got special effects and sound effects. Hey, they're putting on a real play. This isn't like something out of Sunday school."

While five hours may seem like a long time to keep teenagers interested, Walton says the program is "such a creative evening that not only does the time go fast, but finally we have to kick kids out because it's 1 o'clock in the morning."

Walton attributes the program's success to the extra energy put in to it. Often the evening features a drama by the Son Players, the church's high school drama troupe. The productions can be as elaborate as an episode of *Twilight Zone*—complete with special effects.

The program is also a valuable model for the city since it shows that you can have a "creative, exciting evening for Christ." Today the church doesn't even have to publicize a Midnight Special. "All we do is say we have a Midnight Special, and that's all the advertisement we need." Kids come because they know they can expect a fun, quality program.

Soul Liberation Festival. For eight days each July, the parking lot behind Park Avenue United Methodist Church in Minneapolis is transformed into a unique blend of an old-fashioned revival meeting, a gospel music festival and a neighborhood street fair. The goal, youth worker Art Erickson says, is to "gather as many unchurched people as possible." People bring their blankets, chairs and bikes, and listen to the gospel.

Through nationally known speakers and musicians, the church tries to reach teenagers and adults who might otherwise never have contact with a church. Most music is gospel, and speakers are people with particular appeal to the black and Hispanic communities. The program isn't designed as hard-sell evangelism. Rather, it's supposed to show the neighborhood that the church cares.

In addition to the music and speakers, Soul Liberation Festival also includes a "Rap Room" after the outdoor event for junior and senior high kids. The evening's speaker or a musician comes and spends 45 minutes talking with the kids about whatever is on their minds. "It's one of our most effective components of Soul Lib," Erickson says.[4]

Erickson believes Soul Liberation Festival is an important boost for the community. "Most urban communities do not come out," he says. "There's very little that brings them out together and a lot that keeps people inside and afraid. A festival like this brings people out, brings them together—

and if nothing else, gives them a good feeling because they're hearing, in word and in song, a message of hope. That's what the gospel message is: hope."[5]

Camping, Retreats and Conferences

Camps and retreats can be particularly valuable experiences for urban teenagers. Not only do they expose teenagers to other lifestyles and other areas of the country, but they also can provide valuable opportunities for growth and the development of new skills. Let's look at some of the ways camps, retreats and conferences can help urban teenagers:

Develop life skills. Because of their family, economic and educational backgrounds, many urban teenagers haven't learned basic life skills and coping skills. Camping experiences can help overcome these deficiencies, Erickson believes. Each summer, Park Avenue United Methodist Church sponsors an extensive camping program that includes activities such as rock climbing, rafting, canoeing, backpacking and bicycling.

"You really never know yourself until you've pushed yourself as far as you can go," Erickson says. "The physical reality cuts through all the jive."[6] These "stress camping" experiences help young people learn new coping techniques, and they give people a new perspective on life.

He tells about taking teenagers on a bike camp where they have to take care of their bicycles themselves. They must live, work and cooperate as a team. Erickson says: "It's not a lark. It's an important part of life."

Build group unity. Each summer First Chinese Baptist Church in San Antonio sponsors a major youth camp for both its Chinese-speaking and English-speaking youth groups. The camp's main purpose, Jerald Choy says, is to let the two groups interact "for a week, day in and day out." The week at camp helps build bridges between the two groups.

Explore the world. When Cass Community Church in Detroit announced an upcoming series of retreats away from the city, group members were eager to participate. "Some of the kids from the projects had literally not been out of

Detroit," says pastor Bill Wylie-Kellermann. "To see Lake Huron was a big deal . . . Getting out of the city to be together hooked everybody."

Meet different people. First Baptist Church in Los Angeles tries to include its young people in as many national youth events as possible. Jim Hopkins says these experiences are "tremendously important to inner-city kids." He says it's often the first time they've been around lots of teenagers from other backgrounds. It's a broadening experience as they build ties to different people.

Service

Because of the many needs in the city, urban life fosters a sense of mission and service in young people. As Phill Carlos Archbold of Brooklyn, New York, says: "You see all kinds of people. You see the rich, the not-so-rich, the downright poor. And our kids are made to understand that our world is made up of all kinds of people. If you have a loaf of bread, there are those who don't and . . . why don't you share it? They become concerned about their neighbors."

Urban youth workers learn to take advantage of the city's diversity to teach teenagers about Christian service. Calvary Baptist Church's youth group in Denver regularly does service projects around the city—food drives, clothing drives, painting projects. "In a suburb," pastor Deborah Ban says, "you may be sheltered or protected from those needs."

Archbold's youth group regularly collects and distributes food and clothing for the homeless in the community. "It has given them a desire to really take part in making the world a better place for somebody right here in Brooklyn," he says. "You don't have to go to Africa or China to do it."

Public Advocacy

In order for an urban ministry to be well-rounded and meet young people's needs, it must include an element of public advocacy or witness—addressing the political and social concerns that directly affect the teenagers in the youth group. As Buster Soaries says, "Our kids are in trouble simply by virtue of where they are born. We've got to deal with the systemic evils that oppress our kids."

Soaries believes that churches must be aware of local and national policy decisions that affect urban teenagers. Shiloh Baptist Church in Trenton, New Jersey, has two adult volunteers whose only job is to follow the political process. If issues arise that affect the young people, they inform other leaders.

Once the city council was voting on whether to close the only library in the church's neighborhood. The youth workers found out when the vote was scheduled and took the youth group on a "field trip" to city hall that evening. Several young people prepared written statements that outlined how the closing would hurt them and their educations. As a result, the library stayed open and the young people learned an important lesson about working within the political system.

Bryan Stone of Liberation Community of the Church of the Nazarene in Ft. Worth, Texas, says his teenagers often feel helpless in the face of a political system that affects them daily. Cuts in federal college grants, he says, can mean that a young person won't be able to go to college. As a result, his group often gets involved in issues so they can try to make more of a difference in the world.

One effort they made was to have a voter registration drive during a national election. The teenagers spent several Saturdays asking people to register. In the end, the group of 20 to 25 kids registered as many as 500 people for the election. Stone says that most of the young people really felt like they had done something significant, even though they themselves weren't old enough to vote. In a sense, he notes, they did influence the vote.

A Programming Potpourri

Because they don't have extravagant budgets, fancy buildings and large-scale youth programs, many urban youth ministries sometimes forget they can do things that most churches in other settings could never do. Sometimes kids just need to get out of the neighborhood for a group adventure in the city. There they can take advantage of the city's many resources. Or youth groups can discover more about themselves, their church and their community without spending lots of money.

Here are some fun and different activities for urban youth groups that would rarely work in the suburbs or in a small town:

International food fest fund-raiser. One of the real pleasures of an ethnically diverse church is enjoying each culture's unique flavor—literally. The youth group at North Shore Baptist Church in Chicago celebrated the benefits of having a Chinese, Filipino, Korean, Native American, Nigerian, Japanese and Anglo membership in the congregation by sponsoring an international food fest to raise $1,200 for a youth group trip.

Ambassadors for peace. The youth group of First Church of the Brethren in Brooklyn, New York, took advantage of having the United Nations headquarters in the city. The group invited U.N. ambassadors from different countries around the world to attend the church's Peace Emphasis Sunday. Four ambassadors came, including the ambassadors from the Soviet Union, South Africa and Israel. They had a round-table discussion about peace; then they participated in worship. Two young people served as escorts for each ambassador.

Mission accomplished. Flushing, New York, is home to worship centers for religions from around the world. First Baptist Church used this diversity to teach its youth group about different religions and the uniqueness of Christianity.

Group members divided into teams and went to the different worship centers to ask questions and take pictures. For example, they had to take a picture of a group member standing with someone wearing a Jewish yarmulke. And they had to record people saying something in a foreign language. "It was all geared toward getting the kids interacting with the community and the different cultures that they live amongst," says youth worker David Miles.

TV outreach. Manhattan Bible Church needed a creative way to do evangelism in the city. Since the church already has video equipment, youth leaders go to local high schools and junior highs to interview kids as they leave school. They ask the kids about hot issues—suicide, sex, school violence. They tell the students who they are and what they're doing. And they give them an invitation to the next Friday Night Live group meeting—when they show the video with the interviews.

Subway serenades. The subway system under Manhattan Island is noisy, dirty and sometimes scary. Teenagers and adults from Metro Baptist Church in New York City helped change the mood of the underground maze at Christmas by caroling *under* the streets of New York.

Field trips. Many cities use tax dollars to support a variety of public services such as concerts, libraries, fireworks, museums and public recreation facilities. Youth groups can easily take advantage of these close-to-home opportunities for special events or special studies.

Even the city streets offer innovative learning experiences. The youth group at First Presbyterian Church of Crafton Heights in Pittsburgh took a field trip to the city's main "prostitution street." Then group members talked about the things that seduce people and the dangers of those lifestyles.

Around the world in an evening. Progressive dinners are standard youth group fare. But young people at North Shore Baptist Church in Chicago arranged a December progressive dinner with a different flavor. They selected families from a variety of ethnic backgrounds to host the event. At each home, they learned about that culture's Christmas traditions. They exercised between courses by walking from house to house, since they were all close together in the neighborhood.

Parade of shoes. Knowing the importance of shoes to inner-city teenagers, First Church of the Brethren in Brooklyn, New York, sponsored a Thanksgiving worship service to help teenagers see another reason their shoes are significant. Youth worker Phill Carlos Archbold asked young people each to bring to church one shoe that they wear every day. Then he asked them each to tell about some way they lived the Christian life while wearing that shoe. The service concluded with a time of commitment where the teenagers agreed to "walk" in obedience to God. Archbold says that after the evening, kids would call up excited and say, "I was in this shoe today, and you wouldn't believe what happened."

Tour of churches. Because of the great concentration of churches in cities, urban ministry specialist Ray Bakke gives groups one-day whirlwind tours of Chicago churches. Urban youth workers can follow suit. Arrange with diverse congregations in your city for a similar excursion to help young people experience the diversity and richness of the body of Christ. A tour could include, for example, a store-front Pentecostal church, a downtown Roman Catholic cathedral, a Quaker meetinghouse, a mainline congregation and an evangelical house church.

Basketball bonanza. High schools in Pittsburgh have stopped having night basketball games and activities because of fear of violence. But First Presbyterian Church of Crafton Heights in Pittsburgh decided to fill the void by sponsoring a game between the high school faculty (plus a few seniors) and the crew from a popular radio station. The game quickly sold out, adding to the funds for the church's community center. And the first game was such a success that the church now sponsors the game every year.

Neighborhood photo walk. This two-session activity, designed by Brandon I. Cho, helped group members get better acquainted with their neighborhood. The youth group divided into teams of two or three. Each team was given a camera and film, and instructed to explore a part of the neighborhood. They were asked to take pictures that captured the characteristics of their community. The next week, the pictures were shown and the group discussed the question "Who is my neighbor?" This helped them to talk about the community's diversity and needs.[7]

CIA (Christians In Action). First Baptist Church in Flushing, New York, paired up with another congregation for this undercover operation. But neither youth group knew the other one was involved. The youth groups were given instructions to meet an unnamed person at a certain subway station. This person gave the groups packets of information, a tape recorder and Polaroid camera. The packets gave them instructions that took them all over Manhattan to gather clues in different shops and churches. At each stop, they learned something new about their city or their faith.

The last clue was to pick up a packet of pictures at a photo-finishing shop. The pictures showed the other youth group and gave instructions to meet the pictured group at the public library. When everyone was together, the two groups had a joint meeting on reaching out to the poor in the city.

Reflection and Action

1. Evaluate your youth group events based on the keys to effective programming that are explained on page 143. Add your own keys to the list. Then decide ways you can improve in an area that needs the most work.

	We do this well		This could use improvement	
a. Ministry orientation	5	4	3	2	1
b. Openness and acceptance	5	4	3	2	1
c. Emphasis on relationships	5	4	3	2	1
d. Caution with games	5	4	3	2	1
e. Other: _____	5	4	3	2	1
f. Other: _____	5	4	3	2	1

2. List all your youth programming for a normal month in the chart in Diagram 7-2. Discuss with other leaders whether your programs meet the needs and interests of your young people. Ask yourself and other youth leaders:

● Does the program include the type of activities that attract young people in our community? Why or why not?

● Do we schedule our programs so they're most convenient for teenagers and their families? Are there other times that would be more effective?

● Does our programming include growth opportunities for both new Christians and maturing Christians? List the programs that meet the needs of each group.

● Does the programming address the variety of needs and priorities you identified in Chapter 6?

3. Survey the young people who attend your meetings and events. Ask what they like most about different programs and why.

Diagram 7-2
Youth Group Monthly Schedule

	Week 1	Week 2	Week 3	Week 4
Sunday				
Monday				
Tuesday				
Wednesday				
Thursday				
Friday				
Saturday				

What other programs would they like to have at church? What's the best time for them to meet?

4. Look at the programming ideas in the section titled "A Programming Potpourri." Would any of these ideas work with your youth group? If not, what are some other creative ways you can have fun with your youth group while enjoying the city's benefits?

Endnotes

¹Marlene Morrison Pedigo, *New Church in the City* (Richmond, IN: Friends United Press, 1988), 35.

²Ray Bakke with Jim Hart, *The Urban Christian* (Downers Grove, IL: InterVarsity Press, 1987), 86.

³Sam Toperoff, "A Pillar and Backboard of the Riverside Church," Sports Illustrated, (December 22-29, 1986), 156-166.

⁴"Soul Liberation Festival: A Soul-Winning Block Party" (an interview with Art Erickson), Youthworker, (Fall 1987), 62-67.

⁵"Soul Liberation Festival: A Soul-Winning Block Party," 62-67.

⁶Phyllis E. Alsdurf, "A Church That Learned to Bloom Where It Was Planted," World Vision Magazine, (August 1985).

⁷Adapted from Brandon I. Cho, "Discovering Our Neighborhood," in *Asian Pacific American Youth Ministry*, edited by Donald Ng (Valley Forge, PA: Judson Press, 1988), 105-107.

CHAPTER 8

Teaching the Bible to Urban Teenagers

How do you make parables about sowers, sheep and vineyards relevant to teenagers whose world consists of concrete, skyscrapers and subways? How do you get teenagers who rarely read anything to read God's Word?

These questions are common among urban youth workers. A Group Publishing survey found that urban youth workers' top concern is helping teenagers grow in their personal faith. And the top resources they say they need are Bible studies related to urban needs.[1]

Several issues surface when you try bringing the Bible into urban teenagers' lives:

● First, the Bible and its world seem so distant from today's huge, complicated cities. As one youth worker said, "I find it difficult to relate biblical settings—largely a rural society—to youth who are exposed primarily to urban surroundings."

● Second, many urban teenagers come from unchurched backgrounds. Thus they have no basic Bible knowledge when they come to church. "These kids don't know who Moses is. They don't know who Adam and Eve are. Some don't even know who Jesus is," says Tracy Hipps of Inner City Impact in Chicago.

● Third, even if they do know about the Bible, many urban teenagers are either illiterate or read on an elementary school level. "They're not readers, and they're not people of books," says John Carlson of the Evangelical Association for the Promotion of Education in Philadelphia. "And that's a whole struggle in itself."

● Finally, there are few resources available that relate scripture to urban life. As we discovered in Chapter 5, most resources and curricula are designed for suburban, middle-class white congregations.

This chapter will address these issues, offering some ways urban youth workers have begun to deal with these problems.

The City and the Bible

Whether you live in a city, suburb, small town or rural area, it's sometimes hard to relate to life in first-century Palestine. The lifestyle and culture seem alien to the 20th century in general. But the problem seems even more complicated in the city. Nothing in the Bible seems to compare to our modern-day urban centers.

These perceived differences have led many Christians to believe that the Bible is essentially a rural book. And many people would affirm the conclusion of an article published in the mid-1960s: "God builds gardens; men make cities. God prefers shepherds to vine growers and certainly to city dwellers."[2]

Yet recent biblical scholars have questioned that conclusion. Urban ministry expert Ray Bakke—who has popularized much of the academic scholarship—has found 1,200 references to 119 different cities in the Bible.[3]

What scholars have found is that early Christianity was really an urban—*not* a rural—faith. "A second glance reveals that, unlike the rural character of modern Protestantism, the church of the New Testament was urban," William Baird writes in *The Corinthian Church—A Biblical Approach to Urban Culture*. "The locus of Christian strength was to be found in Jerusalem, Antioch, Ephesus, and Rome."[4] In *The First Urban Christians: The Social World of The Apostle Paul*, Wayne A. Meeks adds, "It was in the cities of the Roman Empire that Christianity, though born in the village culture of Palestine, had its greatest successes until well after the time of Constantine."[5]

Think about the major churches of the New Testament—Jerusalem, Corinth, Ephesus, Rome. Those were also the major cities of the day. And the Apostle Paul, the first missionary, was actually an urban missionary. Virtually all his ministry occurred in the world's major cities. Meeks writes: "Paul was a city person. The city breathes through his language . . . He seems more at home with the cliches of Greek rhetoric, drawn from gymnasium, stadium or workshop."[6]

While 2,000 years certainly have brought almost incomprehensible changes in the world, a close look at scripture reveals that Christians in ancient cities dealt with many of the same issues urban Christians deal with today. To discover some of these connections, let's look at some cities in both the Old and New Testament, comparing their concerns to contemporary urban concerns.

Sodom. Sodom was the Las Vegas of the Old Testament. As Bakke writes, "Everything that prejudices anyone against cities everywhere will prejudice you against the city if you look at Sodom."[7] As the writer of Genesis puts it, "The men of Sodom were wicked and were sinning greatly against the Lord" (Genesis 13:13). Yet we see Abraham pleading to God to spare the whole city if there are just a handful of righteous people in it (Genesis 18:16—19:38). Here God shows concern for the city despite the overwhelming odds. The story also shows God's concern for the individual in the midst of the multitude.

Babylon. Babylon epitomizes the evil city in the Bible. It was so bad that the early persecuted church used the city as a code name for Rome. It was described as "the mother of prostitutes and of the abominations of the earth" (Revelation 17:5).

Yet God sent some of Judah's greatest leaders, Daniel and Ezekiel, to serve in Babylon. In Babylon, the Jews learned skills that became essential for the return to Jerusalem. And in Babylon, Daniel had to learn to distinguish between the fundamentals and superficials of his faith—just as many urban Christians must do today (Daniel 6:1-28).

Ephesus. Ephesus was the capital of the Roman province of Asia. Because it was at the intersection of major trade routes, it boasted a diverse population from around the world. It's little wonder that the city became a critical missionary field for the Apostle Paul. From there, the gospel could easily spread around the world. And it's also appropriate that Paul focused much of his letter to the churches there on building unity in the midst of their diversity (see especially Ephesians 2:11-22 and 4:1-6).

Corinth. Corinth was populated by people from all over the known world. Its strategic location made it a major, wealthy trade city. It offered a rich variety of entertainment, sports and drama. At the same time, it experienced the poverty brought on by slavery, which was considered essential to the urban economy.[8]

Corinth also had other similarities with modern-day cities. It was home to a variety of religions. William Baird writes, "Temples and sacred statuaries were to be found on every corner."[9] Yet Corinth was also known for its immorality. At one time, the temple to Aphrodite had a reputation for having 1,000 sacred prostitutes. In Paul's day, it had a street lined with taverns.

Into this setting came the Corinthian church—a church that was particularly special to Paul (1 Corinthians 1:4). The church struggled with many of the same issues today's urban churches face: divisions in the church, moral laxity, questions about worship style and acceptance of differences.

●

It becomes clear from this brief overview of a few cities in the Bible that scripture does, indeed, address urban issues. Yet these messages are sometimes difficult to convey to urban teenagers because of low Bible knowledge and low literacy.

Low Bible Knowledge

People who grow up in the church begin hearing Bible stories in the nursery and later in Sunday school. Even if they don't apply anything they learn, they still have that basic knowledge in the backs of their minds.

Urban youth workers say they don't have that luxury, particularly if they work in low-income communities. For many urban teenagers, even a superficial understanding of scripture is absent. As a result, these teenagers have no clue where to begin when you ask them to do "Bible study."

Because these teenagers don't have much, if any, background in the Bible, urban youth workers find that they must deal with the basics of faith. "I always stay on the basics, because that's what the kids need," Tracy Hipps says. "They don't need to hear all these deep stories. They need to hear the basics and what the Bible says."

Even the basics can be eye-openers for the kids. John Carlson recalls teaching the Ten Commandments at a retreat. "Most of our kids had never heard of the Ten Commandments or understood them before," he says. When he explained the commandment not to commit adultery, "they all freaked out. They'd never heard of that idea before in their lives."

Carlson believes this lack of background in Bible actually has its advantages because the Bible is fresh and intriguing to the kids. "Some of those simple things out of the Bible are challenging and new to them," he says. "It's not hard to shock kids with stuff in the Bible."

He gives the example of Jesus' admonition to turn the other cheek (Matthew 5:38-39). "It's one passage I use over and over again, because they're in a get-even, fight-out-all-your-problems world. And that passage always blows their minds."

An essential characteristic of urban youth ministries is offering different levels of Bible study for teenagers who have progressed to different levels in their spiritual journey. Lawndale Community Church includes a 15-minute devotion in its weekly meeting and recreation night which attracts a lot of non-Christians. But young people who want to dig deeper into scripture can stay afterward for a more intensive Bible study called "Roots." This approach makes sure every teenager's needs are met, whether or not they're used to studying the Bible.

Low Literacy

Bo Nixon, who works with teenagers on Manhattan's Lower East Side in New York, tells a story about a teenager who became a Christian but refused to attend the Bible study. "We would ask him, but he always refused. We wondered why. Then one day he told us with tears in his eyes that he couldn't read. He was embarrassed to admit that was why he wouldn't come to Bible study."[10]

Nixon's story illustrates the other major difficulty in relating the Bible to urban teenagers. These kids live in a culture that doesn't learn things from books—even if one of the books is the Word of God.

As a result, Michael Eastman of Scripture Union House in London, England, writes, "It's nonsense to start with individual Bible reading for those who are non-readers." He continues: "Some people may never understand the Word in print. Other media are necessary. Instead of asking 'How do we help non-readers read the Bible?' we need to concentrate on another question, 'How do people experience an encounter with the living God in their everyday lives?' "[11]

Urban youth workers have discovered that the key to sharing the Bible's truth is to help kids visualize the truth. "Inner-city kids are very visual," John Carlson says. "And so we're finding that . . . any way of presenting the scripture visually works really well." Here are some ways urban youth workers present scripture effectively and visually:

● Carlson says skits and other dramas work well. His high school group presented the musical *Godspell* for the church. "The audience lapped it up," he said, because it was so visual and because it helped them *see* Bible stories come to life.

● Bryan Stone of Ft. Worth, Texas, says his group's Bible studies come alive when the kids are involved in service to their community. "It makes the Bible studies or the devotional times they have . . . always seem to have a mission edge to them. They don't get too much into discussion of theological or biblical points . . . They really don't care much about that. But if it relates to what they're doing, then it's pretty interesting."

● Christ Church in Manhattan has a youth group made up primarily of unchurched teenagers. Leaders asked the youth group to turn scripture into drama. The kids did, and the result was an unusual, pointed Christmas drama about Jesus being born in New York City. A bag lady hears God's voice telling her to watch for the birth of the savior. Then she recognizes the mother as a pregnant, black teenager on a subway. The girl goes into labor on the street, and she's rushed to a nearby hotel, where the owner won't let her come in at first. But eventually she gets in and has the baby in the maid's room. In the final scene, the whole city crowds around to see the baby.

● Ray Bakke once preached a sermon without saying anything. He was preaching about Luke 15—the three parables about lost things (lost sheep, lost coin, lost son)—because several church members had lost children to drugs or other problems. Bakke describes the experience:

> *I started my sermon by sweeping the sanctuary with a broom for seven minutes without saying a thing. Meanwhile Corean was playing Beethoven's "Rage Over a Lost Penny" on the piano. The music ends with a crash and a bang, and just as she finished it, I found a lost penny under the communion table. When I held it up the people broke into spontaneous applause. They finally had figured out what I was doing.*"[12]

● In an effort to address the immediate needs of teenagers, Friendship Baptist Church in Vallejo, California, lets the kids do most of the talking. Youth minister Harold Wright says leaders ask the kids to role play how they'd relate a biblical truth to someone they'd meet on the street. The result is that they discover in the role plays connections with their own lives.

● A general, effective approach to teaching teenagers is experiential learning. Several models of experiential learning are available today. David Ng and John Stevens Kerr outline one model in an essay in *Asian Pacific American Youth Ministry*. It's easy to remember with the acronym DRAG:[13]

Do: Do an experience that brings the scripture to life— a field trip, a game or another experience.

Reflect: Think and talk about the experience—essentially relive it in words.

Analyze: Probe what the experience means, people's reactions and what people learned.

Generalize: Explore how this experience relates to daily life.

Relating the Bible to Urban Issues

In addition to visual teaching methods, it's important to be able to relate scripture to urban teenagers' daily lives. This chapter concludes with a few examples of connections between scripture and the lives of teenagers in the city. Not all the topics will relate to all urban teenagers, but they should introduce you to some of the many possible connections:

Created in God's image (Genesis 1:27). The issue of personal identity is central for teenagers from minority groups. A study of the belief that all people are made in God's image has rich possibilities not only for teenagers' understanding of themselves, but also for their understanding of God.

Immigrants (Genesis 12:1-9). Asian Pacific Americans, Hispanics and other immigrants can relate to the story of Abraham and Sarah being called by God to another land.

Liberation (Exodus 12—13). This Passover and Exodus story has always had meaning for the black church with its history of oppression and slavery. It also has significance for other minorities who have experienced prejudice in this country and persecution in their own homeland.

Ethnic identity (Esther 2:1-21; 4:1-17; 7:1-4). Esther was forced to conceal her ethnic identity in order to win the king's favor. But when her people were persecuted, she decided to stand up for her ethnic heritage, even though she could die for it.

Rebuilding the city (Nehemiah 2:11-20). The whole book of Nehemiah focuses on Nehemiah's effort to rebuild Jerusalem which was in ruins. It makes a provocative study for ways churches and youth groups can participate in rebuilding their own cities.

Peer pressure (Daniel 1; 6). Daniel was an immigrant to Babylon who was pushed to give up what he believed, in order to enjoy more of the power and benefits of the major city.

Avoiding violence (Matthew 5:38-39). In an urban world where rival gangs live by "an eye for an eye," this passage calls teenagers to make their Christian commitment a part of their daily lives.

Ministry to people in need (Matthew 25:31-46). Urban teenagers daily see people who are hungry, sick, thirsty and in need of clothing. This passage becomes a daily reminder that Jesus cares about each person they see.

God's concern for individuals (Luke 8:42b-50; 19:1-10). These two stories (the woman who touched Jesus' garment to be healed and Zacchaeus) illustrate how God notices and reaches out to individuals who might otherwise feel lost in the crowd.

Christian witness in the city (Acts 23:1-11). In a vision, Paul is told not to worry, but to keep speaking in the city. Paul's defense of the gospel and how he was treated will raise interesting parallels for urban teenagers and how they share their faith.

Basic Christianity (Romans 1:18—8:39). This letter was written to new Christians. It outlines the need for redemption, God's saving act in Christ and the Christian life. It's an excellent framework to study with new Christians.

Celebrating diversity (1 Corinthians 12—13). This central passage in Paul's writing focuses on seeing the importance of different people as part of the body of Christ.

Cultural values (Galatians 3:1-25). The letter to the

church in Galatia focuses on the struggles of being a Christian without adopting Jewish practices. It has particular relevancy for minority groups who want to be Christian but don't want to give up their own cultural heritage to accept the values and priorities of middle-class, white Christianity.

Racism (Galatians 3:26-29). Urban teenagers who encounter people of all races sometimes need to hear the gospel message that "you are all one in Christ Jesus."

Unity in diversity (Ephesians 2:11-22 and 4:1-16). The letter to the church at Ephesus (a major city) deals a great deal with the tensions between Jews and Gentiles. It challenges the church to live in unity with all people.

Reflection and Action

1. If you have trouble relating scripture to your youth group, which of the reasons in the beginning of the chapter do you see as the major factor? What other issues make it difficult for you?

2. What city in the Bible seems most like your city? List some similarities and differences.

3. Do a Bible study looking at cities in the early church. Compare the cities where the church thrived with your city. What are the similarities and differences? What issues did the early church face that your church faces today? How can you learn from the experiences of the early church?

4. Do kids in your youth group have little knowledge of the Bible? How has your program tried to address this need?

5. Have you noticed any group members who have difficulty reading? How do you respond when such a problem arises?

6. Think of ways you've seen the Bible come alive for your kids. What do you think made it come alive? How can you recapture that enthusiasm in future Bible studies?

7. Make a list of issues your kids are facing right now. Use a concordance and other Bible study tools to discover Bible stories and passages that relate to those issues.

Endnotes

[1]Unpublished survey of 80 urban youth workers, conducted by Group Publishing, March 1987.

[2]Quoted in Raymond Bakke, "The City and the Scriptures," Christianity Today, (June 15, 1984), 14-17.

[3]Ray Bakke with Jim Hart, *The Urban Christian* (Downers Grove, IL: InterVarsity Press, 1987), 62.

[4]William Baird, *The Corinthian Church—A Biblical Approach to Urban Culture* (Nashville, TN: Abingdon Press, 1964), 23.

[5]Wayne A. Meeks, *The First Urban Christians: The Social World of The Apostle Paul* (New Haven, CT: Yale University Press, 1983), 8.

[6]Meeks, *The First Urban Christians: The Social World of The Apostle Paul*, 9.

[7]Bakke, "The City and the Scriptures," 14-17.

[8]For a detailed description of Corinthian life, see Baird, 20-23.

[9]Baird, *The Corinthian Church—A Biblical Approach to Urban Culture*, 22.

[10]Ron Schmidt and Bo Nixon, "Getting to the Core of the Big Apple," Reaching Out, (1987), 21-23.

[11]Michael Eastman, "Word for the World and Word for the Church," (An unpublished paper), 3. Used by permission of the author.

[12]Bakke with Hart, *The Urban Christian*, 99.

[13]David Ng and John Stevens Kerr, "Effective Methods in Youth Ministry," in *Asian Pacific American Youth Ministry*, edited by Donald Ng (Valley Forge, PA: Judson Press, 1988), 67-69.

CHAPTER 9

Celebrating Diversity in Your Youth Group

*After this I looked down and there before me was
a great multitude that no one could count, from
every nation, tribe, people and language, standing before the throne and in front of the Lamb.*
—*Revelation 7:9a*

Different cities. Different neighborhoods. Different
schools. Different ethnic backgrounds. Different economic brackets. Different religious perspectives. Different needs.

Most church growth specialists would say you can't
minister in the midst of these differences. They'd say: "Your
youth group won't grow if you try to include *everybody*.
People like to be with their own kind. So pick the social,

economic and ethnic strata you want to reach, and leave the rest to someone else."

Such an approach may make sense sociologically, but not theologically. Sure, everyone's more comfortable with other people who all look, dress, act and think alike. But Christians believe that "there is neither Jew nor Greek, slave nor free, male nor female, for you are all one in Christ Jesus" (Galatians 3:28). As George Vander Weit says: "No one can defend keeping a homogeneous group on biblical principles. The struggles we go through to incorporate other groups are no different than the early church struggling with Jews and gentiles."[1]

The Opportunity of Diversity

Diversity in the youth group is challenging. As Stephen Kliewer writes in *How to Live With Diversity in the Local Church*, "All too often, because diversity tends to be uncomfortable, people in the church try to suppress their differences. They pretend that the difficulties aren't there in order to avoid conflict, or something worse."[2]

Yet diversity also contributes a richness to the youth program. A report from the secular youth-serving organization Quest International argues that "one basic ingredient in helping young people to succeed in today's complex, multifaceted society must be a commitment to the value of cultural pluralism . . . It means celebrating differences instead of viewing them as a problem or a deficit."[3]

Diversity also gives the church an opportunity to model God's kingdom. "We talk a lot about celebrating God's world of magnificent differences," says Jim Hopkins of First Baptist Church in Los Angeles. He says his program emphasizes that God doesn't take sides among groups of people. "God's business is the business of reconciliation," Hopkins says, "of pulling people together—people who under other circumstances would have no reason to be together."[4]

Another important biblical image is the story of Peter's vision and encounter with Cornelius (Acts 10). In his dream, a voice from heaven commands Peter to eat from a large sheet filled with animals that the Jews considered to be unclean. " 'Surely not, Lord,' Peter replied. 'I have never eaten anything impure or unclean.' The voice spoke to him a second time, 'Do not call anything impure that God has made clean.' "

Peter was wondering what it meant when messengers from Cornelius—a gentile—arrived, asking Peter to come share the gospel with Cornelius. Peter went to Cornelius, preached to him and Cornelius was converted. In the sermon Peter said: "I now realize how true it is that God does not show favoritism but accepts men from every nation who fear him and do what is right" (Acts 10:34-35).

Different churches across the country are bringing together diverse groups of teenagers. Consider these examples of the many barriers urban youth programs can bridge:

Ethnic diversity. The youth group at First Baptist Church in Flushing, New York, includes African Americans, Eastern Europeans, Hispanics, Anglos, Chinese, Pakistanis and others. Youth worker David Miles talks about the importance of learning about the different cultures. During his first year at the church, he preached a sermon about meditation. He used what he thought was a humorous illustration from an Eastern religion. But it wasn't funny to the Asians in the congregation. They felt insulted that he had made fun of a holy man.

Religious diversity. First Presbyterian Church of Crafton Heights serves a working class, Eastern European community in Pittsburgh. The community's roots are Italian and Polish Catholic, not Presbyterian. As a result, youth worker Dave Carver says most of the kids who visited church events listed something other than "Presbyterian" on their registration cards. As a result, he tried to be ecumenical in his approach, focusing on the fundamentals of faith— "what unites us"—instead of the particulars of Presbyterianism.

Economic diversity. First Chinese Baptist Church in San Francisco's Chinatown has two distinct congregations. One consists primarily of new immigrants who live in low-income housing in the community. The other is primarily made up of middle-class families who have lived several generations in this country. Youth worker Jerald Choy says a major task of his ministry is to bring the two groups together. Each summer he tries to build bridges across the cultural and economic differences through a summer camp.

Geographical diversity. Some youth group members at First United Methodist Church in Houston drive an hour to church. Instead of asking teenagers to come to church two or three times each week, the church has an all-day Sunday program that lasts from morning through the evening. Youth worker Rob Grotheer says: "Our main struggle is having quality fellowship time together. So we make the most out of our Sundays. Kids can be here from 8:45 a.m. until 7:30 that night."

Bridges Across Differences

Most urban youth workers see the need for building bridges across the different barriers. However, it's often difficult to know where to lay the first stones in constructing the bridge. Here are some pieces you need to build the bridge across diversity in your youth group:

Create a Vision

How do you see your youth group? What vision do you have for it? What are the fundamental values you build your youth program around?

These are critical questions in building an inclusive youth ministry. In his book *Bringing Your Church Back to Life: Beyond the Survival Mentality*, Daniel Buttry writes:

> *The vision has to be clear and the visionary mind-set established before how-tos can be applied successfully. In fact, getting clear about the vision will answer many of the practical questions: emphases, priorities and themes to focus on . . . Clear vision takes care of a number of foundational decisions.*[5]

Jim Hopkins, youth minister at First Baptist Church in Los Angeles, says his group has a motto, "One Spirit, Many Expressions." Different youth groups develop different visions. Buttry suggests that a vision should consist of three elements: God, the church and the world.[6] Let's briefly look at each of these in terms of youth ministry:

God. It's important to develop a theology—an understanding of God—that affirms different people as created in God's image. As a result, it affirms the different cultures and peoples and expressions of God's richness. As Buttry writes, "The key is the acceptance of the different cultures by virtue of recognizing Christ in each."[7]

This vision of God also sees that God is the one who builds the church and the youth group. "Holding such a diverse body together is no easy task," Buttry writes. "The centrifugal forces of our different cultures and traditions tend to pull us apart. The living Christ is the centripetal force that pulls us together . . . There is no way we would be together or even know each other if not for our common commitment to Christ, so whatever we do we need continually to center on the person of Jesus."[8]

The church. A diverse church and youth group intentionally sees itself as the "reconciled body of Christ" (1 Corinthians 12:12-13; Colossians 3:11). "What makes youth programming effective," Hopkins says, "is when it's clearly understood that Christianity is not just trying to make sure things are okay between me and God. It's when you learn to get along and learn to respect people who are different from you."

The world. A vision for inclusiveness must reach beyond the youth group room and the church walls into the diverse community around the church. Buttry writes: "The effort foreign missionaries make to learn a new language and enter into a vastly different culture needs to be mirrored by a similar effort in our communities. We need to speak in the languages of our neighbors, not just verbally, but musically, artistically, and with compassion and concern."[9]

Recognize Other Cultures' Value

"If diversity is to be creative," Kliewer writes, "it is imperative that the church and its members learn to accept as valuable and important those who are different from them, and have ideas and ministries which are different from theirs."[10]

Youth workers in multicultural churches find that the different cultures add richness to the youth group. Group life can include a variety of tasty food, good traditional music and dance, and opportunities to learn new languages.

In addition, these youth groups discover how different cultures can enrich their understanding of God, people and the Christian faith. "Different racial ethnic perspectives and resources can help the church to break free from cultural captivity and stale homogeneity," Wesley S. Woo writes in an essay in *Asian Pacific American Youth Ministry.*[11]

For example, let's say you give two white American kids the ends of a rope. You tie a knot in the middle of it, draw two lines on the ground and tell the kids that they get a nickel every time they pull the knot across the line. What would happen?

Most likely, a competitive tug-of-war would ensue. They'd work hard, tugging and pulling—trying to get more nickels than the other one. After 10 minutes, one might have five nickels and feel triumphant.

But give the same rope with the same instructions to two Hispanic teenagers, something entirely different might happen. Instead of working against each other, they'd play together. They'd steadily saw the rope back and forth across the two lines. In 10 minutes they might make $25 each while having a great time working together.[12]

The story's point is not that the Hispanics outwitted the person making the offer to get the money. The point is that American culture assumes competition—beating each other and keeping others from getting something we want. How much can Christians learn from a culture that assumes cooperation and working together?

Ray Bakke suggests several practical ways to learn about and affirm the rich cultures within your community. They're easily adapted for youth ministry:[13]

● Visit other ethnic groups in your community. Listen to their stories, their histories, their concerns. Find out what's important about their tradition and culture, and affirm it.

● Visit other youth groups and churches. Build relationships with churches with a different ethnic makeup from yours, then arrange visits. Ask them to tell your group about their history, traditions and perspectives.

● Visit the schools. Schools have had to learn to cope

with diversity, because they can't move away from different people like churches often do. Educators often have valuable insights and methods for fostering a climate of acceptance.

Affirm Teenagers' Cultural Identity

Adolescence is a critical time in identity formation. During these years, people discover who they are and their place in the world. Part of that identity involves their cultural heritage. What does it mean to be African American, Hispanic American, Asian American or Native American in this culture?

Hopkins says, "You can't go wrong to affirm what's important about ethnic background and culture." He encourages kids to share who they are, then he responds by saying, "Wow, this is wonderful!"

Part of affirming that identity may be to help them learn about their own history, culture and tradition. Bethel African Methodist Episcopal Church in Baltimore has a wall mural in its sanctuary that traces the history of black people. This art reminds the church and its young people of their roots, their story and how God has worked with them in history.

Review Your Programming

As we discussed in Chapter 5, programming can alienate some people if it doesn't take their culture and lifestyle into account. It's important, therefore, to examine your programming from time to time to discover whether it may subconsciously reflect the needs and concerns of one group of teenagers, leaving others out. "You have to be careful," Hopkins says. "Make sure in trying to write a broad base of programming that race groups don't say, 'Oh, this program is for me and no one else.' Or, 'I can't go because I'm not Hispanic.' "

Consider these questions:

● Does your programming reflect your teenagers' cultural diversity? Or does it alienate some group members?

● Do you assume in your plans that all group members come from a middle-income (or low-income) background?

● Does the music you use in youth group and in worship reflect your group's diversity?

● Does your approach to Bible study reflect the needs and interests of the different kids in your group?

Build Community

All effective youth ministries in any setting spend lots of time building friendships and community among group members. But it's a relatively easy task in suburban churches where most of the kids share basically the same economic, educational, religious and ethnic background. They have a lot in common, so they have a lot to talk together about.

But it's tough in the city where group members may not share any of those common bonds. Art Erickson of Park Avenue United Methodist Church in Minneapolis says he has trouble building community because he has two distinct groups of kids. First, he has the low-income neighborhood kids. Then he has middle-class kids who come from across the Twin Cities area. Kids in the latter group come to church with their parents, and they never see the other kids except on Sundays. "Parents know each other because of the history," Erickson says, "but kids don't know each other."

How do you begin building community between teenagers who have nothing in common? "You have to build common experiences," Erickson says, "to build up a reservoir of things to talk about."

Those common experiences can take many forms:

Youth group meetings. Weekly group meetings can create a supportive environment where kids build relationships. First United Methodist Church in Houston breaks its youth group into small family units of five or six teenagers and an adult counselor. This gives the young people a chance to interact together in ways that would be impossible in a large group.

Athletics. Sports are not only a good way for urban churches to reach out to recreation-starved communities, but they also give a setting for building relationships across differences in the youth group. Sports can also provide an excellent bridge to other churches in the community. First Chinese Baptist Church in San Francisco participates in a summer volleyball and basketball league with other churches in Chinatown. After a game, the two teams get together for Bible study and fellowship. "The intent," says youth worker Jerald Choy, "is to know that there are other Christians outside our own church."

Service projects. The youth group at Liberation Community Church in Ft. Worth, Texas, is actively involved in service projects. While their motivation is to serve others as Christ calls us to do, pastor Bryan Stone says an important byproduct is that "they get closer to each other."

Stephen Kliewer believes that bringing different groups together in working relationships and giving them a common goal overcomes polarization. It gives them a comfort zone to work in, he writes, and they learn to depend on each other.[14]

Bridge-Building Leadership

The shape and attitude of a youth program's leadership is a pivotal issue in building bridges between diverse groups. Kliewer writes, "The church leadership must consciously take the lead in the shaping of atmosphere, developing a dynamic that will support the presence of diverse elements within the church."[15]

If leaders intentionally work to create unity, the leaders themselves become a bridge between different groups. "We found our leadership team was the unifying factor," Erickson says. "We were the glue that held the thing together."

For youth group leaders to build bridges, they need to: be conscious of their own heritage; be inclusive; be servants and facilitators; and be willing to learn from mistakes.

Let's look at these in more detail:

Be conscious of your own heritage. No youth leader grows up in a vacuum. Each person has certain preconceptions and biases. These cultural biases can be barriers between leaders and group members. But by being conscious of your own background, you can also become more sensitive to other people's.

Educators believe that no one can really know a student's culture. Instead, they suggest becoming sensitized to your own and your group members' cultural values and assumptions. What's important is to be open to new ways of thinking and behaving. As one educator says, you need to develop a regimen of "unlearning something every day."[16]

Here are some principles to help with this process:

● Be aware of and accept your own ethnic, historical and cultural background—and the cultural background of others.

● Be sensitive to your own communication patterns.

● Learn to switch between cultural channels to establish an acceptable, non-offensive, productive relationship across cultures.

● Be open to communication systems you may not have noticed before.

● Build relationships with individuals from other cultures.[17]

(Diagram 9-1, "Cross-Cultural Ministry," suggests several additional principles for white ministers who serve in cross-cultural settings.)

Be inclusive. Hopkins says one of the greatest dangers of multicultural youth ministry is letting one ethnic group dominate the leadership team at any one time. "It's important to maintain balance," he says. "Otherwise, kids drift away because they feel disenfranchised."

As a result of this perspective, Hopkins' church does have diverse leadership. The youth leader is white, and volunteer youth workers are from Liberia, the Philippines, Brazil and Ohio.

Erickson follows the same principle. "I try to gather a leadership team that reflects the diversity of the community," he explains. "That way I'm working with leaders of different groups."

Another issue of inclusive leadership involves the structure for getting involved in leadership. If a church requires that someone be a church member for a year or two before taking leadership, that person may feel completely unrepresented in a diverse church. For this reason, pastor Daniel Buttry says Dorchester Baptist Temple restructured its committees and leadership team so that newcomers could quickly be integrated into church life and leadership.[18]

Diagram 9-1
Cross-Cultural Ministry

Many white urban youth ministers work in primarily non-white communities. In an essay titled "Ministry Among the Urban Indian," Dr. Leonard P. Rascher suggests nine principles for cross-cultural communication that are appropriate for urban youth ministers:

1. Be informed. Learn about the community, its people's history and culture. "We need to continually be students of the people," Rascher writes. "Find out what they want, then guide them in it."

2. Be yourself. "We need to be real and not try to put on qualities that are not genuine," Rascher asserts. Absolute honesty is essential.

3. Be flexible. Be ready to adapt, modify and/or change.

4. Be sensitive. Learn to observe other people's feelings and ideas. "We have to be careful not to violate cultural customs and differences," Rascher suggests.

5. Emphasize the universality of Christ's atonement. Christianity is not just a white person's religion. It's a relationship with the King of kings and Lord of lords.

6. Learn their language. Even though it takes work, Rascher believes it's essential to communicating the gospel.

7. Learn their value system. Know what's most important to them and what's not so important.

8. Contextualize the message. Relate Christian beliefs to concepts that are familiar to their culture.

9. Communicate according to their thought patterns. Use learning techniques and thought patterns that grow out of the people's own culture and thought patterns. With Native Americans, Rascher says, communicate with illustrations, diagrams and storytelling.[22]

Be servants and facilitators. Working in a multicultural setting requires tremendous sensitivity, says youth minister David Miles of Flushing, New York. Avoid sounding or acting condescending toward other groups. Respect their cultural values and perspectives. And show that you think those values are legitimate and important.

Regardless of good intentions and self-awareness, urban youth workers live with the reality that their own attitudes may be tainted with racism. Unless consciously confronted, this latent racism can destroy a youth worker's effectiveness in an urban environment.

Art Erickson, an Anglo youth worker, believes that too many people have had a "plantation-owner" mentality when entering urban youth ministry. "The problem," he says, "is that you come in and tell people all the answers. You try to control and run it all. You become the owner of the situation." Such an approach can't last, he says. It only leads to deepened bitterness, suspicion and anger.

Erickson says the key to overcoming the racism in your own actions and attitudes is to learn to accept who you are. "You've got to determine who you are," he explains. "Recognize it, and make your contribution. And don't be embarrassed, because you're part of the image of God—as is everyone else."

Be willing to learn from mistakes. Even if you're sensitive and aware, you're going to make mistakes. You'll say something that offends someone. You'll do something that someone considers rude. An idea that you thought would build bridges will backfire, hurting different groups' feelings. Those mistakes are inevitable, Miles says. "The only thing you can do is learn from your mistakes . . . You have to be teachable."

Dealing With Prejudice and Racism

Joey, a white teenager in Los Angeles, was deeply prejudiced against Asians, particularly Koreans. His racism would even take on physical traits as his face became contorted when he was with Koreans. Sometimes he'd have to leave the room just to regain his composure. At school he had conflicts with Asian teachers because he couldn't show them any respect.

Joey's racism is more extreme than most urban youth workers encounter in their groups. But it highlights the problem. If you have a multiracial group, racism and prejudice are almost inevitable given the widespread prejudice that exists in American society.

Dealing directly with this prejudice is critical in maintaining a healthy spirit in the youth group. Here are several ways urban ministers have dealt with racism in the church and youth group:

● "Perhaps the most effective way to counter racism initially is to develop face-to-face encounters, getting people to work, study and pray together," Buttry writes. "Small groups centered around Bible study or a shared mission can help people break down some of their stereotypes and get to know others as Bill or Peter or Ruby or Kathy, not as 'a white' or 'a black.' "[19]

● When Jim Hopkins encountered a difficult case of racism, he first worked with the teenager. Then he met with the family to help them understand the problem. They talked about stereotypes, and how all stereotypes break down when you get to know people. He helped the teenager examine how unfair it is to judge a whole group of people based on what a few people did. And he examined racism in light of the teenager's own faith.

● Another youth worker uses retreats to overcome prejudice in his group. "When kids eat together and live together," he says, "prejudices break down."[20]

Whatever approach you take, remember that prejudice isn't easily overcome—even in the church. Buttry writes: "Cultural stereotypes, unawareness of the different world views and value systems of others, feelings of superiority . . . all lurk in the most caring people and churches. To remove racism is not a one-time, massive effort, but a life-long journey needing humility and grace."[21]

In Joey's case, the teenager went to a denominational conference with Koreans in the group and came to see his own racism. At the end of the event, he said: "I realize I've got this racism in my life, this prejudice. I've got to get it out . . . and fill the void with something important like a commitment to Christ." That wasn't the end of his struggle, but it was the key to overcoming the hate within himself.

Reflection and Action

1. Do you agree with George Vander Weit when he says, "No one can defend keeping a homogeneous group on biblical principles?" Why or why not? Think of some Bible passages and themes to support your answer.

2. Make a list of all your youth group members. Use this list as a prayer guide during the coming week. Think about what each individual contributes to your group, and thank God for the unique gifts he has given your church in your diverse group.

3. Rewrite the story of Peter and Cornelius by substituting your youth group for Peter. With whom do you think God is calling your group to share the gospel?

4. Look at the list of different kinds of diversity (page 174). Which ones do you deal with in your congregation? What issues do they raise for you?

5. What is your youth group's vision of God, itself and the world? Compare your thoughts to the vision suggested beginning on page 175. What differences and similarities do you see?

6. Make a list of the different ethnic, economic or other subgroups within your youth group. Think of ways each group contributes to your ministry. Then think of ways you can affirm people in each group in the coming weeks.

7. Choose one way you'll learn more about a particular ethnic or economic group in your youth group this week. (If you need ideas, see Bakke's suggestions on page 177.) Make time on your calendar to grow in your understanding.

8. Examine your programming calendar for the next few months. Do your plans reflect the needs and interests of the diverse kids in your group? If not, think of ways to make your program more inclusive.

9. What are some ways you've built community in your group across ethnic or economic differences?

10. Write a one-page autobiography telling about your own cultural background. Think of ways your background affects your outreach to other groups.

11. Does your youth group's leadership reflect the congregation and youth group? If not, think of some people you could ask to join your leadership team who would add the missing perspectives.

12. Do you think you have problems with prejudice in your youth group? If so, what are some ways you can begin addressing the problem?

13. Lead a Bible study in your youth group about racism. Chapter 8 suggests several appropriate passages.

Endnotes

[1]Quoted in Jolene L. Roehlkepartain, "Ethnic Diversity: The Face of the Future" GROUP Magazine, (March/April 1988), 64-69.

[2]Stephen Kliewer, *How to Live With Diversity in the Local Church* (Washington, DC: The Alban Institute, 1987), 27.

[3]*Celebrating Differences: Approaches to Hispanic Youth Development* (Columbus, OH: by Quest International and its Hispanic Advisory Committee, 1987), 1.

[4]Quoted in Roehlkepartain, "Ethnic Diversity: The Face of the Future," 64-69.

[5]Daniel Buttry, *Bringing Your Church Back to Life: Beyond the Survival Mentality* (Valley Forge, PA: Judson Press, 1988), 42.

[6]Buttry, *Bringing Your Church Back to Life: Beyond the Survival Mentality*, 43.

[7]Buttry, *Bringing Your Church Back to Life: Beyond the Survival Mentality*, 65.

[8]Daniel Buttry, "One in the Body," The Christian Ministry, (March 1986), 12-15.

[9]Buttry, *Bringing Your Church Back to Life: Beyond the Survival Mentality*, 75.

[10]Kliewer, *How to Live with Diversity in the Local Church*, 39.

[11]Wesley S. Woo, "Theological Dimensions," in *Asian Pacific American Youth Ministry* edited by Donald Ng (Valley Forge, PA: Judson Press, 1988), 17.

[12]Based on an illustration in James E. Dittes, *When Work Goes Sour* (Philadelphia, PA: Westminster Press, 1987), 83.

[13]Ray Bakke with Jim Hart, *The Urban Christian* (Downers Grove, IL: InterVarsity Press, 1987), 139-140.

[14]Kliewer, *How to Live With Diversity in the Local Church*, 37-38.

[15]Kliewer, *How to Live With Diversity in the Local Church*, 41.

[16]Based on Carol Ascher, "Counseling in a Multicultural Educational Setting," ERIC/CUE Fact Sheet Number 9, (New York: Clearinghouse on Urban Education, 1982), 1.

[17]Ascher, "Counseling in a Multicultural Educational Setting," 1.

[18]Buttry, "One in the Body," 12-15.

[19]Buttry, *Bringing Your Church Back to Life: Beyond the Survival Mentality*, 130.

[20]Quoted in Roehlkepartain, "Ethnic Diversity: The Face of the Future," 64-69.

[21]Buttry, *Bringing Your Church Back to Life: Beyond the Survival Mentality*, 129.

[22]Leonard P. Rascher, "Ministry Among the Urban Indian," in *Metro-Ministry*, edited by David Frenchak and Sharrel Keyes (Elgin, IL: David C. Cook Publishing, 1979), 185-186.

CHAPTER 10

Meeting Critical Needs

I f any single characteristic distinguishes urban youth ministry from youth ministry in other settings, it would be the importance of addressing a variety of critical needs—teenage pregnancy, drug abuse, gangs. Though these needs exist in suburbs and rural areas, they may not be as concentrated, visible or widespread.

There are no quick and easy solutions to these problems. Most involve a complex mix of values, economics and self-esteem. Most experts agree, for example, that poverty is an underlying cause of drug abuse, teenage pregnancy and gangs.

Yet, in the face of the complex issues, urban churches across the nation have developed some of the most effective and creative responses to these problems. Their relatively low-budget approaches sometimes confound the high-priced programs developed by "experts." As Sherry Deane of the

Children's Defense Fund says: "Many programs are in small, isolated churches doing fantastic things—the very best they can with the resources they have—which makes their programs as meaningful as any which are heavily funded."[1]

Programs to Meet Needs

This chapter introduces some of the ways different urban churches across the country have responded to urban needs. Dozens of other models could be included as well. If you're interested in starting one of these kinds of ministries, use the process outlined in Chapter 6.

Illiteracy and Dropouts

Any urban inner-city ministry must have a tutorial program. If you just have a Sunday school class, a youth group on Sundays, and no tutorial ministry in the inner city, you're really not committed to helping kids . . . Most of the kids I work with are kids who might come to know Jesus and have their passport from hell to heaven, but they're going to live in hell here if academically they don't achieve, and if they can't find jobs.

This statement by Bruce Wall of Twelfth Baptist Church in Boston captures the intensity of many urban churches' concern about dropouts and illiteracy in this country. National and local statistics reflect the concern. While the national dropout rate is 29 percent, about 40 percent of urban teenagers drop out of school. The rate rises to 50 percent among urban blacks, 80 percent among urban Hispanics and 85 percent among urban Native Americans.[2]

Young people drop out of school for many different reasons. Most common are pregnancy, a feeling that school is unimportant, poverty and working too many hours.[3] But experts tend to agree that living in poverty is the overriding factor. A report by the William T. Grant Foundation Commission on Work, Family and Citizenship argues that "poverty—not minority status alone, or having a working mother, or coming from a single parent family—is highly correlated with school failure. Although black and Hispanic teens are more likely than whites to drop out, when students from the *same* socio-economic situation are compared, blacks, Hispanics and whites are almost equally as likely to be enrolled in school."[4]

The report explained that poverty hurries teenagers into adulthood before they can handle the responsibility. "Without the financial means or the social supports to create real alternatives," the report said, "too many young people living in poverty back into destructive decisions, sometimes in reaction to a sense of futility and limited options."[5]

Even urban teenagers who don't drop out of school often don't get adequate educations. Another study by the Carnegie Foundation for the Advancement of Teaching reported some disturbing statistics regarding illiteracy among urban students:

● Only 10 percent of 10th-graders at one Chicago high school could read effectively.

● In New Orleans, the average high school senior reads at a level exceeded by 80 percent of the nation's seniors.

● Seventy-five percent of Chicago high school freshmen have reading test scores below the national average.

● Of the 1,918 students at one Los Angeles high school, only 229 read at grade level.

● More than 40 percent of the Boston students who stay in school to graduate (44 percent don't) score below the 30th percentile on standardized reading tests.[6]

The Carnegie report concluded: "In large urban schools, we found . . . an atmosphere in which young people are unknown and unsupported by adults. Teenagers in these schools are often socially unattached and feel unconnected to the larger world. For these students, dropping out is easy. Alienated youth, for whom schools have barely made a difference, are flooding into communities where they confront unemployment lines, welfare checks, homelessness and even jails."[7]

Churches that offer tutoring and other educational programs expand teenagers' options, giving them not only skills, but also a vision of doing something better with their lives. And while some programs are elaborate, others are as simple as matching teenagers who need help in school with a high-achieving peer. Programs can be short-term tutoring for the Graduate Equivalency Diploma (GED) or college entrance exams, such as ACT and SAT. Or they can involve a five-year commitment from both young people and the church.

Let's look at several churches' education and tutoring programs:

Peer tutoring. Though simple and inexpensive, peer tutoring is a valuable, effective ministry that urban churches can offer young people. Not only do under-achieving teenagers receive help from a peer, but the tutor builds self-confidence and a feeling of accomplishment.

One congregation that offers this ministry is Bethel African Methodist Episcopal Church in Baltimore. Marietta Ramsey—a public school teacher who coordinates the church's youth ministry—says the church finds out about a need and then matches the need with another student who does well in that class. After the pairing, the church's main contribution is a quiet place where the teenagers can meet for tutoring.

Adult mentoring. The youth ministry at Shiloh Baptist Church in Trenton, New Jersey, has 50 church members who offer to be mentors for young people who have particular career interests or who have difficulty with specific subjects. For example, if a teenager has trouble in chemistry, a chemical engineer in the congregation might be paired with that young person for tutoring and building a relationship.

Adult advocacy. Because urban teenagers' parents sometimes don't take an active role in their children's education, some churches fill that role by working with the school system and supporting the teenagers through school.

One notable example is First Church of the Brethren in Brooklyn, New York. Youth worker Phill Carlos Archbold and the pastor actively encourage young people in the primarily Hispanic community to continue their education through college. Tutoring begins in elementary school and continues all through high school. Often parents encourage their children to quit school to earn money for the family. But the church tries to counter the need for immediate money by emphasizing the long-term benefits of education.

The church also meets specific economic needs of students that might otherwise mean their dropping out of school. The church buys shoes and covers bus fares for kids who have trouble going to school because they don't have enough money. The ministers also help the young people apply for college admission and scholarships.

"They want to go to college, but there are no funds," Archbold says. "We dig up the funds. We check out the books. We write the letters. We help them find the funds from various agencies and we get them through school."

In addition, Sunday school teachers and the pastors check up on kids in school. "We as leaders of the church feel we make our presence felt for these children, so we make periodic visits to the schools," Archbold explains. They check with principals, teachers and counselors about their students' progress. Archbold believes that "these kids have done very well and have received more attention because of the interest we have shown in them."

The church's record backs up Archbold's belief. In a community with a 60-percent dropout rate, the church proudly points to 17 church members who are in or have already graduated from college.

After-school programs. Some churches organize structured after-school tutoring programs to supplement the often weak education in urban public schools. This format not only gives students an educational boost, but it also occupies them in the after-school hours when kids are often unsupervised because parents aren't home from work.

The Congress of National Black Churches, an umbrella organization of five major African American denominations, has organized such a program. Called Project SPIRIT, the after-school tutorial program focuses on serving six- to 12-year-olds. The program supplements the school curriculum with tutoring in reading, writing, math and cultural heritage.

Fifteen churches in Oakland, California; Indianapolis, Indiana; and Atlanta, Georgia, participate in the pilot program. If the program succeeds in the pilot churches, other congregations across the country will use it, says program director Vanella Crawford.[8]

Long-term programs. In addition to basic tutoring programs, some churches have found that they must also commit themselves to long-term programs in order to keep young people in school and to provide them with the skills and vision to break out of the poverty cycle. One such congregation is Lawndale Community Church in Chicago, which sponsors an ambitious College Opportunity Program.

Each year seventh-graders from the community apply to the program, and 15 to 25 are selected to participate. The selections aren't based on achievement but on commitment and need. "If we didn't help them, they probably wouldn't finish high school, let alone go to college," says pastor Wayne Gordon.

The program is intensive, demanding commitment from the teenagers, the parents and the church. Young people meet weekly for computer training, recreation and Bible study. A full-time staff person visits the schools twice a month. And parents come to church once each month for training.

Although this program is new, the church plans to bring in 15 new seventh-graders each year. Then, as the numbers increase, the church will hire another staff person so that each adult will be working full time with no more than 45 kids.

Gordon explains the program's philosophy: "One of the key words in our ministry is empowerment . . . In ministry to the poor, a lot of people try to do what I call 'benevolence ministry' . . . They never help people change. All they do is just give them food and give them this and give them that. One of our goals when we help adults is to empower them so that they don't need our help a year from now . . . With the younger community, we realize it will take more years to empower them."

Sexuality and Teenage Pregnancy

Teenage pregnancy is a national crisis—not just an urban one. Almost 13 percent of the births in the United States are to teenagers (married and unmarried). Moreover, the problem tends to be greater in cities. The Children's Defense Fund reports that 76 of the nation's 108 largest cities have teenage birth rates above the national average. In the 25 worst cities, one out of every six births is by a teenager. The highest ratio is in Newark, New Jersey, where 26.3 percent of all births are by teenage mothers.[9]

Adding to the urgency of the concern, more girls are getting pregnant at earlier ages. Junior high schools are having to refocus their attention on pregnancy in that age group. Of the 350 Washington, D.C., students who became pregnant in 1988, for example, 113 were in junior high school. To respond to the need, one junior high school in the nation's capital has opened a nursery to help young mothers stay in school.[10]

Numerous factors appear to contribute to increased sexual activity among teenagers. For example:

● Half the girls who become pregnant score low in self-esteem.[11]

● Teenagers who become pregnant have significant learning trouble, including poor reading and writing skills.[12]

● These young people distrust authority figures, so they usually are unwilling to listen to health-care providers.[13]

● Young people who don't do well in school are more than twice as likely to be sexually active than high achievers.[14]

● If a kid's parent didn't graduate from college, the teenager is 50 percent more likely to have sex.[15]

● Black young people are almost twice as likely to have sex as their Hispanic or white peers.[16]

● Teenagers from broken homes tend to have sex earlier than kids who live with both biological parents.[17]

In addition to these findings from research, urban youth workers point to another critical factor in the level of sexual activity among urban teenagers: Many young people don't know what love is, and they have no positive role models of healthy relationships between men and women.

"There are some kids who have no sense of integrity in relationships because they don't have any role models," says youth worker Dave Carver of Rochester, New York. "There are guys in the group I worked with who are very promiscuous. They would claim to be devout Christians . . . but they'd be sleeping around with a dozen different girls. And that's because that's a pattern they saw at home."

The only way many urban teenagers have ever seen love expressed is through sex. Carver tells about another youth minister who has an "I don't want in your pants" talk with the girls. "When I love you, it doesn't mean I want something from you," he tells them.

Because many urban teenagers are already sexually active, traditional approaches to sex education in the church are wasted energy. As one married urban youth worker says: "You think about how ludicrous it is to give a talk on sex to a group of high school boys—to urban kids especially. Half of those kids probably have sex on a more regular basis than I do!"

Since traditional approaches to sex education don't work in the city, urban congregations often focus their attention on other related issues—self-esteem, positive peer pressure, communication skills and character-building. Some churches promote birth control if the young people insist on being sexually active. And many congregations have counseling for those who become pregnant. This ministry may include providing prenatal health care, parenting-skills training, tutoring and other forms of training to maximize opportunities for teenage parents.

No other form of urban ministry attracts as much interest and controversy as teenage pregnancy ministries. Yet urban churches don't have the luxury of debating the issues from a distance. They must decide how to reach out sensitively to young people in their own communities and congregations who need the church's healing hand during a difficult time. Here are descriptions of three different approaches to dealing with the teenage pregnancy issue:

Early prevention. Roseland Christian Ministries Center, a Christian Reformed Church on Chicago's South Side, runs Project Hope, a club that works to prevent sexual activity among 10- to 15-year-old girls. "That's young, but later will be too late," says pastor Tony Van Zanten.

Unlike other programs that might deal with sex in passing, Project Hope focuses on the issue. It helps the girls learn how to put sex in perspective with all of life. "Prevention of pregnancy is the intentional focus, not just a 'by the way' or 'also,' " Van Zanten says.

About 25 girls ages 10 to 15 meet two times per week after school for the program. This group setting is important, the pastor says, "because knowledge broadens options, but mutual support brings strength. The girls have a sense of group discipline, a sense of belonging to the group."[18]

Comprehensive training. Other churches offer comprehensive pregnancy-prevention programs aimed at both males and females, as well as their parents. One example is the Teen Pregnancy Prevention Program, jointly run by three Harlem churches—Memorial, Abyssinian and Canaan Baptist churches. With funding from the New York Urban League, this comprehensive program teaches teenagers character-building, identity development and personal communication skills. The program also sponsors workshops on topics such as AIDS, human sexuality, Christian values and family life.

Parents are included in sessions designed to help them better understand teenagers' developmental issues. Parents are challenged to get more involved in their kids' education and to provide a more stable home life.[19]

Counseling programs. Though urban churches hope to prevent pregnancies, they also minister to teenagers who become pregnant. One example is Bethel African Methodist Episcopal Church in Baltimore, which runs a professionally staffed teenage pregnancy program.

The church works with pregnant teenagers and teenagers with young children. The program teaches prenatal and postnatal care, parenting skills, nutrition and other related issues. It also helps the girls get a GED or return to school.

Drug Abuse

Drug abuse continues to be a perplexing problem among urban teenagers. During the 1980s, drug-related juvenile arrests in major cities increased dramatically, spurred primarily by the advent of the deadly cocaine derivative, crack. Diagram 10-1 compares drug-related arrests in four major cities between 1980 and 1987.

"The drug problem is one that touches everyone's lives here daily," says Willie Wilson, pastor of Union Temple Bap-

Diagram 10-1
Drug-Related Arrests

The following chart compares the number of drug-related arrests in major U.S. cities between the beginning and end of the 1980s:[45]

	1980	1987
Detroit	258*	647
New York City	349	1,052
Washington	315	1,894
Los Angeles	41	1,719
*1981 statistic		

tist Church in Washington, D.C. "Everyone has a family member or friend that is either a user or a seller of drugs."[20]

Two very different types of drugs are particularly troubling in the city: crack and inhalants.

Crack. A great deal of media attention focused on crack, beginning in the mid-1980s when the drug hit the city streets. It's cheap and it's highly addictive. Drug specialist Robert Stutman of the Drug Enforcement Administration in New York says: "A sophisticated marketing analysis couldn't have come up with a more perfect drug for kids . . . Five years ago, a kid had to spend $80 for cocaine. Now a kid can get a vial of crack for $3 to $5. The high is instantaneous, the addiction complete."[21]

Perhaps as troubling as crack's addictive power is the money involved in the crack trade. Many teenagers involved with crack never use it. They're drawn to the money. "They can make $1,000 a week dealing," says Blair Miller of the Adolescent Dual Diagnosis Unit in Detroit's Samaritan Health Center. "These kids have no other skills. It's very hard to resist."[22]

Inhalants. Inhalants are cheap and deadly. About 7 million American young people use inhalants, making them the third-most popular drug in the country, behind alcohol and marijuana. About 20 percent of high school seniors say they've tried or use inhalants.[23]

Abusers get their highs from inhaling the fumes from

common aerosols, solvents and anesthetics. They either sniff
the fumes through the nose or "huff" them through the
mouth. The high can last from five to 45 minutes, and can
cause anything from euphoria to violent behavior to acute
brain damage.

Inhalant abuse is a growing urban drug problem, particularly in low-income Hispanic and multi-ethnic communities. It's perpetuated by boredom, peer pressure and poverty.
Inhalants offer an easy and affordable escape. "It's cheaper
than a joint and cheaper than a six-pack of beer," says Juan
Peña, a drug counselor and former huffer. "It's easy to get.
They see it in school, they see it in the streets. Five kids
pitch in $1 each for a street bottle of tolly or a couple of
cans of spray paint and stay high all weekend."[24] ("Tolly" is
street lingo for toluene, a highly explosive petroleum
product.)

Churches' responses. As pervasive as the urban drug
epidemic is, some churches are making a difference. "I have
been told by people that the crack problem is so extensive
that there is nothing anybody can do about it. Nothing!"
says Cecil Williams of Glide United Methodist Church in San
Francisco. But he adds: "I say there is something that some
of us can do. It might not be much, but whatever it is,
we're going to try."[25]

Williams' church takes a high-visibility approach to the
problem. Williams holds daily sessions for current and former crack users at his church. Sometimes the church's Free-
dom Hall is filled with as many as 200 people for the
sessions. Many addicts and ex-users wear "crack caps" to
symbolize their effort to break the habit. These hats are
decorated with anti-drug slogans.

This Facts on Crack program builds on the 12-step approach developed by Alcoholics Anonymous. "This is no
moralistic thing on nobody. This is no heavy trip," Williams
tells the group. "We're like family offering support . . . Even
if you're on it, we're here. If you're slowing down, we're
here."[26]

Union Temple Baptist Church in Washington, D.C., takes
a more traditional two-pronged approach: prevention and rehabilitation. Both prongs emphasize spiritual strength, since

"drug abuse is a spiritual problem first of all," as Willie Wilson says.

The prevention prong focuses on instilling in young people "a sense of self-worth and spiritual strength." The goal, Wilson says, is to enhance spiritual and physical development and to equip kids with the tools to resist drugs. This program also includes rites of passage, such as memorizing scripture and learning marketable skills.

The rehabilitation prong focuses on helping drug abusers kick the habit. It includes a support group for 11- to 17-year-olds, which involves them coming to church twice each week to reinforce rehabilitation. "Prior to this," Wilson says, "there were absolutely no programs in this city for youth at that age once they came out of a drug rehabilitation program."[27]

Gangs

"The future of our nation is being fought for and will be won or lost on the streets of our urban centers," says Gordon McLean, youth guidance director of Metro Chicago Youth for Christ. "We dare not lose this war by indifference or default."[28]

McLean is referring to the gangs that control and dominate many neighborhoods in major cities. Police in 18 of the nation's 20 largest cities report gang activity.[29] While estimates are difficult to make, the cities and their gang populations include:

- Los Angeles, with about 450 gangs[30]
- Chicago, with more than 125 gangs[31]
- New York City, with 66 gangs[32]
- Denver, with about 20 gangs[33]

Gangs control their turf, often making it impossible for even the police to maintain order. And most gangs are also involved in drug trafficking. Their activity makes it frightening and dangerous to walk the streets in some communities. In Los Angeles, for example, gang shootouts caused 387 deaths in 1987. More than half the victims were innocent bystanders.[34]

Urban youth workers tell about group members who are badly beaten because they strayed into a particular gang's turf. Tracy Hipps, junior high coordinator for Inner City Impact in Chicago, tells about a teenager who rode his bike into another neighborhood. He was stopped and beaten up by five gang members who had seen him on another gang's turf.

Yet these gangs also appeal to urban teenagers. "Newspapers talk about kids being 'pressured to join gangs,' " McLean says. "Well, some of that happens. But the sad thing is that, more often than not, kids want to join gangs." He explains: "Kids use gangs as an illegitimate means of meeting legitimate needs. The longing for security, acceptance, someone to talk to and relief from the boredom of the inner city are all powerful appeals."[35]

Addressing gang issues is particularly difficult. Most often, churches and other urban ministries don't try to confront gangs directly. Rather, they provide alternative opportunities—recreation, drama and job-training programs.

Inner City Impact in Chicago, for example, provides an alternate close-knit group that might appeal to gangs, Hipps says. "We try to make the kids feel wanted . . . We don't really work against the gangs; we just offer a positive alternative."

Yet some churches are working directly with the gangs, trying to refocus their energies and to break down the rigid walls of hostility that cause so much violence. One notable example is the Soledad Enrichment Action Program in Los Angeles. It's run by Brother Modesto Leon with the support of the Catholic church. "We've always had drugs in the street gangs, going back 20, 30 or even 40 years," Leon says. "But now drugs are big, big business, and that business is what the gang wars today are all about."

Leon has addressed the problem from several angles:

● He mounted a citizen's movement against gang warfare. The effort is credited with reducing gang-war fatalities in the community from 22 to two in a year.

● Knowing the gangs' fascination with graffiti, Leon said he'd buy gangs paint if they'd paint pictures instead of slogans or threatening, open letters to other gangs. Today the streets of the low-income community are like vast, open-air galleries of graffiti art. Some of it is good; some of it is not. But it all represents a positive redirection of gang activity.

● Leon's main goal is to get different people in the gang wars talking—police, judges, churches, parents, schools and gang members. He uses the church as a "demilitarized zone" to get the different gangs to talk to each other. "We call parents together, usually mothers, and we try to bring some experts from government agencies and churches and other groups, and we just kick things around," he says. "Eventually we get some of the gang members to come and just sit and listen to the people interacting."[36]

Violence

Two students from Jamaica High School in Flushing, New York, fight over a girl at a party. The next day in school, one of the guys pulls out a handgun and kills his rival in front of the whole class. Some class members attend First Baptist Church.

●

Two rival high schools in Baltimore play a traditional Thanksgiving Day game. A tussle breaks out and a youth group member from Bethel African Methodist Episcopal Church is shot with a handgun.

●

Youth group members from Cass Community Church in Detroit are hanging out at one kid's house. His brother deals drugs, so he has a stash of guns. The kids decide to play Russian roulette. One of them shoots himself in the head.

●

Violence is a tragic reality in urban youth culture. And much of that violence involves handguns. Newsweek reports that "city streets have become flooded with unregistered and untraceable handguns which are available to anyone with a bit of cash. In New York, revolvers can be bought on street corners for as little as $25. Some dealers are even willing to 'rent' a gun for an evening, deferring payment until the teenager can raise money through muggings or robberies."[37]

A survey of Baltimore high schoolers (where the problem is severe) found that:

● 64 percent of the kids know someone who has carried a handgun in the past six months;

● 60 percent know someone who has been shot, threatened or robbed at gunpoint at school; and

● almost half of the males say they have carried a handgun at least once themselves.[38]

Some churches address the issue of violence by dealing with gangs, which account for much of the violence. But Cass Community Church in Detroit has taken a different approach. Through a program called Discipleship and Urban Violence, the church has tried to offer young people an alternative to the violence in the world around them.

It's appropriate that such a program take place in Detroit. Teenagers in Detroit are three times as likely to be murdered as teenagers in any of the country's other 10 largest cities. And guns are used in more than half of Detroit's casualties.[39]

The Cass program, facilitated by former pastor Bill Wylie-Kellermann, works on changing young people's attitudes toward violence. "There's just an awful lot of macho," Wylie-Kellermann explains. "To survive in the projects and on the street, you have to throw your feathers up and show you're willing to fight pretty quick. And that's the attitude of most of the kids coming here."

To counter this attitude, youth group members participated in a program of four retreats designed to help them see alternatives to violence. The retreats (see Diagram 10-2) allowed the young people to gain a new perspective on their own situation. It also gave them the opportunity to apply non-violence training techniques to situations they might encounter in school or on the streets.

The young people played simulation games to demonstrate solutions. For example: Suppose you're leaving a basketball game with your team. You encounter a rowdy group from the other school. They start harassing you. You respond, continuing the game of one-upmanship. The teenagers were asked: How could you respond in a way that breaks the escalating verbal violence that could quickly become physical violence?

Wylie-Kellermann says young people want to be able to

Diagram 10-2
Discipleship and Urban Violence

The "Discipleship and Urban Violence" program at Cass Community Church in Detroit revolved around a series of four retreats. Here's what happened at each retreat:

First retreat. The first retreat was devoted almost entirely to journal-keeping. Pastor Bill Wylie-Kellermann says this discipline was an important part of the whole sequence since the program's focus was to change attitudes.

Second retreat. This retreat concentrated on a distant situation—the racism and violence in South Africa—to help young people gain a perspective on violence. "The parallels were kind of obvious," Wylie-Kellermann says. "But it was one way to deal with it at a distance and also get a sense of the energy and hope that even South Africa had." A highlight of the retreat was a session with a South African college student who personalized the issues for the kids.

Third retreat. Moving closer to home, this retreat studied the Sermon on the Mount and the U.S. civil rights movement. Part of the weekend involved an afternoon of non-violence training similar to that used by Dr. Martin Luther King Jr. This retreat ended with pledges of non-violence by those teenagers who wanted to take such a step.

Fourth retreat. This final retreat was a youth-based, youth-directed experience. In the process the kids developed a proposal of how to respond to the violence around them. They proposed that:

● other churches in the city join their church in a regular Sunday morning "Death Toll" on the church bells—one toll for each young person who has been killed during the year by a handgun.

● the church form a small Christian-based theater troupe for the city. Kids would write their own scripts based on their experiences and their Christian faith. Then they'd perform the skits to help other people begin thinking about alternatives to violence.

---

stop the violence without feeling like they've caved in or lost face. "A lot of times the alternative approach to things seems like the most chancy," Wylie-Kellermann admits. "And you really go on faith when you speak up against the flow of violence. It takes some courage. A lot of what we were doing was praying courage into one another."

Sharing the Burden

Taken together, these needs can seem overwhelming. It's important to remember that no one church can address all the needs within the community. And just addressing one of the needs can be emotionally and financially draining. As Art Erickson says, "You need to have much more intensive ministry to these special problems."

Here are a few ways you can ease the burden on your congregation, allowing you to provide more effective ministry:

Referrals. One important way to overcome your own church's limitations is to work closely with other congregations and organizations. Such networking is, in itself, important ministry. "If you're in urban youth ministry," says James DiRaddo, "you've got to know the resources and the referral systems that are available. Because if you're not working hand in hand with all those people, you're not really addressing the needs as effectively as you could."

Allen Temple Baptist Church in Oakland, California, is an excellent example of how churches can work with other organizations. The church maintains an extensive referral directory of social-service agencies in the community. These include health agencies, child care, drug and alcohol abuse counseling, vocational testing and law enforcement. Not only does the church refer people with special needs to other organizations, but those organizations also refer people to Allen Temple. The church also displays a city map that pinpoints all the churches in the community to maintain cooperation.[40]

Churches that have worked through the Seminary Consortium on Urban Pastoral Education (SCUPE) have found that agencies, schools, businesses and other groups are quite open to working with churches, writes Clinton E. Stockwell of SCUPE. He adds: "The agencies visited were equally happy and surprised that churches were concerned about their neighborhood . . . There is no need for the church to duplicate what others are already doing. Resources in the city are too scarce for that."[41] Of course, churches should take *some* precautions before getting involved with another group. Diagram 10-3 offers some suggestions.

Diagram 10-3
Partnerships for Critical Needs

Jim Hopkins, youth minister at First Baptist Church in Los Angeles, has worked with a variety of community organizations in running his church's community center, El Centro. "Anytime you're forming new relationships, you tend to be hopeful and gloss things over," he says. That can lead to problems later on. Hopkins offers these suggestions for making a partnership work:
● Before rushing into anything, meet together. Get things in writing. Have as specific objectives as possible, and know the basics of evaluation.
● Understand that each partner will have different expectations. Be flexible.
● Remember that nothing is ever going to be what you expect it to be.

Prevention. While churches will always need to deal with critical needs when they arise, they can also work to prevent problems. "You can't always be digging people out of the hole," Art Erickson says. Instead, churches must work to develop programs that promote positive mental health.

Stewardship. Stewardship involves working with "systems"—government, laws, law enforcement, policies, business practices, and so forth. David Claerbaut illustrates the difference between "stewardship ministry" and "service ministry":

> *Counseling and befriending neighborhood youth is necessary in building healthy relationships and modeling what adult life can be, but having a youth program that both attempts to reform and redirect the energies of the gangs and also is vigilant about ways in which the city and its officials can provide a more equitable environment for the youngsters is just as important.*[42]

Claerbaut believes it's important that youth ministries work not just with individuals but also with institutions. He illustrates by telling how the "Young Life" program at LaSalle Street Church in Chicago has developed such a good reputation that judges sometimes grant juvenile offenders probation if they get involved in the program.[43]

Other youth workers have similar experiences. Bruce Wall of Twelfth Baptist Church in Boston also works in the city's juvenile justice system. "Knowing about our day-camp ministry and our Friday night youth program," he says, "judges refer teenagers from the court and say, 'I want this 14-year-old to go into the youth program at Twelfth Baptist Church.'"

Offering Hope to the City

Surveying all these critical needs in one chapter can make the problems seem overwhelming and the outlook hopeless. And the issues certainly are challenging and perplexing.

But that's only part of the story. Not all urban teenagers are involved in premarital sex, drug abuse and gang warfare. "Most urban teenagers aren't running around with guns. Most aren't killing people. Most are doing very well—against great odds," says Frances Pitts, chief judge of the juvenile courts in Wayne County, Michigan.[44]

These young people who maintain a healthy lifestyle against the odds are important reminders to churches. God is already at work in the city, giving urban teenagers strength, vision and hope. The church is called to join that work.

Reflection and Action

1. Check with your library, mayor's office or city hall for statistics and information related to the issues in this chapter. Discover what needs are being met and what needs are being overlooked.

2. Using the following chart, evaluate the need for each type of ministry addressed in this chapter. Add any issues that you think are more important in your community.

	A critical need	A moderate need	Not a need
Illiteracy and dropouts	☐	☐	☐
Sexuality and teenage pregnancy	☐	☐	☐
Drug abuse	☐	☐	☐
Gangs	☐	☐	☐

Violence	☐	☐	☐
Poverty	☐	☐	☐
Other: _____	☐	☐	☐
Other: _____	☐	☐	☐

3. Brainstorm ways you could address what you perceive as the top need in your community.

4. Develop a referral list for your community, including: other churches, health agencies, drug and alcohol abuse treatment centers, counseling agencies, vocational testing and training centers, law enforcement agencies—anyone you believe would be useful.

Endnotes

[1]Quoted in Alex Poinsett, "Suffer the Little Children . . ." Ebony, (August 1988), 144-148.

[2]Reported in Eugene C. Roehlkepartain (editor), The Youth Ministry Resource Book (Loveland, CO: Group Books, 1988), 101.

[3]Roehlkepartain, The Youth Ministry Resource Book, 101.

[4]The Forgotten Half: Non-College Youth in America (The William T. Grant Foundation Commission on Work, Family and Citizenship: January 1988), 16.

[5]The Forgotten Half: Non-College Youth in America, 17.

[6]An Imperiled Generation: Saving Urban Schools (Washington, DC: The Carnegie Endowment for the Advancement of Teaching, 1988), x.

[7]An Imperiled Generation: Saving Urban Schools, xi.

[8]Poinsett, "Suffer the Little Children . . .," 144-148.

[9]Karen Pittman and Gina Adams, Teenage Pregnancy: An Advocate's Guide to the Numbers (Washington, DC: Children's Defense Fund, 1988), 41, 43.

[10]McKendree R. Langley, "Jr. High Nursery Opens in D.C." Eternity, (January 1989), 12.

[11]"Poverty and Pregnancy," Youthworker Update, (December 1988), 3.

[12]"Poverty and Pregnancy," Youthworker Update, (December 1988), 3.

[13]"Poverty and Pregnancy," Youthworker Update, (December 1988), 3.

[14]Roehlkepartain, The Youth Ministry Resource Book, 52.

[15]Roehlkepartain, The Youth Ministry Resource Book, 52.

[16]Roehlkepartain, The Youth Ministry Resource Book, 52.

[17]Roehlkepartain, The Youth Ministry Resource Book, 52.

[18]Patricia Alderden, "Chicago's Project Hope: Learning to be Ladies," The Banner, (June 20, 1988), 22-23.

[19]Preston Robert Washington, God's Transforming Spirit: Black Church Renewal (Valley Forge, PA: Judson Press, 1988), 109.

[20]Kim A. Lawton, "Saying No: One Church's War on Drugs," Christianity Today, (October 7, 1988), 46.

[21]Jacob V. Lamar, "Kids Who Sell Crack," Time, (May 9, 1988), 20-33.

[22]Lamar, "Kids Who Sell Crack," 20-33.

[23]Michael Quintanilla, "Huffing: The Breath of Death," The Dallas Morning News, (August 7, 1988), 1F-3F.

[24]Quintanilla, "Huffing: The Breath of Death," 1F-3F.

[25]"How San Francisco Church Fights Crack Cocaine—and Wins," Jet, (May 16, 1988), 52-54.

[26]"How San Francisco Church Fights Crack Cocaine—and Wins," 52-54.

[27]Lawton, "Saying No: One Church's War on Drugs," 46.

[28]"Mean Streets—the Tough Turf of Youth Gangs," (an interview with Gordon McLean), The Rotarian, (January 1989), 16-19, 50.

[29]Carol D. Cellman and Peggy L. Halsey, Children and Youth in Jeopardy: A Mission Concern for United Methodists (Cincinnati, OH: National Program Division, General Board of Global Ministries, United Methodist Church, 1987), 32.

[30]Scott Armstrong, "In L.A., Line Blurs Between Street Gangs and Organized Crime," Christian Science Monitor, (June 12, 1987), 1, 8.

[31]Gregg Lewis, "The Insane Dragons Meet the Unknown Vice Lords," Christianity Today, (November 20, 1987), 10, 14.

[32]Roehlkepartain, The Youth Ministry Resource Book, 175.

[33]"Opinions Differ on Influence of Street Gangs," Rocky Mountain News, (May 12, 1988), 18.

[34]Lamar, "Kids Who Sell Crack," 20-33.

[35]"Mean Streets—the Tough Turf of Youth Gangs," 16-19, 50.

[36]Robert Holton, "Working 'Near Miracles' with L.A.'s Street Gangs," Our Sunday Visitor, (August 28, 1988), 8-9.

[37]George Hackett et al., "Kids: Deadly Force," Newsweek, (January 11, 1988), 18-19.

[38]Hackett, "Kids: Deadly Force," 18-19.

[39]"The Perils of Urban Childhood," Youthworker Update, (November 1988), 3.

[40]G. Willis Bennett, Effective Urban Church Ministry (Nashville, TN: Broadman Press, 1983), 76.

[41]Clinton E. Stockwell, "Barriers and Bridges to Evangelization in Urban Neighborhoods," in Signs of the Kingdom in the Secular City, compiled by David J. Frenchak and Clinton E. Stockwell (Chicago: Covenant Press, 1984), 100.

[42]David Claerbaut, Urban Ministry (Grand Rapids, MI: Zondervan Publishing House, 1983), 186.

[43]Claerbaut, Urban Ministry, 186.

[44]Lamar, "Kids Who Sell Crack," 20-33.

[45]Lamar, "Kids Who Sell Crack," 20-33.

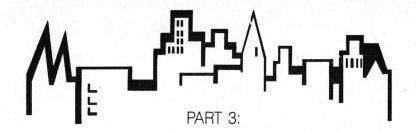

PART 3:

Leading Urban Youth Ministry

CHAPTER 11

Leadership for Urban Youth Ministry

The first Sunday after Rob Grotheer arrived as youth minister at First United Methodist Church in Houston, a young group member walked up to him and said, "Well, how long are *you* going to be here?"

Not quite sure what to say, Grotheer asked, "What grade are you in?"

"Eighth grade."

Grotheer paused. Then he said, "I'll be here when you graduate."

That eighth-grader was articulating a serious problem in urban youth ministry: leaders often don't stay long. They become frustrated and burned out. And they leave.

If they do continue working with the youth group, other problems emerge if they don't really enjoy being with kids. They just lead or teach because nobody else will do it.

Effective, caring leaders are essential to a strong urban youth ministry. Urban kids need positive role models and healthy adult relationships. Effective leaders can be the catalysts for important ministry and growth in young people.

This chapter focuses on several important characteristics of urban youth leaders. It also examines the unique concerns of youth ministry volunteers. The chapter concludes by focusing on the importance of young people themselves taking leadership in your youth ministry.

Quality Urban Leaders

What makes youth leaders effective in the city? When I asked urban youth workers that question no one said, "They have to be dynamic speakers with inspiring, funny and entertaining weekly messages." Or "They need to be former drug pushers who were born-again and now play in a Christian rock band in their spare time." Rather, their answers related much more to who youth leaders *are*, not what they *do*. Let's look at some of the personal characteristics that are particularly important for urban youth leaders.

Compassion and Love

Because urban youth ministry is, above all else, a relational ministry, it's no surprise that compassion and love top the list of characteristics. As Bruce Wall of Twelfth Baptist Church in Boston says: "You have to love young people. Not like them. Not tolerate them. Not want to work with them. But love young people, and see your role as representing Jesus to them."

Other youth workers agree. "They've got to know that you care—and really care," says Michael Walton of First Baptist Congregational Church in Chicago. "Kids in the inner city have been let down in so many ways, even within their own family structure." As a result, he says, "When nobody else was doing anything for kids, they realized they could come down to our church."

This compassion and love undergird all other aspects of the ministry. It's the basis for the relationships that form. It's the foundation for building trust with young people. And it's the motivation for continuing in ministry even when the job is frustrating, difficult and thankless. "God didn't call me to change everybody, but to love them," says Wayne Gordon of Lawndale Community Church in Chicago.

This love is essential to building relationships with urban teenagers. In speaking about his Brooklyn, New York, community, pastor Phill Carlos Archbold of First Church of the Brethren says: "Hispanic youth . . . can spot a fake in a minute. If you're not for real, if you don't really love them for who they are and what they are, then don't start. Because they don't relate to you. They have a sixth sense to know whether you really love them."

Longevity

By its very nature, urban youth ministry demands longevity. It takes time to build relationships anywhere, but it's particularly difficult in the city where kids survive by building a shell around themselves. And it takes longer to figure out what works and what doesn't, since every neighborhood is different.

"You need to be willing to be there for the long haul," says Harold Wright of Friendship Baptist Church in Vallejo, California. "You can't be there for five minutes or five days. You've got to be there for five years. It's taken five or six years just to figure out what to do . . . there are no set models . . . It takes a long time to get a fix on what works here."

Longevity also gives you a right to be heard in the community, explains Steve Pedigo of the Chicago Fellowship of Friends. "You become a viable part of the community . . . But you need to be there a long time to test the waters. They see that you're for real. And once you've earned that right to be heard, then they can hear what you have to say. But prior to that, they just run games all over you."

Jim Hopkins of First Baptist Church in Los Angeles notes that young people don't have a lot they can count on in the city. "They really want something that's going to be there and last a little while," he explains. As a result, consistency and reliability are truer measurements of your ministry than numbers and commendations might be.

Wayne Gordon believes that most ministries and ministers who fail just aren't given enough time. Staff at his church must make at least a two-year commitment, and most are required to commit to five years of ministry.

Incarnational Approach

Many youth workers talk about "incarnational ministry"—dedicating your life to your community and ministry. They point to Jesus' ministry described in 2 Corinthians 8:9: "For you know the grace of our Lord Jesus Christ, that though he was rich, yet for your sakes he became poor, so that you through his poverty might become rich." In the same way, they say, urban youth workers must give their lives to the teenagers and the community, accepting the community's struggles, problems and risks as their own.

This incarnational approach is vital to urban youth ministry, Gordon says. He tells about people "who live in the suburbs and come into the city to tell people what their problems are and show them what the solutions are. And that's so paternalistic." He continues: "The people who come from the outside don't understand what the problems are. They might read books about it. They might think they know. But they don't. The way you understand is to live in it."

Gordon says his church has been able to reach the Lawndale community in west Chicago precisely because almost everyone on staff lives in the community. "If you were to ask me why we are successful, the number one reason is that we live in the community. So it's not their community; it's our community."

When Gordon moved into the community in 1975, he unwittingly chose an apartment on the most dangerous street in the community. His address, he says, gave him credibility he could never have earned if he commuted into the community. "People begin to understand that you live here—you are a part. So we don't say 'your neighborhood.' It's always 'our neighborhood.' "

This incarnational approach also involves a commitment to kids' lives. Urban teenagers have few people they can count on. Larry Gotts, pastor of St. Peter's-in-the-Bronx, puts his ministry philosophy this way: "They can count on me to listen and try to help. No guarantees. But they know I will really share their burden . . . They know I will go anywhere in any building, day or night, even where they wouldn't go themselves."[1]

Living in a community with another ethnic group is not always easy. When Steve and Marlene Pedigo moved into the neighborhood near the Cabrini-Green government housing in Chicago, Marlene writes that "the black community wondered what our ulterior motive might be for coming to Cabrini-Green."[2] She adds that "the burning of property of newcomers with the wrong racial background is not uncommon." In her family's case, the garage was set on fire twice.[3]

Wayne Gordon's family stopped counting burglaries at 10, he says. And when the Chicago teachers go on strike, his own children attend tutoring programs at church along with kids from the community. Yet, despite the trouble, he doesn't regret living there. In fact, he says, it has helped his family learn to confront problems, while many suburban families simply run from them.

This contrast between "your neighborhood" and "our neighborhood" is sensitive and critical in the city, particularly in cross-cultural situations. John M. Perkins, president of Voice of Calvary Ministries, expresses the problem's intensity when he writes: "Blacks move in and whites move out, and six months later, the whites send their kids back to the neighborhood with the Four Spiritual Laws and try to tell those folks that God loves them. The black people cannot help but wonder why those Christians didn't show love when they had a real opportunity to do so."[4]

Modeling

A persistent problem in the city—particularly in low-income communities—is a lack of positive role models. The main reason is quite simple: When people become "successful," they move into wealthier communities. "In a poor urban community," sociologist David Claerbaut writes, "a youngster is likely to grow up without a single well-educated person with whom he can identify . . . The role models of the poor are from the ranks of the unemployed, unskilled, alcoholic, disabled and criminal. Ironically, the criminal group includes the most affluent of the lot: the three P's—prostitutes, pimps and pushers."[5]

Also, the cycle of poverty often traps people into unhealthy and destructive lifestyles. They never see any other patterns. Art Erickson of Minneapolis, Minnesota, says only one couple is still married from the high school class that graduated 10 years ago. So he invites married couples to youth camp "so kids can see couples relating, because they never see it."

In many cases, the youth worker can be a positive role model for urban teenagers. Glandion Carney writes: "One of the most effective ways to build positive values into young people is to serve as a model. Let teens see you in a natural environment, where you fail and succeed, work and play, laugh and cry."[6] Carney says this modeling and relationship-building helps young people learn basic life skills and relationships—money management, household chores and healthy family interaction.

Phill Carlos Archbold says his young people are involved in social ministries in the city because the whole church is. "We're involved in it, so they're involved in it," he says. "You just can't begin overnight. You have to start somewhere, and you have to be consistent . . . For us it's a way of life."

Bruce Wall sees a similar need. "How can I challenge these young people . . . to serve Christ if I'm walking on the edge of compromising my own lifestyle—things I do, things I say, people I hang out with, what I'm reading?" he asks. "Watching them watch me challenged me to try to be Christlike."

Self-Confidence

Buster Soaries says that a significant problem in urban youth ministry leadership is that youth workers don't have much confidence in themselves. As a result, they don't have as great an impact on their communities as they could.

"We are the ones who have the answers," he says. "Newspaper reporters and TV newspeople should come to urban youth workers when they want to know how to deal with youth riots in Miami, violence in Detroit or teenage pregnancy in Atlanta." To do this, he says, youth workers must "adequately describe who you are and what you do." They must position themselves as community leaders, not as "lowly urban youth workers." He concludes, "Our self-concept has got to improve significantly . . . or we'll never make a difference."

Psychological Attributes

Attitudes about the city and about urban youth ministry make up the final quality that is important for urban youth ministers. Urban ministry expert David Claerbaut identifies eight important "psychological attributes" for urban ministers. Decide whether each description fits you:

	This fits me	**This doesn't fit me**
1. I enjoy the different cultures I encounter in the city. I love learning about kids' backgrounds.	☐	☐
2. When I do something for young people, I expect them to notice. And I expect them to respond positively to my ministry.	☐	☐
3. I believe issues I confront in urban youth ministry are too complex to have clear-cut answers. Sometimes I believe it's impossible to know exactly what's "right" in a particular situation.	☐	☐
4. I don't understand why kids in my youth group get caught up in negative behaviors. I usually come down hard on them when they do.	☐	☐
5. I won't make a decision about something unless I'm sure I have the proper Christian answer to the question.	☐	☐
6. When people criticize me, I don't let it		

get to me much. I understand that other
people see things differently from me—
and that's okay.   □   □
7. I'm always frustrated when people have
so far to go, and they just inch along,
not making much progress and not
changing much for the better.   □   □
8. I'm one of those people who always sees
the funny side of the story when things
don't go exactly as I planned.   □   □

Now, let's see why Claerbaut says various attributes are
particularly important for urban ministers:

*1. I enjoy the different cultures I encounter in the city. I
love learning about kids' backgrounds.*

Respect for and appreciation of cultural diversity is essential to reaching the city. The city is so diverse that no
one can be effective without understanding this diversity.

*2. When I do something for young people, I expect
them to notice. And I expect them to respond positively to
my ministry.*

Part of being a servant is serving young people because
you're called to serve them, not because of what you'll get
out of it. A servant attitude frees you from feeling like every
"investment" has to have a good return. God calls you
regardless of the response of the person being served.

*3. I believe issues I confront in urban youth ministry
are too complex to have clear-cut answers. Sometimes I believe it's impossible to know exactly what's "right" in a
particular situation.*

Issues, conflicts and choices aren't simple in the city.
Understanding and accepting the ambiguity that comes from
living in a world with "no easy answers" is essential.

*4. I don't understand why kids in my youth group get
caught up in negative behaviors. I usually come down hard
on them when they do.*

Urban teenagers face a myriad of choices, many of them
negative. Youth workers must have understanding and compassion about why kids get involved in negative behaviors,
instead of just condemning their behavior.

5. I won't make a decision about something unless I'm

sure I have the proper Christian answer to the question.

Theologians and suburbanites may have plenty of time to argue about and debate homosexuality, sex outside marriage, AIDS, abortion and various other social issues. But in the city, those are real-life concerns that urban youth ministers must respond to in faith, even if they aren't sure of the "right" answer.

6. When people criticize me, I don't let it get to me much. I understand that other people see things differently from me—and that's okay.

There are too many different people in the city to please everyone. Urban youth ministers will be criticized for different things from different people. They must learn to deal with that criticism without being debilitated by it.

7. I'm always frustrated when people have so far to go, and they just inch along, not making much progress and not changing much for the better.

There are too many important needs to meet all of them. Urban youth workers must compromise, knowing that a little progress may not be what they want, but it's better than no progress at all. Often the obstacles are so great that you have to celebrate the few forward footsteps you take, even if you hoped to move miles.

8. I'm one of those people who always sees the funny side of the story when things don't go exactly as I planned.

Claerbaut writes: "Humor is the guardian of sanity. If one cannot laugh, one will be left only to cry . . . Laughter is a therapeutic gift, and finding as many ways as possible to exploit its use will be in the best interest of the urban pastor."[7]

Volunteers and Sponsors

Finding good youth ministry volunteers (called "sponsors" or "supervisors" in many churches) is a constant problem for youth ministry everywhere. But it's often an even bigger problem in the city. A survey of junior high ministers by Group's JR. HIGH MINISTRY Magazine found that finding volunteers tied for the second greatest concern of urban people—higher than in either suburban or rural settings.

Many factors contribute to the difficulty of finding volunteers:

Lack of time. Jim Hopkins says many adults in his church work six or seven days a week in low-paying jobs just to survive. And they can't volunteer for special events such as camp because they don't get vacation time.

Lack of understanding. In church traditions without a strong emphasis on youth ministry, adults often don't see the importance of working with young people. Thus you have to educate these adults about the need before getting their leadership.

Lack of leadership experience. In some communities, people have never had the opportunity to lead anything. As a result, they haven't developed any leadership skills.

Yet cultivating adult leaders in the congregation is essential both for the church and the youth group. "Too often," urban ministry expert Ray Bakke charges, "a new pastor rushes in with programs and recruits students from nearby Bible colleges, first to supplement, and then to replace local people who cannot measure up to the requirements and expectations of the program."[8] While he agrees that such an approach has value—particularly as training for the students—it generally "is a stop-gap solution at best, and it may retard the emergence of local leadership even further."[9]

Bakke believes that God has given people in the congregation the gifts the congregation needs for its ministry. The challenge is to convince them that they can act and make decisions themselves. He writes: "People cannot jump from paternalized, welfare-state dependency to democracy in one stride. You must have incremental steps going on for several years to change the climate and build leadership."[10]

Recognizing the great need for training, the Archdiocese of Philadelphia initiated its Hispanic Youth Ministry Training Program. The program included three retreats plus nine weeks of workshops designed to help adults learn to articulate their faith, to build an understanding of youth ministry and to teach basic leadership skills. Here's the outline of the training program's format, which can be used as a structure for training volunteers in your church:[11]

First session. This session consists of a weekend workshop about youth ministry. It introduces the goals and objectives of youth ministry and outlines the place of youth ministry in the church.

Second session. Leadership techniques are taught in this weekend session. These include basic leadership skills, communication skills and public speaking skills.

Third session. This session is a retreat designed for leaders-in-training to focus on themselves and build community as a team.

Fourth session. This final session is really a nine-week series of intensive studies. It covers:

● Understanding teenagers, their world and the urban world

● Understanding faith, discipleship and the church— valuable information for adults who may not have had much training themselves in these areas

● How to do peer counseling—a valuable tool for relational ministry

Of course, people won't be completely skilled when they first come out of the training. Yet giving them responsibility has benefits that far outweigh the disadvantages.

Ray Bakke remembers when he began building a volunteer base at Fairfield Avenue Baptist Church. He told the church secretary to stop typing the church bulletin. Instead, she was to train church members to type it. It took much longer and the quality was never as good as what the secretary could do. "The bulletin sometimes went this way and sometimes that, and there were a few misspelled words," Bakke recalls, "but it was the product of the members, and each issue bore the names of the women who had done the typing. Suddenly there was pride in the bulletin, and church members were glad to give it out on Sundays. It was a true reflection of our congregation."[12]

Cultivating a volunteer base isn't easy, and it doesn't happen overnight. Indeed, Wayne Gordon believes that it takes 15 years to build "a new generation of indigenous Christian leadership." However, sharing your ministry with people in the community ensures its long-term health.

As he was leaving First Presbyterian Church of Crafton

Heights in Pittsburgh, Dave Carver reflected on what he would do differently if he were starting again. "I'd pour my life into four or five adults who were going to stay in Crafton Heights all their lives," he said. "If we can give the ministry to the adults, then our ministry will stay forever."

Youth as Leaders

If adults in the city have few opportunities to lead, it's even more true for teenagers. They have few, if any, leadership opportunities at school. There are rarely extracurricular clubs or community organizations where they can take leadership. And because there are so many teenagers around, only the most exceptional kids have the few opportunities that do exist.

The church provides a valuable ministry by building leadership in its community through the youth program. "One of the purposes of youth ministry is to help young persons grow in their ability to serve others in the name of Christ," David Ng writes. "When young people assume leadership, they learn as they serve . . . Any church would be concerned about developing young leaders, persons who will accept the mantle of leadership and decision-making in the church today and in years to come."[13]

Many churches have found that urban teenagers not only learn a great deal from leading, but they also do important and creative work. Let's look at four examples of different ways you can get kids involved in leadership:

Leading in the church. New Hope Lutheran Church in Chicago participated in the Doulos Program, a denominational effort designed to build church leadership in young people. The program's goal, says pastor Karen Battle, was to "create leadership in the church minority youth." Young people who were selected for the program were required to participate in regular meetings. They helped lead in worship. And they had regular jobs and responsibilities in the church. Battle says the program "gave them a sense of maturity and responsibility."

Leading within the youth program. When First Presbyterian Church of Crafton Heights in Pittsburgh decided to rehabilitate an old movie theater as a community recreation center, a central goal was to have kids involved in the whole process, says Dave Carver. Kids sponsored fund-raisers and went along when Carver sought grant money. Then they helped with renovation by hauling cement and busting down old walls. Altogether, they spent 18 months on the project.

"Kids most appreciated the fact that they could make a positive contribution," Carver remembers. "The church gave those kids the chance to do something right."

Leading special ministries. The "Discipleship and Urban Violence" program at Cass Community Church in Detroit is a youth-led program designed to address the critical issue of youth homicide in Detroit. Young people were involved in writing a grant proposal for funding, says Bill Wylie-Kellermann, the pastor who oversaw the program. When the request was granted, they were involved in leadership throughout the training process.

Leading younger kids. Each summer, First Chinese Baptist Church in San Francisco sponsors a day camp for children in the Chinatown community. About 100 children attend, and most of the leaders are youth group members. Youth leader Jerald Choy says the day camp is "where they first learn to be more responsible . . . as part of the church."

The program's success is partly due to its progressive training structure, which is based on experience. The first year kids are "counselors in training." The next year they become "junior counselors." "By the time they've been in the program three years, they're ready to be senior counselors," Choy says. "They can take a whole group of kids and plan the program with the junior counselors and counselors in training."

How do you find teenage leaders? Suburban youth ministries sometimes watch for leaders at school or in the community, then they attract that person to the youth group. An instant leader! But urban churches don't have that luxury. Instead, they must discover and nurture the natural leadership abilities God has given individuals. That may not be as easy as finding ready-made leaders, but it's an important ministry.

Looking for Leaders

Perhaps you agree that developing a leadership base is important. And perhaps you agree that it's important to find leaders in the community. But how do you do it when no one seems like a strong candidate?

It's appropriate to remember that many leaders in the Bible didn't seem like strong candidates either. Moses came from a non-traditional family. And he wasn't a very good speaker. Ruth was an impoverished immigrant who relied on the soup kitchens of her time—gleaning food from other people's fields. And Mary, the mother of Jesus, was an unwed teenage mother.

The Bible is filled with examples of God turning unlikely people into leaders. And God continues to raise up unlikely leaders. Urban youth workers must discover the Moseses, Ruths and Marys within their own congregations—people whom God has blessed for significant ministries in the city.

Reflection and Action

1. If you have a job description, examine it. If you don't, create one based on what you do in youth ministry. What would you say are the most important qualities you bring to your ministry?

2. Do you agree with Wayne Gordon when he says people who drive in from the suburbs to minister are being paternalistic? Why or why not? Give examples to support your answer.

3. Think about the most effective urban youth ministers you know. Do they possess the qualities listed in the first section of this chapter? If not, what do you think makes their ministry effective? What other qualities would you add to this list?

4. Think about your answers to the self-test on page 217. Do you agree with David Claerbaut's list of psychological attributes? Which ones make the most sense? the least sense? What particular area do you think you need to work on? Make a plan for beginning to address that issue during the coming week.

5. If you have trouble getting volunteers, look through your church membership to discover people who might have hidden gifts. Approach these people about volunteering. Offer them training and support.

6. Meet with your youth ministry volunteers. Find out their concerns and needs. Plan training sessions to address their needs and interests.

7. Think of three things you do now that would be appropriate to turn over to volunteers so they'll feel more pride and ownership in your youth ministry.

8. List the ways young people are involved in leadership in the congregation. If the list is short, think of ways they could contribute to your church and the youth group.

Endnotes

[1]Bonny Vaught, ''A South Bronx Ministry: Symbol and Reality,'' The Christian Century, (June 22-29, 1983), 616-618.

[2]Marlene Morrison Pedigo, New Church in the City (Richmond, IN: Friends United Press, 1988), 23.

[3]Pedigo, New Church in the City, 23.

[4]John Perkins, ''Urban Church/Urban Poor,'' in Metro-Ministry, edited by David Frenchak and Sharrel Keyes (Elgin, IL: David C. Cook Publishing Company, 1979), 49-59.

[5]David Claerbaut, Urban Ministry (Grand Rapids, MI: Zondervan Publishing House, 1983), 78-79.

[6]Glandion Carney, Creative Urban Youth Ministry (Elgin, IL: David C. Cook Publishing Company, 1984), 50.

[7]Claerbaut, Urban Ministry, 198-203.

[8]Ray Bakke with Jim Hart, The Urban Christian (Downers Grove, IL: InterVarsity Press, 1987), 93.

[9]Bakke with Hart, The Urban Christian, 94.

[10]Bakke with Hart, The Urban Christian, 95.

[11]Adapted from Maria Torres-Riviera, an unpublished paper, ''Hispanic Youth Ministry Training Program,'' (March 1988). Used by permission of the author.

[12]Bakke with Hart, The Urban Christian, 92.

[13]David Ng, ''Planning to Meet Specific Needs,'' in Asian Pacific American Youth Ministry, edited by Donald Ng, (Valley Forge, PA: Judson Press, 1988), 61.

An Impossible Job Description?

Position: *Urban youth worker*
Qualifications:

- *Commitment to Christian service*
- *Desire to minister to young people*
- *Genuine concern for urban teenagers*

Necessary Experience:

- *Coaching experience in basketball, softball or volleyball—preferably all three*
- *Administration with working knowledge of how to run outreach and recreation centers, fund-raising campaigns and computer literacy programs*
- *Counseling experience with particular expertise in drug abuse, gangs and violence, dysfunctional families and low self-esteem counseling*

Job Requirements:

- *Work 16 hours a day, seven days a week*
- *Ability to speak several languages (including street talk)*
- *Thrive on the city's pace, lifestyle and culture*
- *Low salary, if any (may need to work full time in another job)*

•

C an a normal human being survive in urban youth ministry? The problems are so big, so diverse, so challenging. Is anyone qualified? Is urban youth ministry humanly possible?

Urban youth workers struggle daily with these kinds of questions. They minister to young people with tremendous needs. The work is long on hours and short on recognition. Success is difficult to measure. Many church traditions have no history of youth work, leaving the urban youth worker with little support.

While specific statistics aren't available, urban youth workers agree that the burnout rate is much higher for youth workers in the city than in other settings. While longevity is an important key to successful city ministry, few youth workers survive long enough to enjoy the benefits.

David Frenchak, director of studies for the Seminary Consortium for Urban Pastoral Education (SCUPE), tells about a 16-year-old inner-city teenager who stopped going to church after being an every-Sunday attender for years. When asked why, she said she didn't go anymore because four of her five pastors had suffered emotional breakdowns.[1]

In spite of the struggles, urban youth work and city life can be particularly rewarding. Veteran urban youth workers can point to lives they've seen changed, challenges they've met and growth they've experienced as a result of working in cities.

This chapter examines both the personal challenges and the opportunities for urban youth ministers. It also suggests some ways urban youth workers have learned to survive and thrive in urban youth ministry.

The Challenges to the Youth Worker

Many of urban youth ministry's challenges are inherent in the work—ministering in a difficult environment, addressing tough issues, convincing the congregation of the need to reach teenagers, operating with little or no budget. But how do these challenges affect the person in ministry? Let's look at some of the personal challenges urban youth workers face:

Urgency of the Task

People enter youth ministry out of a sense of God's calling in their lives. Yet urban teenagers' needs are so urgent and so complex they can overwhelm even the strongest sense of calling. As a result, youth workers who feel called to reach and help urban teenagers discover that it's impossible to meet every need. The result is a constant tension between stark need and human limitations.

Art Erickson, associate pastor of Park Avenue United Methodist Church in Minneapolis, Minnesota, illustrates the overwhelming needs by recounting incidents that had touched his ministry within the past four-week period: "One high school kid had a 3-year-old daughter who was raped and left in a dumpster. A 13-year-old was kidnapped and raped 12 times in a basement within 24 hours. One kid had homosexual relationships with three of his nephews. And now he was sexually molesting the 4-year-old daughter of the girl he's living with. And the list goes on."

Such needs can easily overwhelm anyone who tries to help. Youth minister Michael Walton of First Baptist Congregational Church in Chicago struggles with the tension between his own limitations and the great needs he sees among urban kids. "Personally it's a struggle," he says. "I can't save all the kids . . . There are so many problems with the kids; I cannot solve all of them. I probably will not get them all in a youth group either."

Failure

Closely related to the challenge of overwhelming needs are inevitable failures youth workers experience in dealing with urban teenagers. As Frenchak writes: "Anyone who has worked very long in the city knows that the occasions for celebration do not come along very often . . . The problems are simply massive. For every 10 people you help, there are at least 1,000 more who need help, and perhaps more desperately than the 10 you helped."[2]

Phill Carlos Archbold, associate pastor of First Church of the Brethren in Brooklyn, New York, says failure is the most difficult issue he struggles with as well. He tells about standing over the open grave of a teenager who died of a drug overdose. His church had tried to reach the young person, and now it was too late. Such failures are ever-present, he says. "We have sent many community residents to drug programs. We have buried many. We have buried 260 with AIDS since the epidemic began. But what can you do? . . . You can only do so much in a 24-hour day. And we say, 'Lord, help us not to burn out' . . . We just keep going. It hurts, but we have to keep going."

Youth worker Dave Carver of Rochester, New York, also says living with failure is perhaps the most difficult issue he must personally deal with in urban youth work. He remembers one girl who was almost like a daughter to him. Both her parents were in jail. Away from their negative influence, she had become a straight-A student in sixth grade and was active in his youth group. Then her parents were released, and she went back to live with them. Her life completely fell apart. She became involved in drug abuse, was sexually active and was picked up for shoplifting. She had to repeat ninth grade three times.

Such perceived failures can drain youth workers of their enthusiasm and their sense of purpose—the hope that they can make a difference for urban kids. Unless they discover other ways to assess their ministries, they find themselves frustrated, cynical and burned out. And they leave.

Lack of Support and Understanding

"Urban youth ministry may be the loneliest ministry in the country," asserts Paul Tarro. That assessment is based on his own experience as director of Urban Youth Ministries in Kansas City, Missouri, and his conversations with other urban youth workers. Too often, urban youth workers feel little support from those whom they should lean on most: their congregations, their youth ministry colleagues and their denominations.

Their congregation. Because many urban churches have little or no history of youth ministry, many urban youth workers face the ongoing challenge of repeatedly convincing the congregation of the importance of youth work.

One urban youth minister says he constantly has to answer the church leaders' complaint: "We didn't have all these fancy, expensive programs when we were kids. Why do these kids need them?" Constantly having to defend the youth program drains youth workers' energy—when they desperately need the congregation's support and encouragement.

A lack of tradition in youth ministry can also affect the urban youth worker's sense of ministry. Because youth ministry hasn't been a priority in the black church, Walton says he thinks he'll "probably always be considered a second-class pastor." He continues: "I'm always called a youth minister—but not in terms of what a youth minister is. Just someone young. I've been in the ministry for 15 years. I have a wife. I've been married nine years. I have two kids. I'm not a kid anymore. But that's how many of these 'senior pastors' feel—that I'm just a young minister with a lot of crazy ideas that they don't need."

Their youth ministry colleagues. Urban youth workers also feel isolated from their ministry colleagues. While urban ministers may develop a small support network in their city, it's difficult for them to develop support relationships with suburban and rural youth workers. First, their needs and ministries are different. As Tarro says, "Working with a child prostitute is not a typical youth worker problem." Yet urban youth ministers deal with such problems regularly.

Furthermore, urban concerns aren't on the agendas of many regional and national youth ministry gatherings and training events. As a result, unlike others, urban workers don't have forums where they can discuss concerns, challenges and ideas—and be supported in their concerns by their peers. Because these events don't address their specific concerns, they find it difficult to justify the cost of attending them.

Their denominations. Urban youth ministry is rarely a priority for denominations. Either the denomination has little or no emphasis on youth ministry in general (as is true with most traditionally black denominations), or the denomination emphasizes traditional suburban youth ministries. In the latter case, the youth ministry executives most often were trained in traditional youth ministry and gained their experience in a suburban youth program. Thus the denominational leaders have trouble relating to the dynamics and struggles of urban youth work.

Demands on Time

Urban youth ministry isn't a full-time job. It's a round-the-clock job. Because city life continues late into the night, ministry often does too. As Paul Tarro says, "Urban ministry can begin at 5 a.m. and end at 2 a.m."

Such time pressures are not only physically draining, but they eat away at family life. Walton says he's working to spend more time with his wife and two children, but "right now they're not getting half the time they should be getting." He continues: "The time that has to be put into it can get out of control . . . There will always be kids with problems." Walton is on call at all times—and young people call him at all times. In fact, he finally installed two phones at home—one for his family and one for church calls.

Adding to the time pressure is a reality of city life: Everything takes longer. There are longer lines, heavier traffic, more bureaucracy that urban youth workers must deal with daily. "It takes 10 times more effort to do anything in the city," says David Miles, youth minister at First Baptist Church in Flushing, New York. "By the time I get to work, I have to have a prayer meeting just to get my heart right."

Low Salaries

If urban youth workers receive salaries (which many do not), those salaries are often low—even for youth ministry. One full-time youth minister in a large Chicago church receives only $11,000 per year. He wouldn't be able to stay in ministry if his wife didn't earn a comfortable salary to support their family.

Many urban churches simply cannot afford to pay a youth minister more—they hardly have funds to keep their buildings maintained. But the lack of financial support from the church puts particular stress on youth ministers who have to pay their own bills too.

Prejudice and Racism

When David Miles first began youth ministry in Flushing, he rented an apartment from a landlord who hated Asians and Hispanics—the very groups who form a large part of Miles' youth group. If he wanted youth group members to come to his house (an important part of his ministry), he had to move.

Despite the civil rights advances in our country and despite the Christian belief that Christ breaks down all barriers, racism remains a pervasive—even growing—problem across the country and in churches. And while homogeneous suburban churches may seldom deal directly with the issue, it's a central concern in diverse urban congregations.

In addition to racism's effect on young people in the church, the problem arises as a personal concern for youth workers. If they minister with people from backgrounds other than their own, they often must deal with suspicion, mistrust and prejudice.

Miles—a white who ministers in a community that's mostly Asian American—says some families don't like him simply because he's white. And Walton—an African American youth worker—says he's often not taken seriously in youth ministry circles simply because he's black.

It's important to note that some suspicion and mistrust of white ministers by minority groups is understandable and justified. Minorities, particularly blacks, have experienced a long history of oppression, abuse and patronizing attitudes from whites, including whites in the church.

Yet sometimes the race issue becomes so dominant that it destroys any possibility of healthy, intercultural ministries. "I think there are a lot of false ideas . . . about a white guy working in a minority group," says Wendell Fisher, who ministers in a primarily Hispanic congregation in New York City. He says seminaries sometimes discourage whites from considering churches in minority communities because church growth research indicates that people want to be with "their own kind." Fisher rejects such logic as theologically unsound. He says the choice of ministry positions should be based on the question "What does God want you to do with your life?"

Thriving in the City

The stresses and challenges of urban youth ministry are undeniable and unavoidable. The question is, how can youth workers respond to the challenges in healthy ways, enhancing both their ministries and their personal lives?

Unfortunately, many youth workers don't react in healthy ways. Paul Tarro laments that too many youth workers respond to the stress of their task by becoming even more deeply involved in their work—which doesn't help. Instead, it hurts both them and their ministry. They think of the stresses and frustrations of their ministries as their "thorn in the flesh." Instead of trying to heal the wounds, they ignore the pain until it saps their energy, enthusiasm and vision for ministry.

Daniel Buttry tells his own story of burning out in urban ministry—a story that rings true for many urban youth workers:

> *When I came to Dorchester Temple, I was filled with ideas, youthful zeal, boundless energy, and a vision I was eager to proclaim. I worked hard for 13 months in the church and in the community. Then I had a physical breakdown. A normal hay-fever allergy put me out of commission for two months.*
>
> *Behind my burnout was a messiah complex . . . I was going to save Dorchester Temple. I was going to save Codman Square, our decaying neighborhood . . . My vision was very good and biblical. But my faith was actually in myself . . . I was the messiah in my own mind, but I discovered that I was utterly inadequate for the task.*[3]

A more healthy response to the challenges of urban ministry involves finding a balanced perspective that allows you to continue in ministry while also taking care of the only body, mind and spirit God gave you. Urban ministers who have overcome the challenges see a number of keys to thriving in urban youth ministry:

Set Priorities

Youth minister Jim Hopkins of First Baptist Church in Los Angeles says that one of the more prevalent aspects of urban youth ministry is that "so many things demand your attention." You have to reach the point, he says, when you can say, "This is what I can do; this is what I can't do."

Setting priorities is necessary to be effective in ministry and to maintain balance in life. Even Jesus had to set priorities for himself. After all, even he didn't heal every sick person who came to him. Mark 3:10 tells how he healed *many*—not *all*—who were sick. And usually after being with the crowds, he went away to pray and rejuvenate (Mark 6:46). Instead of burning out solving every problem, Jesus chose to spend time alone in prayer, as well as time in recreation. His life presents a healthy model for anyone in ministry.

Each person's priorities will vary depending on personal and family needs, ministry emphases, professional responsibilities and other factors. For example, if your youth program focuses primarily on building relationships with unchurched teenagers, your priorities will be different from the youth minister whose program focuses on building up and challenging young people who are already committed to the church.

In establishing your priorities, talk with your family members to discover their needs. Make sure you know congregational expectations. And make sure the congregation understands your need to limit your efforts in some areas in order to concentrate on more important ministries and your own personal life.

Keeping priorities is never easy in urban youth work. When you give time to one need or person, another need or person won't be addressed. And when you take time to care for yourself or nurture your family life, you can't simultaneously meet the needs of every teenager who calls.

In order to keep from becoming overwhelmed by the need, long-term urban youth workers remind themselves that their task is not to save every teenager, to solve every problem or to meet every need. The youth worker's calling is to know God and serve him as faithfully as possible within the limitations of a 24-hour day and a human body. As Erickson points out, "You're in this ministry not for human needs, but out of obedience to Jesus Christ."

Deepen Your Spiritual Life

Art Erickson believes that "if you can master that first hour, you can master the rest of the day. But if you let that go, you just get 'behinder and behinder.' " He points to the critical need for spending daily time in scripture and prayer for spiritual insight, guidance and nurture.

David Miles has also found that personal spiritual growth is critical to his personal success. By developing a relationship with God, he says, he can maintain his perspective and priorities. "I had to learn to enjoy God—really enjoy God," he explains. "If I can enjoy my God, then I can enjoy my life. I don't care if I'm in a jail cell . . . or if I'm in the midst of graffiti or if there's a crack dealer down the street from me like there is, I can still enjoy my life because I can enjoy my God."

Share Leadership

One important way to maximize your effectiveness in urban youth ministry is to develop lay leaders in the church who take responsibility for much of the youth program. Ray Bakke argues that "the purpose of the staff should not be to run the programs but to be resources for multiplying the gifts of others."[4] Such a vision of shared ministry is crucial in order to meet the diverse needs of urban teenagers.

Twelfth Baptist Church in Boston doesn't have a paid youth minister, but volunteer leader Bruce Wall relies on a team of 14 lay leaders to lead the church's 14 different program emphases. In addition, the church emphasizes youth leadership in the church. Teenagers serve as counselors in the children's day camp program, and they're active worship leaders in the church.

Beyond the immediate benefit of sharing the workload, sharing leadership has important long-term benefits. After 15 years of encouraging youth leadership, Wall says that people who used to be leaders in the youth group are now leaders in the congregation and community. In fact, most of the people on the youth program's current adult leadership team used to be members of the youth group.

Find Opportunities for Growth

Urban youth ministry involves constant giving. Youth workers need opportunities to learn and grow themselves—to rejuvenate—in order to remain fresh and vital. "Cities are very rich in learning possibilities, both formal and informal," Ray Bakke writes. "There is no excuse for becoming stifled and intellectually bankrupt; you must take on responsibility for learning and make it a structured priority."[5]

Paul Tarro encourages urban youth ministers to make a personal commitment to self-improvement. This could involve a goal of reading a specific number of books or periodicals each month or year—some related to work; some purely for personal pleasure. Or it could involve a continuing education program. Bakke also suggests studying in one specialized area to give you the satisfaction of doing at least one thing exceptionally well.[6]

Inner City Impact, a parachurch urban ministry in Chicago, encourages its staff members to visit other urban ministries to learn new ideas and perspectives. Youth workers are also encouraged to participate in continuing education through colleges and seminaries in the Chicago area. They also try to attend youth ministry conferences and workshops in the area.

Build a Support Network

Building and maintaining a personal support group is the most important key to maintaining perspective and utilizing the resources available in urban youth work. "In the urban setting, you die if you don't network," says Harold Wright, minister of youth and family services at Friendship Baptist Church in Vallejo, California. He says networking is essential to sharing ideas and to challenging and supporting colleagues.

Any number of people can be part of your support group—other staff people, pastors, laypeople, other youth workers. It's important, though, that the people understand and respect your work, Paul Tarro urges. They need to be people who will hold you accountable for your finances, time and spiritual life.

One of the richest opportunities for networking and

growth may be with youth workers from other denominations who serve your community or nearby neighborhoods. Not only are you likely to share common concerns, but you can learn from each other about the richness and diversity of Christ's body. Often theological, ethnic and linguistic barriers are overcome as you work together toward the mutual goal of reaching and ministering to young people in Christ's name.

Harold Wright participates in a regional network called the Coalition for Urban Youth Leadership. Groups meet weekly or quarterly, and build a commitment to support each other. Urban Youth Ministries also has as a central mission the opportunity for urban youth workers to network together and support each other. (For more about both organizations, see the resource listing on page 245.)

Love the City

Urban youth ministry veterans love their cities. Sure, they see problems—they complain about the traffic and the hassles. But they love the city. That love is an important secret to their longevity. As Bakke writes, "If I do not love my city, I cannot work effectively there."[7]

This was a difficult lesson for youth worker David Miles. He moved to Flushing from a suburban church. The city seemed dirty and dangerous—and he didn't like it. But then he began examining what he disliked most, and discovered that almost everything grew out of his middle-class, white values—keeping a neat yard, not having dents in the car. His biggest complaints had little to do with his theology.

That self-examination challenged Miles to look for the benefits of city life and to ask God to open his heart to accept the city. As a result, he says he has discovered a rich community that he can call home.

One of the greatest concerns many people express about living in a city is: "What about the kids? You're not going to raise them there, are you?" When he hears that question, Wayne Gordon doesn't hesitate—even though he lives in a west Chicago neighborhood that's been classified as the 15th worst in the nation. "I think this is the best place on Earth to raise my family," he says. "And I mean that sincerely. There are a lot of hard times, but, boy, do we have a great family."

Ray Bakke tells about some of the things his children learned by living in the city. By going to Chicago's public schools, Bakke writes, they got to know and appreciate people from many different cultures and backgrounds. When they went to college, "they saw the parochialism of their student colleagues who had never had black or oriental friends, and they didn't feel sorry for all the material resources they may have lacked."[8]

Bakke also tried to overcome some of the shortcomings of city life by intentionally enriching his children's lives in a number of ways. His experiences serve as a useful model for urban youth ministers:

● He took an active part in his children's school. He went to games, lectured to classes, coached teams and worked for changes as a parent representative to the school.

● His family took advantage of the numerous cultural opportunities in the city—museums, art galleries, concerts.

● To help his children form positive friendships, he started a Fairfield Kids' Club each summer. He organized activities for kids his own children's age and invited neighborhood kids to join in the wholesome fun. Not only did the program help protect his own children from negative influences, but it became a great community outreach![9]

Get Away

Regardless of how much you love the city or how dedicated you are to youth ministry, you need to get away to rest and regain perspective. "The heat and concrete, the pains and the problems, the noises and the nuisances, and the pace and pressure of the city have a wearing effect," David Claerbaut writes. "Time for reflection and rest can reenergize a person who takes a week or a weekend or even a day off on a regular basis."[10]

Phill Carlos Archbold agrees: "You have to get away—in a different atmosphere, a different ambiance . . . I try to get away—get out of the neighborhood and just relax," he says.

Different urban youth ministers take different approaches to getting away:

● Recognizing the high burnout rate among urban youth workers, Inner City Impact in Chicago instituted a furlough program similar to the furloughs foreign missionaries take. The furloughs give youth workers a chance to get away from the city and its overwhelming needs for a short time. After three years, workers get a three-month furlough. The furlough length increases the longer someone serves.

● Each summer Art Erickson takes his family on a two-week family vacation when everyone sits, reads and does almost nothing. Then he and his wife also take a winter vacation without the children because "we've got to get away for us."

● David Miles gets away from the city by going rock climbing in the Allegheny Mountains or surfing in the Atlantic—both of which are within easy driving distance of his community.

● Phill Carlos Archbold takes a break from his Brooklyn community by going off somewhere by himself for a day. Sometimes he just rides a train to Washington, D.C., and eats a light meal in the train station. Then he returns to Brooklyn. He says the train trip gives him a change of scenery and time to think without going to a lot of trouble or expense.

Learn to Live With the Failures

By most measures of success, many urban youth ministries will never be "successful." To be sure, some teenagers' lives will change dramatically and many lives will be touched. But the challenges are so great that to expect 100 percent success is unrealistic.

Before Erickson went to Park Avenue Church, he was a successful Young Life leader. He says that failure was the first personal issue he had to deal with after his move to urban youth ministry. "I left success in the suburbs," he says. "I was used to a large number of kids . . . And I came to Park to work with 23 kids." Erickson continues: "If I tried to measure myself by my previous successes, I would lose my mind. You have to say every corner is different, and you're responsible for your own corner."

More is at stake than psychological well-being when we

learn to live with failure. Christianity is not, in the end, a "success-oriented" faith. It is a faith in which "the last shall be first" and in which the meek shall inherit the Earth. Like Jesus, Christians are called not to success but to faithfulness.

The Reluctant Prophet Revisited

Urban youth ministry is indeed difficult. But it's not impossible. And with God's help, it offers the potential of rich, rewarding ministry.

Chapter 1 introduced Jonah, the reluctant prophet who resisted the Lord's command to preach to the great city of Nineveh because he saw only the city's wickedness. Jonah was caught in a trap similar to one many urban youth workers fall in to. He looked at the city's crime and other problems, and saw no chance for success. He failed to see the vast supply of grace that God wanted to pour on the troubled people of Nineveh.

Yet, despite all the problems Jonah saw, all the evil he faced, and the weakness of his own faith, God used Jonah. Through this one man, God changed the lives of more than 120,000 people. And all because Jonah, in the end, was faithful to his call.

Just as God cared for Nineveh in Jonah's day, so he is concerned about *your* "great city." And God still works through faithful people!

Reflection and Action

1. What's expected of you in your ministry? Make a list of your responsibilities in the coming week. Are these expectations realistic? If not, what would it take to make them realistic?

2. Make a list of your five greatest struggles in urban youth ministry. Ask a colleague or a friend to pray for you about each of those struggles. Think of ways you can ease the stress in those areas.

3. Rate how well you do in each of the keys to thriving in urban youth ministry:

	Very well				**Not well**
Setting priorities	5	4	3	2	1
Deepening your spiritual life	5	4	3	2	1
Sharing leadership	5	4	3	2	1
Finding opportunities for growth	5	4	3	2	1
Building a support network	5	4	3	2	1
Loving the city	5	4	3	2	1
Getting away	5	4	3	2	1
Living with the failures	5	4	3	2	1

Which one would you like to work on this week? Write it on a 3×5 card and post it near your desk. As you make progress, jot notes on the back of the card. Then at the end of the week, celebrate your progress with your spouse or a close friend.

4. Reread the story of the "reluctant prophet." Do you think this is an accurate analogy for today's church? Why or why not?

5. If you were Jonah and God called you to the city as he called Jonah to Nineveh, would you go? Why or why not?

6. If Jonah were to come preach in your city today, what do you think he would say?

Endnotes

[1]David I. Frenchak, "Urban Fatigue," in *Metro-Ministry*, edited by David Frenchak and Sharrell Keyes (Elgin, IL: David C. Cook Publishing, 1979), 115.

[2]Frenchak, "Urban Fatigue," 117.

[3]Daniel Buttry, *Bringing Your Church Back to Life: Beyond the Survival Mentality* (Valley Forge, PA: Judson Press, 1988), 89.

[4]Ray Bakke with Jim Hart, *The Urban Christian* (Downers Grove, IL: InterVarsity Press, 1987), 122.

[5]Bakke with Hart, *The Urban Christian*, 124-125.

[6]Bakke with Hart, *The Urban Christian*, 124.

[7]Bakke with Hart, *The Urban Christian*, 51.

[8]Bakke with Hart, *The Urban Christian*, 171.

[9]Bakke with Hart, *The Urban Christian*, 161-167.

[10]David Claerbaut, *Urban Ministry* (Grand Rapids, MI: Zondervan Publishing House, 1983), 209.

Turning the Tables

Since mid century, churches have generally looked to the suburbs for their youth ministry models. Those models generally assume stable, traditional families, decent incomes, adequate education, homogeneous ethnicity and a church background. If the models dealt with problems, it was in the privacy of the counseling office.

But youth workers in every setting are discovering that those models are inadequate for the end of the century. The assumptions behind the models are no longer valid. Problems formerly seen as uniquely urban are becoming widespread. Even the suburbs—the idyllic locus of the "American Dream"—are experiencing broken and abusive families, homelessness, illiteracy, ethnic diversity and unchurched teenagers. Essentially—as we said in Chapter 1—the whole world is becoming more urbanized.

As Ray Bakke and Samuel K. Roberts write in *The Ex-panded Mission of "Old First" Churches*: "Until recently the American suburbs were exempt, but now almost every problem that was called 'urban' can be found there also . . . While there are differences still between rural and urban environments, the differences are of degree and not primarily of substance."[1]

And the traditional youth ministry models aren't sure how to respond.

Urban youth workers have a response: Come to the city. We've been struggling with these issues for years. "It becomes clear," Bakke and Roberts write, "that we should study ministry in large cities—not to see how unique or different it is—but so it can show us where the whole country is moving or will be 20 years hence."[2]

To respond to the new needs in their own communities, suburban, rural and small-town youth workers can learn from the Art Ericksons, Buster Soaries, Phill Carlos Archbolds, Marietta Ramseys, Jerald Choys and many others in cities across the country. These are the youth workers who are providing innovative models for youth ministry for the coming century.

Implications for the Future

This trend has several positive implications for urban youth ministry in the future. Consider these possibilities:

● It will be respected. Instead of being considered a stepping-stone to more prestigious youth ministry positions in large suburban churches, urban youth ministry will be valued for the important ministry that it is.

● It will have new visibility. Urban youth workers won't feel isolated and neglected, since the whole church will be looking to the city to learn how to deal with "urban" concerns.

● More resources will become available. Because urban youth ministry will no longer be seen as an isolated, specialized concern, youth ministry publishers and organizations will begin providing resources that specifically address urban concerns.

● More networking will begin happening. As urban

youth ministry becomes more prominent, new opportunities for networking will develop. Numerous national, regional and local organizations have begun forming, signaling the beginning of this trend.

Welcoming the Future

The future is ripe with possibility for urban youth ministry. But these possibilities won't happen automatically. The church must hear the stories of urban youth ministries. Urban youth workers must make themselves available to the church to share their stories and ideas. And they must develop the disciplines of writing, teaching and speaking in order to share those stories effectively.

In other words, the future will require dedication and patience. But those are two characteristics that urban youth workers have already developed. So—in the words of the Apostle Paul to Christians in the city of Philippi—"Forgetting what is behind and straining toward what is ahead, I press on toward the goal to win the prize for which God has called me heavenward in Christ Jesus" (Philippians 3:13b-14).

Endnotes

[1]Raymond J. Bakke and Samuel K. Roberts, *The Expanded Mission of "Old First" Churches*, (Valley Forge, PA: Judson Press, 1986), 45, 50.
[2]Bakke and Roberts, *The Expanded Mission of "Old First" Churches*, 50.

Urban Youth Ministry Resources

This listing includes many resources for urban youth ministers. Many resources are available through your local Christian bookstore, or they may be ordered directly from the publisher. In addition to the organizations listed, several colleges, seminaries, denominations and parachurch organizations provide resources, training and leadership for urban ministry issues.

Urban Ministry

Bringing Your Church Back to Life: Beyond Survival Mentality. Daniel Buttry. Judson Press, Valley Forge, PA 19482. Based on the story of Dorchester Temple Baptist Church in Boston, this book examines many of the struggles of urban churches. Buttry challenges churches to develop a vision that will reinvigorate their ministries.

The Church in the Life of the Black Family. Wallace Charles Smith. Judson Press, Valley Forge, PA 19482. Provides an important foundation for understanding the unique dynamics of the black family. Suggests guidelines for establishing a ministry to families in black congregations.

City Streets, City People: A Call for Compassion. Michael J. Christensen. Abingdon Press, 201 Eighth Ave., South, Box 801, Nashville, TN

37202. Focuses on the need for reaching the city's poorest residents—street dwellers. Includes ideas for starting and running an urban ministry. Based on the experiences of Golden Gate Ministries in the Haight Ashbury district of San Francisco.

A Clarified Vision for Urban Mission. Harvie M. Conn. Zondervan Publishing House, 1415 Lake Dr., Southeast, Grand Rapids, MI 49506. A pivotal book that dispels the stereotypes of the city and its people. Deals with such issues as the "depersonalization misunderstanding," the "crime generalization," the "secularization myth" and the "monoclass generalization."

Discipline and the Urban/Disadvantaged Youth. James M. Harriger (compiler). International Union of Gospel Missions, Box 10780, Kansas City, MO 64118. A collection of discipline policies and procedures from urban youth ministries around the country. Includes information on camp discipline, crowd control and age group characteristics.

Effective Urban Church Ministry. G. Willis Bennett. Broadman Press, 127 Ninth Ave., North, Nashville, TN 37234. Based on a case study of Allen Temple Baptist Church in Oakland, California, a major black church with an innovative ministry. Suggests practical ways churches can effectively serve the city.

Evangelizing Blacks. Glenn C. Smith (editor). Tyndale House Publishers, 336 Gundersen Dr., Box 80, Wheaton, IL 60189. Produced in cooperation with the Paulist National Catholic Evangelization Association, this book provides valuable insights into understanding and reaching black Americans.

The Expanded Mission of "Old First" Churches. Raymond J. Bakke and Samuel K. Roberts. Judson Press, Valley Forge, PA 19482. Based on research in established congregations across the country that are faced with transition, this book suggests the unique roles these churches can play in their communities.

God's Inner-City Address: Crossing the Boundaries. Mark E. Van Houten. Zondervan Publishing House, 1415 Lake Dr., Southeast, Grand Rapids, MI 49506. A practical and realistic book that examines the elements of an urban ministry. Written by a pastor of homeless young people on Chicago's north side.

God's Transforming Spirit: Black Church Renewal. Preston Robert Washington. Judson Press, Valley Forge, PA 19482. Tells the story of Memorial Baptist Church in Harlem, New York. Offers practical strategies for renewing urban congregations (of any ethnic group) and for providing important ministries to the community.

Hear the Cry: A Latino Pastor Challenges the Church. Harold J. Recinos. Westminster/John Knox, 100 Witherspoon St., Louisville, KY 40202. Written by a former high school dropout who is now a seminary professor, the book builds on the author's experiences as a pastor of a Puerto Rican congregation in New York City.

Hispanic Ministry in North America. Alex D. Montoya. Zondervan Publishing House, 1415 Lake Dr., Southeast, Grand Rapids, MI 49506. Provides a basis for understanding the Hispanic community and the Hispanic church.

How to Live With Diversity in the Local Church. Stephen Kliewer. Alban Institute, 4125 Nebraska Ave., Northwest, Washington, DC 20016. Suggests practical principles for building an inclusive congregation. The principles are easily adapted to youth ministry.

New Church in the City: The Work of the Chicago Fellowship of Friends. Marlene Morrison Pedigo. Friends United Press, 101 Quaker Hill Dr., Richmond, IN 47374. Tells the inspiring story of the Chicago Fellowship of Friends, which serves in the midst of government housing on Chicago's north side. The church began as a youth ministry, thus its struggles parallel the struggles of other urban youth ministries.

Signs of the Kingdom in the Secular City. David J. Frenchak and Clinton E. Stockwell (editors). Covenant Press, 3200 West Foster Ave., Chicago, IL 60625. A collection of speeches from the 1980 SCUPE Congress on Urban Ministry, this book provides valuable essays on understanding the city, evangelism strategies in the city and various ethnic groups.

Soul Theology: The Heart of American Black Culture. Henry Mitchell and Nicholas Cooper Lewter. Harper & Row, Icehouse One—401, 151 Union Street, San Francisco, CA 94111. An important study that pulls together black culture and theology, focusing on the nourishing spirituality of a folk faith.

Tell Me City Stories: A Journey for Urban Congregations. Philip Amerson. SCUPE Urban Church Resource Exchange Center, 30 W. Chicago Ave., Chicago, IL 60610. A practical manual for urban churches to examine their own history and context as a basis for exploring directions for the future.

The Urban Christian: Effective Ministry in Today's Urban World. Ray Bakke with Jim Hart. InterVarsity Press, P.O. Box 1400, Downers Grove, IL 60515. Pulls together years of practical and insightful wisdom from one of the world's leading urban ministry experts. Provides practical tools for urban churches to evaluate and revitalize their ministries.

Urban Ministry. David Claerbaut. Zondervan Publishing House, 1415 Lake Dr., Southeast, Grand Rapids, MI 49506. The foundational text for understanding the dynamics and needs of the city. Written from a Christian sociologist's perspective, the book is "must" reading for anyone involved in urban ministry.

Youth Ministry

Asian Pacific American Youth Ministry. Donald Ng (editor). Judson Press, Valley Forge, PA 19482. A ground-breaking book that addresses the specific needs of this rapidly growing urban youth population. Includes both foundational articles about understanding Asian Pacific American young people as well as practical programming ideas on topics such as identity, culture, racism, Christian beliefs and God's will.

Beating Burnout in Youth Ministry. Dean Feldmeyer. Group Books, Box 481, Loveland, CO 80539. A humorous and practical look at the issue that plagues urban youth ministry. Suggests practical ways to get control of your youth ministry such as running effective meetings, taking time off, setting goals and learning to say "no."

The Bridgebook: Youth Group Ideas for Cross-Cultural Contacts. Dale Dieleman (editor). Baker Book House, Grand Rapids, MI 49506. Discusses cross-cultural issues such as prejudice, stereotypes and personal identity. Includes information about various ethnic groups, and describes a variety of programs that build bridges.

Building Attendance in Your Youth Ministry. Scott C. Noon. Group Books, Box 481, Loveland, CO 80539. Draws on several principles of church growth to describe a model of youth ministry that maintains integrity and attracts young people. The principles and approaches that focus on building a variety of ministries to meet a variety of needs are particularly relevant to the urban setting.

Building Community in Youth Groups. Denny Rydberg. Group Books, Box 481, Loveland, CO 80539. Practical ideas for developing a caring youth group using a five-stage plan that involves bond-building, opening up, affirmation, stretching, deeper sharing and goal setting.

Controversial Topics for Youth Groups. Edward N. McNulty. Group Books, Box 481, Loveland, CO 80539. Gives youth workers the tools they need to help their young people deal with controversial issues. In addition to an introduction on how to handle controversial topics, it includes programming ideas on topics such as drugs, premarital sex, politics, pornography and abortion.

Counseling Teenagers. Dr. G. Keith Olson. Group Books, Box 481, Loveland, CO 80539. The most important available resource for counseling teenagers. Deals with developmental issues, Christian counseling techniques and various youth issues such as identity, sexuality issues, delinquency and spiritual issues.

Dennis Benson's Creative Bible Studies: Matthew—Acts and *Romans—Revelation.* Dennis C. Benson. Group Books, Box 481, Loveland, CO 80539. Together, these two volumes cover the entire New Testament, offering a total of 550 Bible studies for youth groups.

Determining Needs in Your Youth Ministry. Dr. Peter L. Benson and Dorothy L. Williams. Group Books, Box 481, Loveland, CO 80539. A scientifically designed survey to give to teenagers to discover their needs and concerns. Includes tools for analyzing the results as well as ways for using the results in future planning.

Drugs, God & Me. Kathleen Hamilton Eschner and Nancy G. Nelson. Group Books, Box 481, Loveland, CO 80539. A unique drug and alcohol abuse-prevention curriculum designed for junior highers and their parents. Focuses on building self-esteem, overcoming ignorance and developing refusal skills. Opens communication between parents and their children about this critical urban issue.

Intensive Care: Helping Teenagers in Crisis. Rich Van Pelt. Youth Specialities/Zondervan Publishing House, 1415 Lake Dr., Southeast, Grand Rapids, MI 49506. Written by an urban youth worker, the book examines the sensitive dynamics and issues of crisis intervention with teenagers. Addresses such issues as disrupted families, sexual abuse and substance abuse.

The Youth Group Meeting Guide. Richard Bimler and others. Group Books, Box 481, Loveland, CO 80539. An essential resource for planning, leading and evaluating youth group meetings. Includes 88 ready-to-use program designs, many of which can be adapted for urban youth groups.

Youth Ministry Drama and Comedy. Chuck Bolte and Paul McCusker. Group Books, Box 481, Loveland, CO 80539. A foundational resource for creating and planning drama with teenagers. Discusses developing goals, choosing or writing scripts, directing, acting, rehearsing and many other subjects. Includes 20 ready-to-use scripts.

The Youth Ministry Resource Book. Eugene C. Roehlkepartain (editor). Group Books, Box 481, Loveland, CO 80539. The most complete collection of data and information about youth ministry available. Includes statistics about teenagers and youth ministry, listings of denominations and organizations involved in youth work, and annotated listings of resources for youth ministry.

Urban Theology and Biblical Studies

The Corinthian Church: A Biblical Approach to Urban Culture. William Baird. Abingdon Press, 201 Eighth Ave., South, Box 801, Nashville, TN 37202. A foundational book for drawing parallels between the New Testament urban world and today's urban world.

The First Urban Christians: The Social World of the Apostle Paul. Wayne A. Meeks. Yale University Press, 302 Temple St., New Haven, CT 06520. An academic text that analyzes Paul's letters and other New Testament passages to make a strong case that Christianity began as an urban faith. Provides a provocative reinterpretation of passages that relate to contemporary urban issues.

The Meaning of the City. Jacques Ellul. William B. Eerdmans Publishing Company, 255 Jefferson Ave., Southeast, Grand Rapids, MI 49503. Ellul examines cities in scripture, interpreting the passages to say that the city is a cursed human invention. While few urban ministers will accept Ellul's approach, he provides a provocative interpretation of the city that is echoed in many people's assumptions about the urban world.

The Secular City (revised edition). Harvey Cox. MacMillan Company, 866 Third Ave., New York, NY 10022. This is a controversial and provocative re-evaluation of the city that originally appeared in the mid-1960s. While few readers will accept Cox's whole package, he provides valuable insights into the rich possibilities of urban life and ministry.

Urban Ministry Organizations

Center for Urban Theological Studies (CUTS), 1300 W. Hunting Park Ave., Philadelphia, PA 19140. Offers a variety of degrees in urban ministry in cooperation with area schools.

Coalition for Urban Youth Leadership, Box 12231, Portland, OR 97212. A cooperative network of urban youth workers who serve to build leadership in urban teenagers in primarily black and Hispanic communities. Offers training for youth workers, local support networks and an annual national leadership event for young people.

ERIC Clearinghouse on Urban Education, Box 40, Teachers College, Columbia University, New York, NY 10027. Funded by the U.S. Department of Education, this information clearinghouse provides valuable and inexpensive research reports and program descriptions related to urban education and multiracial education. Though geared for public schools, the research and educational techniques provide important insights for urban youth ministry.

The Grantsmanship Center, 1015 W. Olympic Blvd., Los Angeles, CA 90015. This is a non-profit educational institution that provides training, workshops and resources for resource development. It provides valuable information on requesting and receiving funding for specific ministry programs.

Open Door Ministries, Box 4248, Seminole, FL 34642. Publishes a variety of curricula, books, videos and other resources specifically for black churches.

PROMESA, Box 15140, San Antonio, TX 78212. PROMESA is an acronym for Proyectos Y Ministerios Evangelicos Hispanos. This national organization works with churches, denominations and other organizations to reach Hispanic Americans in urban areas. It offers workshops, consultations and conferences. It may begin publishing a newsletter.

Seminary Consortium for Urban Pastoral Education (SCUPE), 30 W. Chicago Ave., Chicago, IL 60610. The best-known and most comprehensive urban ministry education program in the nation. Sponsored jointly by seminaries in the Chicago area, it provides pastoral training specifically for urban ministry. Provides resources for urban ministry through its Urban Church Resource Center. Sponsors a biennial SCUPE Congress on Urban Ministry that brings together the leading thinkers and practitioners in urban ministry.

Urban Life Center, 5004 S. Blackstone Ave., Chicago, IL 60615. This center offers a unique approach to urban education that uses the city of Chicago as its classroom for internships and study experiences. A variety of options are offered—from semester-long study to weekend experiences—

that deal with such issues as urban ministry, arts, urban problems and ethnic diversity.

Urban Ministries Inc., 1439 W. 103rd St., Chicago, IL 60643. An interdenominational organization that publishes and distributes a wide variety of resources for urban black congregations. Produces curricula for all age levels as well as books and videos.

Urban Youth Ministries, Box 10780, Kansas City, MO 64118. Formed in 1988, this organization's goal is to be a national network of urban youth workers in evangelical congregations and parachurch organizations. The organization plans to provide support, training, networking and resources.